Acknowledgements

This study was completed with the help of two local authorities and many staff in other organisations concerned with child protection. For the sake of confidentiality, we cannot name individuals, but it should be clear that research in an area as sensitive as suspected child abuse can only be mounted with a great deal of help from others. We are especially indebted to the children and families who participated in the research. They let us into their homes in difficult situations and answered searching questions fully and honestly.

The research was funded by the Department of Health and copyright rests with the Crown. We would like to thank the members of the Research and Development Divisions, Community Services Division and Social Service Inspectorate for their help. On behalf of their staff, we would thank Professor Michael Peckham, Tom Luce and Herbert Laming. Special thanks must go however to Carolyn Davies for her liaison work on behalf of the Unit.

We would also like to thank the numerous research colleagues who have discussed issues with us and read drafts. Finally, we would thank the Dartington Hall Trust and members of the Social Research Unit for their essential help. We are deeply grateful to them all.

Contents

List of Tables

List of Diagrams

Chapter 1

Introduction

During the 1980s a series of child abuse scandals in the United Kingdom caused widespread public concern. While the underlying anxieties were not new and certainly not peculiar to Britain, social work improprieties in Cleveland and the Orkneys were exhaustively reported. Had the professionals been over zealous? How serious were the abuse problems faced by the children? Subsequent public inquiries drew attention to the paucity of knowledge in the area of child abuse and detected confusion in the reactions of investigative agencies. As part of its response, the Department of Health launched a programme of research studies to explore different aspects of child abuse which, in combination, would help to provide a more comprehensive assessment. The initiative is unusual because its focus is not restricted to the deviant behaviour of children and families. It includes studies of behaviour in normal families, agency processes and decision making. In each study there has been a concern for short and long-term outcomes.

The aims of this study

This study, which is part of the programme just described, explores parental perspectives in the context of suspected abuse. It looks at the interaction between these perspectives and the intervention of child protection agencies. It then considers whether and how the perspectives and the intervention, separately or in combination, influence the well-being of children and families. A model incorporating the different dimensions of parental perspectives is developed.

We examine the progress of an intervention from the moment a suspicion of child abuse is brought to the notice of a statutory agency, through the various stages in the inquiry process when the suspicion gathers momentum and becomes the subject of official scrutiny. We consider how professionals make their suspicions known to parents and the conditions in which the relationship between suspect and investigators is negotiated. The central focus of the study is the degree of concordance between the perspectives of parents and professionals at various stages in the investigation.

To explain why there should be an interest in the perspectives of suspected abusers, we need first to consider the historical and intellectual background to the emergence of child abuse as an important issue.

The historical and intellectual background to the child abuse problem

Strategies for dealing with unwanted, unloved or destitute children inevitably reflect cultural, historical, economic and religious forces. In Britain, although legislation to protect children was continuously debated throughout the nineteenth century, intervention was largely confined to situations outside the family. Thomas Coram was moved to charity by the number of babies he found dead or abandoned on the London streets in the late eighteenth century; in 1802 the concern was to protect apprentices; in 1872 the worst excesses of child minding and baby farming were outlawed (Pinchbeck and Hewitt, 1973). Of periodic concern was the sexual exploitation of girls and the extent of child prostitution, but while larger social issues, such as anxiety about the ravages of venereal disease, influenced attempts to control vice in the metropolis, the focus continued to be on extra-familiar activities. Not until 1889, when the National Society for the Prevention of Cruelty to Children was formed, did the family cease to be regarded as an entirely inviolable institution, and thereafter legislation permitting the scrutiny of personal family relations was slow in coming and grudgingly enacted.

The role of the State in child care was governed by the Poor Law which emphasised parents' legal obligation to maintain their children without government assistance. Any form of State support was thought to weaken family ties and encourage dependency. It was also costly. As a result, intervention was kept to a minimum and only considered an acceptable recourse in order to rescue children from the absolute extremes of poverty and degradation. Indeed, the emphasis on parental obligation occasionally resulted in the Poor Law guardians returning children to clearly abusive relatives who were liable for their maintenance (Ward, 1990); a corollary was the practice of severing all connections between those children placed in care and the evil influence of their 'bad' parents.

It was left to writers such as Dickens and Kingsley to draw attention to the cruelty to and exploitation of the young, while venerable parliamentarians such as Lord Shaftesbury recited the reasons for not interfering in the private domain. He stated in 1880:

> The evils are enormous and indisputable, but they are of so private, internal and domestic a character as to be beyond the reach of legislation and the subject would not, I think, be entertained in either House of Parliament.

The Victorian diarist, the Rev. Francis Kilvert, writing in 1871, alluded to the predicament in which a humanitarian of the time was likely to find himself – aware of a grave cruelty but prevented by conventional morality from intervening (Plomer, 1973).

Annie Corfield is better but we fear that she and her sisters, the twins Phoebe and Lizzie, are very miserable and badly treated by their father since their dear mother's death. What would she say if she could see them now, ragged, dirty, thin and half-clad and hungry? How unkindly their father uses them. The neighbours hear the sound of the whip on their naked flesh and the poor girls crying and screaming sadly sometimes when their father comes home late at night. It seems that when he comes home late he makes the girls get out of bed and strip themselves naked and then he flogs them severely or else he pulls the bedclothes off them and whips them all three as they lie in bed together writhing and screaming under the castigation. It is said that sometimes Corfield strips the poor girls naked, holds them face downwards across his knees on a bed or chair and whips their bare bottoms so cruelly that the blood runs down their legs.

Concern for the welfare of children persisted long after Kilvert had made this entry, as did the conditioning argument that beatings and backboards were a legitimate means of 'correcting' the innate waywardness of children. As the voluntary associations gained strength and enabling legislation was enacted, the needs of children within families became more salient, but as late as 1970 the main point at issue was neglect rather than physical or sexual abuse as we now define it. Why this should have been is unclear. Perhaps, as Parker (1990) has suggested, the improvement in material conditions after the First World War and the accompanying fall in infant mortality tended to make families who were both poor and neglectful more conspicuous. On the other hand, there is much to suggest that a child's allegation of sexual assault was simply not to be believed.

Even in the 1960s and 70s sexualised 'acting out' was interpreted as signifying wider psychological disturbance, and there was a middle-class assumption, even among psychiatrists and social workers, that incest was so much a common practice in working class and rural areas as to be considered normal – and harmless. Whatever the reasons, child abuse as we now perceive it is of relatively recent recognition; in the writings of Bowlby, Winnicott and Anna Freud, otherwise so profuse in their acknowledgement of every bonding nuance and weaning trauma, there is no mention of it.

Policy has been influenced by a succession of child-care scandals, which in retrospect can be regarded as the indicators of changing public preoccupations. Just as the 'baby farming' of the nineteenth century reflected anxiety over private child care arrangements, the infamous case of Dennis O'Neill, who died in 1945 while in a foster home, focused public attention on the shortcomings of substitute care. In contrast, the death of Maria Colwell as a result of parental cruelty in 1973 revealed the consequences of poor inter-agency liaison and the failure of swift intervention. Further, the Cleveland affair, which provoked this and numerous other studies, raised questions about the rights of parents under investigation for suspected child abuse. Thus, professionals have been made increasingly aware of the vagaries of risk assessment and the difficulties of respecting parents' and children's rights.

Since the late 1960s cases of parental cruelty have attracted a great deal of media attention. The tragedies of Jasmine Beckford, Kimberley Carlile and Doreen Mason all gained national coverage and their names became watchwords for the distress they experienced. Public awareness that parents can and do inflict pain and suffering on their children has been so heightened that in 1986, in association with the broadcasting media, Childline was launched, making it possible for children to report allegations confidentially by telephone. Just as significantly, considering the state of affairs 20 years previously, in 1989 the *Annual Report of the NSPCC*, was called *Listening to Children*.

Anxiety that victims of parental abuse should not suffer in silence still needs to be reconciled with the view that family life should be free from interference and invasion. Reports of official inquiries reflect the incompatibility of these polarised positions as they oscillate between criticism of neglectful parents and reproaches against doctors and social workers for interfering in the private lives of families. The highly emotive Cleveland and Orkney cases were clear illustrations of a public initially scandalised at what seemed over-zealous social work; the Jasmine Beckford inquiry exposed the consequences of leaving children in dangerous circumstances.

It is in this climate of uncertainty that interest in the perspectives of parents has grown. The realisation that they, too, can be the victims of abuse investigations has led to greater consideration of their views and to closer scrutiny of relationships within the wider family. These practice changes reflect in part new ideas and better knowledge.

A number of disciplines and ideologies have something to contribute to an understanding of the dynamics at work inside families and in the relations between parents and their children. The first to mention is the feminist critique, by which domestic violence is regarded as an indicator of the disposal of power in the relationship between men and women, not merely as the symptom of pathological behaviour. Previously, the private worlds of home were frequently ignored by sociologists and neglected by legislators (Billington, Strawbridge, Greensides and Fitzsimons, 1991), and thinkers such as Foucault highlighted this weakness in explorations of the relationship between power structures in society and personal behaviour and beliefs in contexts such as those that interest us.

As relevant is the accumulation of research findings and clinical work which has established the opinion that abuse is damaging. Longitudinal studies, especially in the field of psychiatry, have underlined the need to protect children by suggesting that abuse in childhood is to be regarded as a risk factor every bit as dangerous as serious childhood illness (Sroufe and Rutter 1984, Bentovim 1987). The experience of childhood abuse may predispose the victim to problems relating to his or her mental health, social competence or sexual adjustment. However, it is also the case that responding precipitately and removing the child into the care of the State may actually increase the risk of other long-term problems. Recent child-care research shows that children in long-term care often experience placement break-down, drift and increasing isolation from family and home neighbourhood (Bullock, Little and Millham, 1993). Thus the haunting possibility always exists, and must be taken into account, that the abused infant rescued in good faith may become the isolated and suicidal adolescent in custody.

Definition of the problem

As a result of three decades of research we know that child abuse is multi-faceted and has physical, sexual and emotional aspects for which the terminology of neglect is quite inadequate. Initially, research from North America was responsible for alerting British readers to the differences; the momentum of inquiry increased after Kempe and colleagues (1962) had provided the first comprehensive description of the 'battered child syn-drome', which revealed the extent of the physical damage young children could suffer as a result of deliberate acts of parental cruelty. Kempe and Kempe (1978) and later Finkelhor (1979, 1984) highlighted the equally serious plight of sexually abused children; rather later, emotional maltreat-ment of children became established as a category of abuse (Garbarino, Guttmann and Wilson Seeley, 1986). Each abuse category also varies in terms of the seriousness of injury or violation.

This heterogeneity, coupled with the fact that categories are not mutually exclusive – the Cleveland Report, for example, found that a third of children referred for physical and emotional abuse had also been abused sexually – complicates attempts to assess the prevalence of abuse, since calculations are bound to be influenced by the definition and the threshold for notification. For example, Besharov (1982) demonstrates that estimates of child abuse incidents in the United States range from 60,000 to 4,500,000 a year according to the definition used.

Nevertheless, there is no doubt that the rate of reported child abuse has increased significantly since Kempe's definitive paper; indeed, American authorities suggest that between 1963 and 1985 the incidence of reported abuse increased twelve-fold (Besharov, 1987). While cynical commentators might argue that this explosion has been stage-managed in order to buttress the social work profession (Brewer, 1980), there is evidence that more frequent reporting and the establishment of specialised child protection agencies have saved many thousands of children from death or severe injury.

Crittenden (1988) in the United States and Creighton (1988) in the United Kingdom both found a preponderance of less severe injuries in their examination of reports during the past decade. NSPCC figures for physical abuse in Britain between 1979 and 1986 indicate a decline from 17% to 8% in the proportion of serious or fatal injuries. Pritchard (1992, 1993), in a study of rates in 15 countries, is even more sanguine, showing that the fall of 61% in baby homicides in Britain between 1973 and 1988 was a return for sound investment in child protection work. In the light of this evidence, the expansion in the number of reported abuse cases may be said to reflect an increasing preoccupation with less serious cases.

The discrepancy between the popular view of widespread serious abuse and the reality influences the perspectives of everyone involved. We shall see that there are some 160,000 child abuse suspicions in Britain each year. Most of the abuse is relatively mild, but within that group there are 100 or so child homicides and 6,000 children who need to be looked after away from home. Thus, social workers fear that every case is a Jasmine Beckford tragedy and parents worry that their children will be taken away, when the greatest likelihood is that, even if abuse is confirmed, children will remain at home and the family will receive help. Even those children removed from their families are not usually away for long (Pritchard, 1991; Bullock, Little and Millham, 1993).

The high profile given to child abuse in recent years has other implications for accused parents. It has created an atmosphere of suspicion in which some reports and accusations are inevitably unfounded or malicious. Besharov (1982) argues that the desire to avoid scandal over child abuse has led to over-investigation and to too great an emphasis on sexual abuse (Wressell, Kaplan and Kolvin, 1989). It can also lead to a poorer service for non-abused children in need, particularly as anxiety about appropriate behaviour in foster and residential placements may deter carers from exerting control and displaying affection.

Child abuse procedures

Before Cleveland, the official response to clear-cut cases of abuse varied but most passed through several stages of inquiry: suspicion, referral, consul-tation, investigation and resolution. Depending on the circumstances, children entered the child protection system at different stages. Child and family may already have been well known to the social services; on the other hand, suspected abuse may have come to light when the child visited a hospital or when neighbours contacted the NSPCC.

Clear procedures and a definition of child abuse were introduced by the Government in 1988 and the revised guidance *Working Together* (Home Office et al, 1991) states that Social Services have a statutory duty:

to investigate reports of children suffering, or likely to suffer, significant harm and to take appropriate action to safeguard or promote the child's welfare. These duties and responsibilities apply to all children in the community whether the child is living at home with parents, in residential care in either a children's home or a residential school, or living with another carer (who may be a local authority foster parent).

As a result of such investigation, a child may:

a) remain at home, because there seems little future risk or there is a lack of evidence. No formal action is taken although the situation may be carefully monitored and since the implementation of the 1989 *Children Act* the child may be examined under a child assessment order;

b) remain at home under scrutiny because he or she is the subject of a supervision or care order or recorded on the Child Protection Register;

c) be removed on an emergency protection order and, subsequently, made the subject of interim and full care orders. The local authority is then responsible for finding the most suitable alternative placement. The child may also be looked after elsewhere under voluntary arrangements.

Our survey of 583 abuse referrals, described in Chapter Five, will further illustrate these routes.

In practice, however, research has shown that professionals still resort to personal, even idiosyncratic interpretation of the law (Hallett and Birchall, 1992). For example, it has been difficult to compile a national picture of the incidence of abuse and account for regional variations. In the two local authorities we scrutinised, one identified five categories of abuse: (1) neglect, (2) physical injury, (3) sexual abuse, (4) emotional abuse and (5) grave concern; while the other local authority recognised six: (1) physical injury, (2) physical neglect, (3) failure to thrive and emotional abuse, (4) children in the same household as a person previously involved in child abuse, (5) suspected or actual child sexual abuse and (6) potential child abuse. In the former, incidents of 'failure to thrive' or the arrival of a known sexual offender in the family would be subsumed under more general risk headings. In both, attribution to any category of maltreatment could lead to a child's name being placed on the Protection Register. *Working Together* has abandoned the category of 'grave concern' as a basis for registration. Those current are (1) neglect, (2) physical injury, (3) sexual abuse, (4) emotional abuse.

Differences in definition have posed problems for research dealing with the use of Child Protection Registers. For example, there is a tenfold variation among local authorities in the numbers of children placed on the register proportional to the total population of children. This disparity cannot be explained by different application of risk or deprivation indicators (Little and Gibbons, 1993); on the contrary, Gibbons and her colleagues (1993) have demonstrated that operational factors in local authorities are the most significant.

Notwithstanding such problems, the Department of Health has collected data on the numbers of children registered for all forms of abuse since 1988. For the year ending March 31st 1992 there were estimated to be 38,600 children and young people on Child Protection Registers in England, a figure which represents 3.5 per thousand of the child population under the age of 18 years. During that year about 24,500 names were added and 31,300 de-registered. It is noteworthy that only 5,700 of the children were looked after away from home by local authorities.

The contribution of this study

Since the majority of abused children remain at home or eventually return, it is important that parents should feel their views have been respected by professionals, particularly when the suspicion of abuse is first investigated. The treatment a family receives is likely to determine the extent of co-operation with welfare agencies; indeed, the quality of such an experience may be a governing factor in any attempt to monitor the welfare of vulnerable children. There is little to suggest that in their dealings with families social workers discuss appropriate parenting behaviour (DHSS, 1986), an interaction which may help create a favourable view of the intervention. Increased family participation in the process might even reduce the high level of re-abuse indicated by several research studies (Skinner and Castle, 1969; Friedman and Morse, 1974; Gibbons, Gallagher and Bell, 1992).

Furthermore, this approach has relevance to rights issues. The Cleveland Report criticised the professionals' handling of children and parents. It recommended that children should be given clear explanations of what was happening and that interviews and medical examinations should be sensitively conducted. Finally, it was recommended that parents should be made aware of their rights and substantial support should be given to the family during any investigation.

This study contributes to an understanding of how good relationships can be maintained in taxing circumstances by examining parental perspectives during the investigation and over the following two years. But charting such responses proved a complicated business, because any individual's perception of any set of circumstances will be based on shifting sand. Parents' attitudes change according to the stresses of the moment; professionals, similarly, bring preconceptions to bear on each case. With these dimensions in mind we developed the concept of an operational perspective, which we describe in Chapter Six. We shall see how the operational perspectives of parents and professionals alter and what can be done to promote greater concordance.

Conclusions

This preliminary discussion suggests that in any investigation of suspected child maltreatment it is necessary to examine the context in which concerns about child abuse arise. As the level of public concern fluctuates, the definition of what constitutes abuse is revised. The reasons for this fluidity are complex and variations due to social change, shifts in cultural values and the accumulation of clinical evidence make it difficult to compare the incidence and effects of abuse in different localities or to chart statistical trends accurately. Nevertheless, in the light of encouraging empirical evidence, and heeding the recommendations of official reports and current guidance, it is necessary to explore the child protection system in more detail in order to determine whether procedures at the outset of an investigation can be made more humane and conducive to work with families and children. Particularly important in this is an understanding of the perspectives of those involved and the measures by which conflict may be reduced.

Summary Points

1 This study, part of a wider initiative which explores different dimensions of child abuse and protection procedures, focuses on parental perspectives in the context of suspected child abuse. How does the accusation of child abuse, however delicately made, affect families? Is the compliance and co-operation of some family members negotiated to the detriment of others? We shall consider the role of different agencies at various points in the investigation and whether parental perceptions influence the outcome of the case.

2 Since the late 1960s, public and professional sensitivity to awareness of child abuse has been heightened by a series of much publicised child deaths and subsequent official inquiries.

3 Understanding of child abuse has been enhanced by theories which link family behaviour to wider social structures and by clinical evidence highlighting the long-term risks associated with abuse in childhood.

4 Attempts to assess accurately the nature and extent of child abuse and any trend towards lesser or greater prevalence have been hindered by problems of definition.

5 Once child abuse is suspected, procedures for dealing with cases vary considerably. Research would indicate that the majority of children remain at home or return home quickly, emphasising the need to work sensitively with families and gain their co-operation. Failure to share care with parents puts vulnerable children at greater risk.

Chapter 2

The contexts in which perspectives are fashioned

In the opening Chapter we considered the history of child protection legislation and the surge of interest in the problem of child abuse. Having suggested reasons why parental perspectives have become an important consideration, we now examine the cultural context in which they are fashioned. In particular we look at anthropological evidence, sociological studies of moral panics, the significance of suspicion and studies of trauma.

The cultural context of family life

Very few societies deliberately set out to harm children and there is broad agreement across races and cultures that neglect, sickness and death among the young are undesirable and socially destructive (Parker and colleagues, 1991). But beyond this simple principle, societal perception of what constitutes desirable child behaviour varies according to expectations in areas such as obedience to elders, religious observance and adolescent social life. Similarly, differences in values and beliefs, family structures and views on collective responsibility generate distinct patterns of parenting behaviour (Giovannoni and Becerra, 1979). Moreover, certain conventional Western practices, such as the stern toilet-training of infants, the use of 'outsider' baby-sitters and child-minders or the dismissal of children to their own bedrooms at night would cause offence elsewhere just as we are appalled by impoverished families in the Third World who maim their children in order to enhance their 'begging' potential (Benedict, 1938, Korbin, 1981, Levinson, 1989). Even within a particular culture, certain categories of children will be regarded and treated unfairly and societies which place a high value on children may nevertheless relegate the adopted, the illegitimate or the handicapped (Agathonos, 1992).

In looking at the contexts in which families operate we also need to be aware of the wider political framework. In certain circumstances a preoccupation with child abuse may be used to divert attention from wider issues of poverty, housing and poor family health or in an attempt to redefine 'normal' or 'acceptable' standards of social or sexual behaviour (Robin, 1989). This point is emphasised by the structural explanations of child abuse offered by Korbin (1991), who suggests that the pace of social change in societies undergoing industrialisation may destroy established relationships and aggravate family violence. Studies of the effect of long-term unemployment likewise indicate that marital relations can be disrupted and that domestic violence, divorce, and even suicide may follow the loss of a job (Kaplan, 1977). There is also evidence to suggest a link between poverty and child abuse and neglect (Brown and Madge, 1982). However, because only a minority of families exposed to adverse conditions abuse their children, such findings are not easily incorporated into any protective strategy. Nevertheless, explanations that weigh psychological and social stressers against protective factors, such as good relationships within the family, offer a possible way forward (Browne and Saqi, 1988).

Changing definitions of good parenting

The significance of the cultural context is brought home when we try to define good parenting. It is salutary to consider that were they alive today and had they refused to conform, the distinguished Victorian 'flogging' headmasters, Keate and Vaughan, would be languishing in prison, segregated under Section 43 rules. Beatings, once part of the underpinning fabric of the British education system and thus of the social structure they maintained, are no longer generally condoned in Britain. The use of quarantine to isolate children with infectious diseases has likewise been abandoned, nor do we brand sexually precocious adolescents as 'promiscuous' or 'morally defective' or lock them up them in institutions (Parker, 1988). Thus, as with much else in an advanced society, not only do definitions of child abuse change with time but there is a tendency for the movement to be cyclical. The attitudes of the 1960s towards teenage sexuality would have been unthinkable 50 years before, but during the last decade anxieties about AIDS, venereal disease and infertility have been influential in the revision of moral values and appropriate sexual behaviour (Mellanby, Phelps and Tripp, 1992).

Empirical studies of parenting behaviour available in Britain suggest marked social class differences. For example, nearly 20 years ago Newson and Newson (1976) showed that physical punishment was inflicted more frequently on children from working-class homes, but it was left open to conjecture whether the cold silences and isolation endured by the children of the more affluent might be regarded as any less painful or harmful. So, while it may be generally believed that parents should and do control their children by exhortation and mild punishment and by rewarding or ridiculing certain behaviours, and that this measured technique transcends class, education and cultural distinctions, plainly the interpretation of child-rearing practices has to be conducted in a theoretical context that takes issues of class, race, religion, age and gender into account.

The consequence of this variability is that the perspectives of families on child-rearing and parenting behaviour are frequently at odds with agencies responsible for investigating child abuse. Those under scrutiny often feel misunderstood (Giovannoni and Becerra, 1979). Mothers may explain 'I always clip my children when they're naughty, doesn't everybody?' or argue, 'if they don't eat their tea then they can go without'. Judged by the 'objective' criteria of the health visitor or social worker, such attitudes, colloquially expressed, may be considered unacceptable, sowing the seeds of parental bewilderment, anger and distress. Furthermore, the tendency for agencies to overlook the strengths that may exist in an abusing family is an extra irritation for parents.

Moral panics and suspected child abuse

A discussion of general social and historical context does not adequately explain why child abuse should have become the focus of so much concern in recent years. In any era some parents inflict pain and suffering on their children and regard them cruelly as their possessions. This much is well documented in studies of the grudging and slow development of child protection in the 19th century. We have noted, too, that as the visibility of child abuse has increased, organisations have responded accordingly and that a series of scandals surrounding private care, state care and, more recently, parents' and children's rights has acted as the catalyst. Of a different order has been the furore generated by reports of organised or satanic sexual abuse. There was a period when scarcely a week passed without some new incident or allegation being luridly described.

With hindsight, the temperature of social and political opinion concerning child abuse may be said to have amounted to a moral panic, to that state which exists when 'a condition, episode, person, or group of persons emerges to become defined as a threat to societal values and interests' (Cohen, 1972). The scenario is of considerable vintage. From a safe distance on the boardwalk of the old pier, in the company of Sussex gentlefolk, television cameramen and frothy sociologists, Cohen watched 'Mods and Rockers' fighting it out on Brighton beach. He subsequently argued that particular groups become agents of society's moral indignation and that, in order to maintain general orthodoxy, the deviants are cast into outer darkness, into the role of 'folk devils' which then serve as a 'visible reminder of what we should not be'. Groups which are rejected in this way are also highlighted by Becker (1963) when he talks of the 'outsiders' who threaten the consensus of society.

Very stimulating and insightful this literature remains. It suggests that society needs to legitimise its own control mechanisms, and thus reinforces the argument that the current interest in child abuse serves some ulterior purpose. Roaring motorbikes, skidding stolen cars and raucous acid house parties threaten those of us whose glazed eyes result not from amphetamines but from an overdose of *Coronation Street*. Something has to be done, preferably by someone else. Sensational press coverage reflects our baser perceptions and feeds instinctual terrors; on our behalf simplistic remedies are re-invented, whether 'short, sharp shock', tagging, forced emigration or secure schools. Thus, in an unguarded moment, we will fulminate against pathological parents, whom we believe dance in quarries dressed as Beelzebub, and the next we will froth at the violation of cosy family values by high-handed and intrusive social workers. Most moral panics have concerned the behaviour of adolescents and drug abusers, but the mechanism is as relevant to an understanding of the fear of child molesters and all the consequences of child abuse, in particular the early media coverage of suspected child abuse in Cleveland, Rochdale and the Orkneys.

Psychologists have also described how group aggression acts as a displacement mechanism which helps make scapegoats of vulnerable groups (Allport, 1924). What Littlewood and Lipsedge (1982) term 'cultural paranoia' has been manifest in Europe from mediaeval times, initially taking the form of witch-hunting. The most famous case occurred in Puritan New England, culminating in the Salem witch trials of 1692, when the combination of political and socio-economic uncertainty, the threat of small-pox and a freezing winter convinced the community that the Devil and his witches were meddling in their affairs. False accusations, public confessions, torture, trials and many executions followed. As illuminating as the historical incident itself is Arthur Miller's play *The Crucible*, which used the Salem witch trials as a vehicle for anatomising another moral panic, the anti-Communist fever generated by McCarthyism in the 1940s and 1950s. As a correspondent suggested in a letter to *The Times* at the time of the Cleveland inquiry, 'the best training social workers could have is to read *The Crucible*'.

What does such cautionary evidence have to offer those about to embark on child abuse research? First, it shows that most of the population will be influenced by the general anxiety and subscribe to the prejudices that prevail. Should an individual, however, fall prey to those prejudices, his or her sense of outrage is extreme. Secondly, it warns researchers to remain sceptical of evidence collected in difficult circumstances and make proper allowance for the obstacles children and adults face in trying to get a fair hearing. Under pressure, victim or accused may hasten to provide proof in order to satisfy their interrogators. Indeed, the moral panic surrounding suspected child abuse may have lowered the threshold of suspicion to such an extent that, under scrutiny, innocent child-rearing activities, such as children sharing the bath with adults, seem to be invested with furtive and forbidden pleasure. A French colleague recently observed 'Now I don't stop to watch children on the roundabouts in the Tuilleries Gardens. The gendarme looks at me suspiciously, so I hurry on – and a sense of deprivation engulfs me, robs the children of an audience and should sadden all at lost innocence.'

The impact of suspicion

Central to the context we are considering in this Chapter is suspicion – that partial or unconfirmed belief that something is wrong or someone guilty. Suspicion, too, has a history, gathering momentum inside an agency or community, ebbing and flowing at different organisational levels until an investigation becomes inevitable. Intrinsic to the process are betrayal, denial, false allegation, paranoia and the need for concealment, and all of these will shape the perspectives that are the focus of this study.

However, research literature devoted to the workings of suspicion is scarce. The instrumental cousins of suspicion, deception and distrust, have more often attracted the attention of psychologists, because they are articulated more clearly in interpersonal behaviour and body-language. Suspicion is more reflective – and possibly considered too romantic in its overtones and psychological associations to warrant analysis. In *Othello* and *The Winter's Tale* Shakespeare explored the dangerous situations that occur when suspicion is complicated by other emotions, such as jealousy. Other Elizabethan writers were as preoccupied with suspicion as a pervading social and political influence, reflecting steamy conditions in which intrigue, espionage and calumny flourished. Francis Bacon wrote an essay on the subject. 'Suspicions amongst thoughts,' he decided, 'are like bats amongst birds; they ever fly by twilight'. Acknowledging the perils of rumour he said, 'suspicion that the mind itself gathers are but buzzes, but suspicions that are artificially nourished by others are stings'. By both writers we are reminded of the consequences of public intervention in private affairs and that in the eyes of a suspecting audience, denial merely compounds guilt.

Secrecy is highly likely to be a feature of cases of suspected child abuse. All involved face an ethical dilemma of whether to conceal or reveal. A range of emotions, such as jealousy, disgust, revenge or despair, can motivate 'whistle blowers' (Bok, 1978, 1982). Open secrets contained within a small community can leak into wider circulation through chance events and accidents, such as taking the wrong roll of holiday snaps to the chemist for processing. Even when an abuse inquiry is under way, parents will frequently conceal an accusation from the wider family and the outside world. Unblemished though they may be, mothers, child victims and the wider family may be left with a sense of having been betrayed by those they trusted. Children also conceal the progress of suspicion from friends and feel uneasy under the knowing gaze of schoolteachers. Who knows and thinks what?

Suspicion is rarely perceived as a fleeting, isolated episode; it is a process, a contagion whose progress along different routes will depend upon how and with respect to whom it is incubated. In order to stay alive it must spread; it may be inflamed by local gossip or it may catch fire in the hot wind of a national scare. Just as the 'Careless Talk Costs Lives' campaign of 1940 introduced paranoia to the country post office, so, today, child molesters lurk outside every school gate. An important part of this study has been to understand how the perspectives of parents and professionals are enshrouded by this miasma of suspicion.

The relationship between perspectives and 'meaning'

In seeking to define social and behavioural processes, ethnographic researchers and social psychologists have tended to focus on the mechanisms by which individuals interact, communicate and influence one another, rather than attempting to assess the importance of individual perspectives. The way parents define, interpret and give social meaning to their situation at any moment is closely related to previous experience, even to the peculiarities of their own upbringing, so that faced with any unexpected difficulty they will bring to bear familiar, previously successful strategies. In most cases an allegation of child abuse will introduce such trauma into parents' lives that they will have no strategy adequate to cope with it. In fraught domestic circumstances professionals must learn to distinguish between information or facts and the perspectives participants bring to bear on that information (Hammersley and Atkinson, 1983). As we shall see, misconceptions may endure throughout the entire process of a child abuse inquiry.

Faced with such trauma, parents may respond by defending their lifestyle or by using careless arguments to counter the accusation. Schatzman and Strauss (1955, 1973) suggest that coping in traumatic situations is assisted by attributing events to external causes, for example by considering them someone else's responsibility. Difficulties arise, however, when society rejects such explanations and a different stance has to be adopted. These manoeuvres may involve attempts to deny and conceal behaviour and may result in self-induced paranoia, as Lemert (1962) shows in his study of alcoholism. Those involved in deviant behaviour develop strategies for managing uncertain situations by comparing their own position with others they identify as 'like-minded' (Becker 1963).

Criminological studies of deviance have also explored adaptation in stressful situations, particularly those used by young offenders. Matza and Sykes (1957) describe several 'techniques of neutralisation' adopted by delinquents to excuse or justify anti-social behaviour. A similar analysis has been applied by Mary de Young (1988) to American paedophiles whom she demonstrates acknowledge that their behaviour is illegal, but engage in sophisticated techniques to mask their deviance and present themselves as orthodox.

Goffman (1963) explores the defensive strategies employed by those who feel flawed and degraded. Avoidance strategies may involve blocking communication, pleading ignorance or trivialising the significance of an action (so that shooting so-and-so didn't much matter, 'because he was old anyway'). Specific to child abuse, Bentovim (1987) reminds us that accused parents may be struggling with the effects of 'psychic numbing' which can follow the trauma of an investigation, as well as the more common expressions of anxiety, depression and a feeling of worthlessness.

These contexts will inevitably affect the views of those accused of child abuse. The combination of social and psychological factors and ambivalence about their situation in a damning climate makes parents' perspectives complicated and fluid. The concepts used to explore the issue in question must therefore reflect this complexity, but before fashioning them we need to consider the strengths, weaknesses and usefulness to our purpose of previous studies.

The relevance of other studies

There has been a growing interest in parents' experiences and perceptions of social work generally, but few studies have focused on incidents of suspected child abuse (Fisher, Marsh and Phillips, 1986). One exception is Brown (1986) who examined parental perceptions in such situations and found that parents were highly critical of the performance of social workers. They felt they were given too little information, that social workers were insufficiently honest and that too slight account had been taken of the difficulties families faced. Visits often left parents feeling anxious, fearful and low in self-esteem. On the other hand, the consequence of developing a warm relationship with the social worker was anxiety that the social worker might abandon families once the abuse inquiry was over, leaving them without effective help. The studies of trauma previously discussed emphasise the need to deal sensitively with people in order to mitigate long-term risk; the structure of child abuse inquiries may be usefully considered in this light (Bourne, 1970; Raw, 1989).

Corby (1987) studied a large northern metropolitan social services department and interviewed parents who were the subject of child abuse investigations. He found that the route suspicion followed influenced parental perspectives. Initial referral by a hospital was highly stigmatising and contact with the police particularly distressing. However, he identified as most worrying the lack of information parents received from social workers, a finding which echoes the previous study as well as those by the Social Services Inspectorate (DHSS, 1986) and Prosser (1992) who demonstrated that parents considered themselves to be guilty until proved innocent. In short, many parents felt they were kept in the dark. Although these issues have also been highlighted in the *Cleveland Report,* as subsequent abuse inquires in Rochdale and the Orkneys have shown, the messages are slow getting home .

Information problems seem to be a common feature of child-care services. In marked contrast, parental participation in the field of health and education is now viewed as beneficial to children's development and hospitalised children are tended, wherever possible, by parents (Plowden, 1967; Menzies-Lyth, 1988). But, while recent child care legislation has emphasised the role of natural parents in the care of absent children and encouraged 'shared care', little has been done to discover whether clients are satisfied or how much they know about what is going on. One suspects that 'could do better' might be scrawled on much social work activity. There are, of course, some exceptions: Thoburn (1980) was able to demonstrate a high degree of consensus between parents and social workers about perceptible improvements in a family situation when children went 'home on trial', but, in contrast, Shaw (1987) examined the perspectives of prisoners' children and their families and came to the conclusion that everyone was caught 'in a web of punishment'. Packman, Randall and Jacques (1986) also scrutinised the problems faced by parents as consumers of social services' intervention, noting a feeling of powerlessness even when arrangements were 'voluntary'.

At Dartington, we have consistently stressed the importance of the client's perspective. In *Lost in Care,* which scrutinised 450 children passing through local authority care, we found that parental participation diminished over time and that their uneasy relationship with social services reflected previous, often stressful, confrontations. In *Access Disputes in Child-Care,* events were examined from the parental viewpoint and it was demonstrated that it was possible for families to feel satisfied with social services' intervention even when decisions were not in their favour. Although the experience was frequently painful, parents saw the value of a court appearance when seeking an access order. It left them with the sense that their views had been properly considered.

A number of studies have examined the extent to which parents actually participate in child abuse inquiries. One London Borough which encourages parents to attend child abuse meetings concluded that both parents and professionals found participation useful and informative (London Borough of Greenwich 1986). However, such participation can only be fruitful if social work practice is much improved, especially with regard to the chairing of meetings, giving parents information and permitting them to take an active part in the proceedings. These conclusions are supported by more recent evidence (Brazil and Steward, 1990; Shemmings and Thoburn, 1990).

Two studies of more relevance to us in that they compare aspects of parents' and professionals' perspectives in abuse situations are those under-taken in York by Bell and Sinclair (1993) and in Oregon by Shireman, Grossnickle, Hinsey and White (1990). Bell and Sinclair looked at 50 cases in which families were invited to attend case conferences and 33 in which they were not. It emerged from interviews with parents and relatives that those participating felt they had better relations with individual social workers and were more likely to regard the system as fair. However, they were no more enamoured of social services and their plans than were those who had been excluded from the process. For the professionals, the experience of parents attending conferences served to reduce general anxieties about participation, but it was a source of continuing concern that professional discussion tended to be inhibited and the interests of the child less central.

The Oregon study looked at the differences in information gathered from social work records and from interviews with families that had received protective services. They found a high degree of agreement on factual matters, such as the identity of perpetrators and placements of children, but less similarity where judgements and impressions were concerned, such as whether families had problems or what services had been provided. Key practice distinctions, such as between counselling and family therapy, were not recognised at all by parents. In terms of continued risk to children, records noted more cause for concern than was acknowledged by parents. In follow-up interviews, researchers heard no parental reports of further abuse, whereas official records showed that 19% of the families had received further services and another 18% had been scrutinised following concern for the children's welfare. Thus social workers are more likely than parents to view the child as being 'at risk' and to regard preventative action as having been taken.

While the research literature indicates the kinds of responses expected from parents and professionals, only two of the studies cited compare perspectives, and only one explores the changing patterns among participants as the abuse enquiry proceeds. This study seeks to fill the gaps by making a wider comparison than the York and Oregon research and by analysing shifts in perception over time.

Conclusions

The review of the contexts in which parental perspectives are fashioned indicates some of the issues we are likely to encounter in examining the perspectives of parents suspected of child abuse. Cross-cultural and historical studies highlight the changing and varied definitions of abuse and the importance of the conditions in which child rearing takes place. The ways children are brought up will reflect the socio-economic structure, values and beliefs of particular societies. Irrespective of the suspicion, therefore, we need to ask, would the outcomes of an abuse investigation be identical for families from ethnic groups or socio-economic backgrounds similar to those of the investigating professionals?

The literature also suggests that we need to be aware of the climate of moral panic created by recent child abuse scandals and their subsequent investigations. In this atmosphere of fear, social workers conducting investigations not only dread discovering something unsavoury within the family but fear a public scandal if cases are mismanaged. General anxiety also encourages suspicion to light upon innocent or ambiguous parenting behaviour. The uncertainty surrounding any investigation will, therefore, influence not only how social workers and other professionals approach parents but also affect the willingness of agencies to co-operate with one another and view the contribution of others sympathetically.

On the other hand, coping with an accusation of child abuse is fraught with difficulties, irrespective of whether the suspicion is well-founded or not. Even if a parent is articulate and experienced in confronting professionals, the intervention and monitoring of his or her private life can have many repercussions. Few of us could throw open our most private and intimate territories without some slight unease as to what a stranger might think. The rubber wet-suit hanging behind the bedroom door or the ribald rhymes on *his* and *hers* bathing suits bring forth apologetic giggles. For those with much to hide, the defensive strategies against unwelcome intrusions may be numerous, varied and sometimes unexpected. Even innocent parents, caught unawares, may resort to lying, while the guilty may reveal 'truths' in coded or hidden messages. The main problem posed for agency intervention is the interpretation of such reactions.

Finally, the area of parental and children's rights is highly emotive, nowhere more than in child abuse situations. Decision making requires the skills of Machiavelli, the wisdom of Solomon, the compassion of Augustine and the hide of a tax inspector. Making decisions proves to be something of a balancing act for professionals. Taking into account parental perspectives involves surrendering a degree of control to the powerless. It is clear that there may be considerable contrasts between what actually happens when agencies intervene in a family and what parents perceive to be happening. Satisfaction with the outcome of a case may not be the best indicator of a good resolution and parents may feel they have had a fair deal even if their wishes are overruled. Conversely, others may rejoice in professional impotence and frustration. Mishandling by professionals may so antagonise families from the start of an intervention that the prospect of co-operation is always slender; the outcome of a case, in terms of what will happen to the child and to parental well-being and the chances of 'working together' may be irredeemably prejudiced from the first.

Summary Points

1 Parenting behaviour in different societies varies considerably. Even within communities, class, race and religious belief will affect the way children and adolescents are reared. Each societal group applies its own criteria when identifying behaviour which is violating to children. What constitutes desirable behaviour among the young may be hotly debated, but the experience of sexual violation or physical violence is rarely condoned.

2 Research has suggested that family poverty and situational stress which help precipitate child abuse can be remedied by good relationships within the family. Certain factors precipitate abuse, but in identical circumstances others protect children from violation.

3 Definitions of child abuse change over time. Poor parenting behaviour attracts attention, but little is written about good parental practice or what constitutes family strength.

4 Anxieties over child abuse lend themselves to interpretation in terms of 'moral panic'. Such an analysis serves as a reminder that cool objectivity, wariness of accepted explanations and tolerance of different lifestyles should inform any investigation.

5 Suspicion, 'the partial or unconfirmed belief that something is wrong or someone is guilty', is viewed as a social process, with its own dynamics. Suspicion is triggered, gathers momentum, is fanned by gossip and anxiety, ebbs and flows, becomes public and compels even the disbelieving to investigate.

6 Parents' responses to abuse accusations will vary. Events may be attributed to external causes, the seriousness of incidents may be neutralised.

7 All the contexts discussed will affect the views of those involved in a child abuse investigation. Thus, parental perspectives will be complex and changeable.

8 While research literature indicates the kinds of responses expected from professionals and parents involved in child abuse structures, few studies compare perspectives over time.

Chapter 3

Negotiating research access to child protection agencies

Negotiations to set up a child abuse research project are of little interest in themselves. But in a context where there is a mandatory requirement for inter-agency work and where uncertainties about good practice abound, the difficulties of mounting such investigations have wider implications. They illuminate the contrasting ideologies of the professions involved, highlight the problems of achieving co-operation and further elaborate the context in which investigations are undertaken.

In order to conduct the research, we needed to contact parents suspected of child abuse and recently confronted. For access to families we were heavily dependent on the co-operation of all involved in child protection work, at a time when the increasing demands of students and statisticians were making agencies extremely cautious about granting research requests. Indeed, a failure to secure such co-operation has delayed or curtailed many studies. Such hesitancy is also attributable to the strain the business of research can sometimes place on already over-stretched resources, difficulties compounded in this study because we wished to work simultaneously with more than one agency. Further, co-operation among professional groups is affected by the different perspectives each one holds regarding the value of research and the methods thought appropriate for the task. For example, doctors feel comfortable with treatment and 'client' based inquiries, but many senior social workers prefer organisational and management studies.

In the case of this particular study, the multiplicity of agencies involved created additional problems because each erected a different obstacle to access for us to negotiate, each of which indicated much about the ideologies and foibles of the profession responsible for it. It soon became apparent that scaling one hurdle did not make life any easier at the next. How, then, did we gain access to the information we sought?

Initial optimism about gaining access

Two local authorities participated in the study. In each, we held meetings with senior social services staff during which we explained our intentions and sought co-operation. A clear outline of the research aims and methods was made available and we stressed the limited demands the work would place on staff once cases had been identified.

Fortunately, in both cases the directors of social services and middle management quickly became committed to the study and their support proved crucial in securing the co-operation of other agencies less familiar with research demands, particularly the Area Child Protection Committee. This multi-disciplinary group, responsible for co-ordinating child protection work within a geographical area, proved significant since it created a forum for professionals to voice their concerns about our study as well as to propose ways forward. For example, some disquiet was expressed regarding the value of the project: would a qualitative study of 30 cases be sufficient to produce general findings? Would the research condition procedures and performance, generating a 'Hawthorne' effect?

There was also anxiety about methodological issues. Some Committee members doubted that parents suspected of child abuse would unburden themselves on such a sensitive subject; indeed some professionals felt the study would simply prove impractical, particularly if we attempted to interview minority ethnic families. Some practitioners were concerned that the study would upset the fragile relationship between families and agency staff. In particular, it was feared that parents might manipulate the researchers into an advisory, counselling or adversarial role, thus making the already harassed professional's job even more difficult.

Practical concerns were compounded by ethical worries, particularly over the issue of confidentiality. For example, both medical and social workers were uneasy that we might unearth fresh information concerning child abuse, and that unsavoury findings might be allowed to shelter behind research anonymity. They sought assurances that the relevant authorities would be informed of any new revelations of that sort. Social services, as well as the legal and medical representatives, were also worried about the ways in which families would be identified and referred to us for scrutiny. In particular, they were anxious that their clients' rights to privacy would be upheld and that names of parents under suspicion of child abuse would be kept private.

Finally, the police raised a different issue, namely that the research should not interfere with their ability to obtain evidence or in any way prejudice investigations. They feared that the research presence could alert the guilty to the need to disguise their behaviour or change their statements, thus hindering efforts to gain convictions.

Of course, there were no fool-proof procedures by which these difficulties might be obviated, but by involving the Area Child Protection Committee in the design of our procedures for approaching families and by developing a policy of limited confidentiality, at least it was possible to secure support for the study and acknowledgement of its value for practitioners. Confidence was also bolstered by the success of previous Dartington studies in sensitive child-care areas, such as maximum security, access disputes and residential care. Indeed, the Committee members in both local authorities not only came to support the research but shouldered the task of persuading and briefing colleagues 'back at the ranch'.

Despite these auspicious beginnings, however, several months into the research we were still struggling to comply with the request from the Area Child Protection Committee that we should gain the understanding and co-operation of all agencies involved in child abuse inquiries. We encountered different organisational structures as well as variations in procedures and practices within each service. These differences affected the ability of senior management to ensure the collaboration of more junior staff, so that for all services, with the exception of the police, agreement and directives from on high were no guarantee of individual staff co-operation. If we were to gain access to families, much more was necessary. The next stage was to convince local agency staff of the integrity of the research, the efficacy and value of the study and the importance of referring cases to us.

Agency involvement: social services

Social services were, of course, key to the study as they play such a pivotal role in child abuse work. We spent much time with them setting up the research. However, we were to find that the reasons for selecting the two authorities, that is their contrasting geographical areas and organisational structures, militated against a swift start. In the inner city area, a dense population and cultural diversity had encouraged the development of a decentralised service. Neighbourhood offices were scattered within walking distance of their clients, and housing, health and education departments sheltered under the same roof. The price of these gains in local accessibility, however, was the relative isolation of small social work teams, who were all too easily overwhelmed by the rising tide of child protection work, a situation exacerbated by staffing problems which frequently resulted in cases remaining unallocated. Indeed, some neighbourhood offices used private agency social workers.

Because child abuse referrals were so numerous, it was thought that sufficient cases would be forthcoming if we focused on just one neighbour-hood office, a decision which had the additional bonus for social workers of minimising the disruptive effect of the study. Although the first office we selected would have yielded many child abuse cases, staffing difficulties proved greater than we had anticipated and the research initiative began to crumble. Staff became divided in their support for the study: some keen for new knowledge, others fearing scrutiny of their practice and the possibility that our involvement would jeopardise their relationship with families. Industrial action and high levels of staff stress and sickness created worse problems, with the result that we were eventually driven back to senior social services management in search of a new and more co-operative location. These frustrations delayed by six months the start of the inner city study, until two nearby neighbourhood offices came to our rescue.

The Shire county differed considerably from the urban authority. For example, although committed to a policy of decentralisation, the wide scattering of its settlements meant there was no basis for a neighbourhood office system, and instead the area was divided into eight large social work teams. Cases of suspected child abuse did not dominate social workers' case loads to the same extent as in the city, so that to generate sufficient referrals, we were recommended to work with two contrasting district offices, one urban the other rural, as well as with the social work department of the local hospital. This arrangement yielded sufficient cases and a wide range of referrals.

Having gained the co-operation of senior management in both local authorities, we needed to persuade area managers and local staff to refer cases to us and allow us to read their case files. We needed to know not only the agencies' formal procedures but their informal working methods. For example, it was important to discover how much discretion individuals exercised, whether some suspected abuse cases were monitored informally or whether all were referred to social services. How would a health visitor react to rejection and emotional abuse springing from faulty bonding between a mother and new baby? What would be a probation officer's reaction if anxieties were raised because a client's eight year old son appeared listless, inactive, unresponsive and never smiled? What would a teacher do on reading a pupil's essay which described 'questionable' sexual activity? Would any of these professionals speak of their concern with the parents before referring the case to social services or the police? If they did, how could the research become involved at this early stage?

To answer these questions, we examined each local authority's policy documents and formal procedures and held discussions on the ways in which cases were handled. Scrutiny of child protection manuals for the two local authorities revealed contrasting procedures. The inner city area had already rewritten its manual incorporating the Government guidelines, while the Shire county was still using their 1984 handbook, although it was updated during the study period. The inner city borough's manual was unequivocal on the course of action that care workers should follow when child abuse was suspected and gave a directive that both the neighbourhood office social work team and the police should be informed. Could we then assume that initial concerns of child abuse were always dealt with by social services or police and that referrals for our study would all come through these two agencies? In contrast, the handbook used by the Shire county gave individual agencies considerable discretion, particularly when concern about child abuse was minimal.

These complexities not only reflect the sensitive nature of cases and amount of work involved, they were frequently presented as barriers to co-operation. But there is more to it (Hallett and Birchall, 1992): social workers are, after all, perfectly familiar with child protection – as Gibbons and colleagues (1993) have found, there are 160,000 investigations each year – but they are less confident about their professional status and responsibilities in such a delicate area. Social work has no discrete domain of expertise; it has an eclectic knowledge base and relies on a management structure that removes senior personnel from direct work with clients. Thus, social work's role *vis à vis* children's families can be unclear and a tension exists in its interaction with other more powerful agencies.

Certain aspects of our negotiations with social services reflected this situation. It is significant that commitment to the research varied considerably among individuals, that the initiative collapsed altogether in one area office and that the arguments used to resist participation centred upon the risks research posed to the special relationship between practitioner and client, the need for confidentiality to protect clients' rights and the fear of opening files to wider scrutiny. These problems seem to be increasing and should be kept in mind when sensitive research investigations are envisaged. Access cannot be guaranteed nor sophisticated methodologies maintained.

We now consider the working practices of the other agencies involved in the identification of suspected child abuse and the difficulties these posed for the research. Did they share the initial reluctance of some social workers?

Agency involvement: the medical profession

Health visitors

The health visitor service was created in 1946 by the *National Health Service Act* when local health authorities were obliged to recruit and train nurses 'for the purpose of giving advice as to the care of young children'. Their duties included visiting and monitoring the development of all children from birth to school entry and, by informing and assisting parents, promoting sound health care practices.

Health visitors, although linked either to a health centre or a general practitioner, are supervised by a nurse manager who also supervises the work of school nurses. Health visitors' case loads vary but responsibility for anything between 300 to 500 families is not uncommon. The majority of children and their families raise few child protection concerns, although, if suspicions are aroused, it becomes the responsibility of the nurse manager to refer the case to the relevant agency.

The general public have come to acknowledge and value the work of health visitors and readily accept them into their homes. As a result, this professional group is frequently able to identify very early indicators of child abuse, neglect or failure to thrive.

School nurses

School nurses are also part of the health visiting service and take over the role of screening children's health and development when children enter the school system. The duties of the school nurse range from advising and informing children on general health issues to administering routine medical examinations. Caring nurses offer a safe haven for children at school should they need an aspirin or a comforting shoulder to cry on. In this way, the school nurse may become the receptor of children's closely guarded secrets.

Unlike health visitors, school nurses have an opportunity to share any anxieties about a child's welfare and safety with teachers. In fact, staff room gossip may serve to heighten or dissipate suspicions of child abuse and thus act as a filtering process prior to any referral to social services or the police.

When seeking the co-operation of health visitors and school nurses for our research, we encountered practice differences within the two local authorities. For example, the nurse adviser for child protection in the inner city borough emphasised the official procedures. It was argued that health visitors and school nurses should never personally discuss their suspicions of child abuse with the parent before consulting social services. We were assured these practice guidelines were always closely followed. Such a situation would mean no research referrals coming directly from the health visitors or school nurses in that neighbourhood.

In contrast, health visitors and school nurses in the Shire county were expected to react more cautiously depending on the degree of suspicion aroused, although any concern was to be reported to the nurse adviser. Thus, the nurse adviser decided on what action was to be taken and was to a considerable extent autonomous. She or he decided whether to remain silent while monitoring a child's behaviour, whether to explore concerns with parents, whether to refer the case to social services or whether to convene a child protection meeting. Thus, in the Shire county, health visitors allowed our study early access to families under suspicion since they frequently referred cases to us.

Doctors

> Child abuse is now a medical diagnosis and doctors are taking responsibility not only for repairing the broken bones but also for ensuring, in a wider context, the child's protection and safety (Hobbs, 1992).

It is a doctor's responsibility to recognise child abuse and decide when to involve other agencies in the investigation. Doctors' involvement starts early in a child's life, indeed, in some cases before conception. Their role is wide ranging and includes preventative work, such as working with drug, alcohol and tobacco abusing mothers, as well as identifying and treating all types of abuse once children are born.

Some doctors have a more specialised role. For example, in the inner city community, paediatricians based in health centres liaised closely with health visitors, schools, social services and general practitioners. This cohesion of professionals was not achieved in the Shire county where general practitioners took a supervisory role.

Hospitals

Whilst paediatricians, radiologists and urologists may be foremost in identifying abuse or neglect, physical abuse is the commonest pattern of violation seen by hospital doctors. In fact, one in ten of pre-school children attending accident and emergency departments present injuries which result from maltreatment (Hobbs, 1992). But hospital personnel referring a case to other agencies rarely raise their suspicions directly with parents. Doctors shy away from confrontation and it is left to hospital social workers to discuss concerns with parents, hence their involvement in the study.

Child psychiatric and psychological services

We were also aware that early suspicions of child abuse may surface or be referred to the child psychological and psychiatric services. Discussions with educationalists revealed that both local authorities ran a school psychological service responsible for children with learning difficulties. The educational psychologist's involvement in suspected child abuse was restricted to providing the social services with an assessment of a child's cognitive and behavioural development. Child psychiatrists, on the other hand, can be involved in all stages of child abuse proceedings. For example, they frequently carry out delicate disclosure work with children and run family therapy, as well as working with child and adult victims. In addition, they may be called to act as expert witnesses during court proceedings.

The child psychiatric provision differed between the two local authorities. Facilities in the city were hospital centred, whereas in the Shire county locally based child guidance clinics provided a psychiatric service for children and families. Child guidance personnel agreed to refer cases of suspected abuse for our scrutiny.

Having got this far and in the process obtained the support of the Area Child Protection Committees as well as the enthusiastic commitment of health visitors, school nurses, hospital consultants, general practitioners and community paediatricians it was somewhat galling to discover that there was still another hurdle to overcome. The approval of the local Medical Ethical Committee was essential, and, before they would give it, they required us to adapt our approach. The Shire county adhered to formal procedures and, after our initial presentation to the Committee, sought written clarification on a number of issues before final approval was given. In the inner city, our research request was presented on our behalf by the senior clinical medical officer and, in due course, we were informed that we had been successful.

Once again, it can be seen how the negotiations we had to undertake and the arguments used to encourage and deter the research reflect the position of the particular profession in child abuse work. Problems are created in a medical context less out of professional insecurity than as a result of the contrast between child protection and more ordinary medical practice. The hierarchical structure of the medical profession is antipathetic to sharing information with other agencies; the lack of accurate and reliable diagnostic methods, the need for haste and the fact that patients' records may be designed to conceal rather than illustrate the issues at stake, all present doctors and nurses with unfamiliar problems.

Having secured the co-operation of the medical practitioners, we turned our attention to the probation officers and the police.

Agency involvement: the probation service

Probation officers are agents of the court system and may become involved in cases of suspected child abuse by a number of routes. For example, once an individual convicted of offences against children is discharged from prison, it is the responsibility of the probation service to inform the local authority about his or her proposed residence. Probation officers are also involved in supervising offenders and, in this way, may bring to light behaviour which places children at risk, for instance, when a convicted perpetrator moves into a household that includes children. The probation service is also responsible to the court for the supervision of children following contested custody cases. This is often a time of acute distress for both parents and allegations of child abuse may be identified or, indeed, used as a weapon by one party against the other. When this arises, the court welfare officer, who is part of the probation service, involves other agencies to ensure the safety of the child.

Discussions with the probation service management and staff in both local authorities showed the procedure in handling suspicions of abuse to be similar. Once probation officers became suspicious, cases were referred to social services and from that source our referrals were obtained.

Agency involvement: the police and the crown prosecution service

Increasingly, child protection procedures cross the boundary between criminal and family law, and, since there are considerable differences in the way case material is handled in each arena (not least because the burden of proof in criminal law remains much greater than in civil law) great sensitivity is nowadays demanded of those child protection agencies whose work crosses the old divide.

For example, the primary role of the police is to enforce the criminal law, protect the community and bring offenders to justice, but they are directly involved in family life, particularly in incidents of domestic violence, and also become aware of suspected child abuse when other professionals refer cases to them. Members of the public approach them directly or as a result of their routine duties.

Once possible abuse has been identified, the police seek to determine whether a criminal offence has been committed, to identify whoever is responsible and to secure the best possible evidence for a conviction. A decision must be made about whether information which might possibly lead to prosecution is passed to the Crown Prosecution Service or handled solely in conjunction with social services. If the former, the Prosecution Service must decide whether there is sufficient evidence for prosecution and whether it is in the public interest and in the interest of the child. Mishandling of information at this stage can wreck the chances of a successful prosecution.

To ensure the safety of the child, some information gathered by the police during an investigation is shared with other agencies, including social services. If criminal procedures are pending, the police must ensure that the prosecution case is not prejudiced and social services must take care that new information, for example generated during child therapy, does not undermine Prosecution Service efforts to deal with the alleged offender. The range of information gathered in such cases may be considerable, including medical evidence gathered by the police surgeon, photographs of physical injuries and transcripts of interviews.

The police in both local authorities held social services in considerable esteem and expressed a commitment to the guidance offered in *Working Together* and the Home Office Circular 52/1988. However, there were some differences in practice. In the Shire county, the police were worried that the research would interfere with their ability to gather 'good enough' evidence for criminal prosecutions. As a result, we were advised not to become involved early in any case under police investigation as we would consequently be liable to be subpoenaed to give evidence. In fact, the police in this authority were unwilling to refer families, irrespective of whether or not their investigation was completed, although they did provide information on individual cases referred to us from other sources.

In contrast, the police in the inner city, while recognising the importance of preserving evidence, had recently changed their policy from being offender-oriented to being victim-centred. Consequently, research intended to improve services for abuse victims was highly valued and full co-operation for case referrals and file scrutiny was given. As the police force is a highly structured organisation, securing the agreement of senior management meant that local offices participated. We left our meeting with them feeling that, for one agency at least, gaining acceptance for the research and establishing a referral process was not an issue.

By comparison with social services and the medical professions, the interests of the police and probation in child abuse cases are more clear cut. Their principal interest is in prosecution of abusive acts and the provision of services for offenders and victims. Hence it was possible for them to be far more consistent in their response to our research interest. Decisions were routed through a hierarchical structure, often from a central office, although there was some scope for individuals at the local level to interpret them as they chose. The issue of confidentiality in these conditions was seen more as a matter of protecting the integrity of any criminal investigation than defending clients' privacy.

Agency involvement: education

Finally, we needed to examine the role of the schools. Because children spend the greater part of their lives in the classroom, teachers are in a good position to act as observers and confidantes. But what happens when teachers become concerned as to a child's welfare and some form of abuse is suspected? Were anxieties raised directly with parents, and if so, would schools refer cases to the research study? Here again there was considerable variety between schools in each local authority and those in any one area. Some employ counsellors who are specifically trained to listen to children and act as their advocate in dealing with adults or in enabling and empowering children themselves to deal with them. School counsellors are involved in identifying and working with all forms of suspected abuse, covering the whole process from disclosure to therapy.

Once again, discussions with the area education officers uncovered similarities and differences between the two local authorities. For example, there was a concern in both about the unevenness of child abuse referrals to social services: some schools referring high numbers, others very few. Differences in school organisation clearly affected the way suspicions of abuse were being dealt with. For instance, at the outset, the inner city borough employed social workers within the schools who worked with parents. In the course of the research, local government in the inner city area was reorganised and the schools participating in our study resurrected the practice of using educational welfare officers as part of system similar to that in the Shire county. Educational welfare officers have a wide range of responsibility, much of which lies outside the school. However, three schools in the Shire county also employed the services of a school counsellor and here issues of child abuse assumed a high profile. We were assured that members of the teaching staff would follow the Department for Education circular (4/88) and would not be expected to discuss with parents the possibility of child abuse although, in talking to head-teachers, we found practice was occasionally idiosyncratic.

The main problem we faced in enjoining the co-operation of teachers was their reluctance to appreciate the significance of the study for their own profession. Of course, teachers are concerned about abused children and take strong action when necessary but abuse is only one of several problems they have to deal with. Children's poor attendance, general neglect, learning difficulties and disturbed behaviour tend to be regarded more seriously than mild abuse and, of course, are far more common phenomena. Thus, for teachers, it was their ideology that became the source of resistance to our research. Was abuse and our research worth the time, given its marginal significance to the daily work of teachers? In primary schools, there was a further serious worry: would information given to researchers damage relations between school and parents? Interestingly, of all of the professional groups involved, primary school head teachers were the most reluctant to release the names of pupils at risk. As schools tend to be autonomous institutions, they presented particular difficulties. A number of primary school heads refused to co-operate and there was little we could do to circumvent their refusal. Secondary schools, in contrast, were more pragmatic and securing co-operation here was easier.

The breakthrough

At the end of each of these many meetings, we were frequently left with a huge sense of relief, certain that all the problems had at last been ironed out and referrals would start to arrive within a matter of days. But no: weeks went by between an agency receiving their batch of research notification cards and a case being referred to us. We were to discover that management lacked confidence to proceed and that agency staff wanted a lot of time in which to reassure themselves that our research would do no harm.

Eventually a pattern emerged. One day the telephone would ring and a case would very tentatively be handed over. Gradually, in whichever agency had made that contact, confidence would increase and more referrals would follow. On the other hand, in offices where there was greater reluctance to participate or where child abuse claimed only a fraction of their time, extra persuasion was needed to maintain the high profile of the project. Once an agency had referred a family, the follow-up interviews with staff tended to reinforce their commitment.

Among individual members of agency staff the pattern was similar: those brave enough to refer one family were eager to refer more. The importance of the first referral was clear for it signalled a significant breakthrough for the research process; thereafter, the continuing contact with agencies was itself sufficient to guarantee an enduring interest.

The barriers one expects are seldom those that materialise. In this paper, we have picked our way through the forest of child protection services and described the obstacles to our research we had to overcome. In the planning stages we had expected resistance not from professionals but from the parents accused of abusing their children. These fears were misplaced; fewer than a third of parents eventually contacted for inclusion failed to participate. We, therefore, found ourselves asking a different question. Why were professionals so reluctant to participate and why did the focus of their anxiety vary so greatly?

Conclusions

This lengthy exploration of the difficulties experienced in establishing a study of suspected child abuse is offered not just because it catalogues the obstacles but because it furthers our discussion of the context in which abuse investigations are conducted. The complexity of interagency co-operation in the early identification and investigation of abuse illustrates the different interpretations of need and parents' rights held by different agencies and the ways that those accused receive conflicting messages. The arrival of researchers with an interest in child abuse is far more threatening. The consequences of a lacklustre strategy or signal deficiency in child protection work are more serious in terms of potential public outcry than in almost any other area of social work; naturally, therefore, there was a deep-seated wariness of the consequences of our research .

Our diary of negotiations shows how sophisticated are the methods used by organisations to dissipate threats and reduce anxiety. They have been well charted, not least by Menzies-Lyth (1988) in a study of how nurses cope with stress in their daily interaction with patients. In previous studies, we have noted how research is often dismissed by practitioners as being of little practical relevance or is said to be based on situations that have since changed. In addition, a stalling policy can cause the threat of any investigation to recede. However, the response in this case was slightly different. The research was welcomed at one level in the organisation, usually at the most senior, but the logistics of referral were made extremely cumbersome.

We have argued that difficulties arise from ideological differences between agencies. Teachers, for example, are trained to take a broad view of children's lives and often claimed not to understand why minor bruising should cause such concern when illiteracy, delinquency and disturbed behaviour did not. Equally to be reckoned with is each profession's need for security and strength and the extent to which ideology, membership and organisation correspond. The police, for example, appeared confident and consistent, had a clear if limited focus on the problem and gave definite answers. Social workers, while strong on ideology, espouse a more participatory professional ethic and as a consequence were dogged by role conflicts.

The conclusion from our experience in setting up the project are that, in child protection work, every group faces problems of professional insecurity and appropriate role. Child abuse is a difficult area for everybody. But the source of the problem is different in each case. Thus, inter-agency co-operation in the early stages of abuse investigations is not what it seems. The police stress the dangers of contaminating evidence. The medical profession is unfamiliar with situations where diagnosis has no clear research base, where case notes are expected to be shared with others and where a patient's history may be designed to conceal rather than to reveal. Social workers, on the other hand, are familiar with protection work but are insecure about their professional status. They are, to use Etzioni's (1969) term, a semi-profession with an ambiguous area of expertise based on eclectic knowledge. Child protection work has done much to bring definition to their area of competence and responsibility but they have still to learn to cope with the fear of failure.

Summary points

1 For the research to be mounted, negotiations with several agencies were necessary. The nature of the difficulties that had to be overcome illumi-nates the contrasting ideologies of the professions involved, highlights the problems of achieving co-operation and elaborates the context in which investigations are conducted.

2 All agencies expressed concern about the research but the focus of the anxiety varied in each case. Social workers were worried about client confidentiality and relationships with clients; police emphasised the dangers of contaminated evidence; medical staff drew attention to their unfamiliarity with the situations to which abuse gives rise ; teachers questioned definitions and thresholds.

3 The barriers erected to setting up the research reflect the sophisticated methods used by organisations to dilute threat and reduce anxiety. The focus of each agency's concern reflected its professional ideology and sense of security.

Chapter 4

Research methods and design

The methodology we devised for this research takes into account the social and cultural contexts described in the opening Chapters and seeks to minimise the difficulty of assessing an individual's perceptions in a climate of moral panic. We deal with the conditions in which suspicions of child abuse incubate, which agencies are involved in an investigation and how the suspicion is made known to parents. We intend to explore whether some strategies of intervention are better than others and whether the early stages of an investigation can affect the subsequent outcome of a case. Here we describe the considerations that influenced our analytical approach.

Developing a study design

Several ways of studying parents' perceptions of what is happening in any given set of circumstances are possible. Most obviously, in the case of an abuse investigation, one might canvass all the agencies involved, as well as parents, and attempt to determine how different strategic approaches to abuse affect parents' attitudes and the degree of their willingness to co-operate. However, we knew from our studies of access terminations and from research in which agency policy was examined in relation to client response that there was no evidence of a clear connection between professional method and customer satisfaction (Millham, Bullock, Hosie and Little, 1989). The resistance to classification of the differences between the strategies adopted by local authorities was a further obstacle, and, in any event, it was realised that such an approach would produce no detailed information about the way parents' attitudes changed over time. Past experience, therefore, suggested a qualitative approach.

We were anxious to take a broad view of the family. Rather to their detriment, many previous studies of child neglect and abuse have concentrated on the child's mother (Browne and Saqi, 1987): fathers, siblings and other family members have received much less attention. We wanted to consider the views of any adult who had assumed a parenting role – the natural father, step-father or cohabitee – as well as others closely involved with the child, such as a grandparent or older sibling. We decided foster parents might also be regarded as parents in certain circumstances. As a result, allegations of abuse concerning either their own or fostered children were included. This widening of the definition of abusive parent in order to deal with individual adaptations also tended to justify an intensive, qualitative study.

Other factors went in favour of an extensive approach. We have indicated how definitions of child abuse vary according to historical setting and cultural context, but there are also administrative criteria to be taken into account. Agencies frequently make use of established categories, such as physical violence/non-accidental injury; neglect; emotional abuse; non-organic failure to thrive and sexual exploitation, and many hold data on the characteristics of the children referred to the child protection system. We would have been remiss to ignore this information.

To make the most of the wealth of recorded data and to be able to assess the frequency and depth of agencies' involvement in investigations, also to examine the dissimilarities between cases and consider how parents responded to the scrutiny of outsiders, we decided to incorporate both an extensive and an intensive dimension into the study. This two-handed approach had the further advantage of enabling us to gather follow-up evidence as an indicator of the outcome of any intervention and to see whether parental perceptions affected what happened in the longer term.

Other research into child abuse has shown that agencies have different and contrasting policies with regard to parental participation in abuse investigations. Procedures have been allowed to evolve in particular social and geographical settings, and have been adapted according to the ideologies of individual members of staff. Policy and practice thus tend to vary on different levels within an organisation. There is disparity, too, at the inter-agency level, such as between police and social services, and within one neighbourhood there may be differences between individual hospitals and day nurseries.

For all those reasons, we chose to concentrate on two local authorities of contrasting geography, demographic profile, administrative and professional organisation, child-care population and child abuse investigation procedures. In selecting them, we looked for areas where the proportion of children on the Child Protection Register was typical, given their socio-demographic make-up and organisational procedures (Little and Gibbons, 1993).

For the research to succeed, it was vital to gain the co-operation and support of all the relevant agencies. Access to cases was understandably difficult to arrange, but, once inside the system, in each agency we were permitted to examine practice guidelines and policy directives as well as staff training programmes. We explored the routes by which an agency became aware of possible child abuse, the extent to which parents were involved and encouraged to participate, and the informal procedures within organisations for dealing with suspected cases, particularly those governing preliminary consultations between agency staff. In addition, we looked at the referral of cases between agencies.

The extensive study

In the extensive study we monitored the progress in one of the participating authorities of a large number of suspected abuse victims through the child protection system. Case files were scrutinised to discover when and where cases surfaced, how different professions compared in their approach and where the burden of work fell. It was a useful exercise in its own right because there was a shortage of information on families suspected of child abuse which extended to how and with what consequences early suspicions were managed. The result is a survey of suspected child abuse which is indicative of national patterns.

We took account of all cases 'seriously considered' by the police, health visitors, social services or probation in one calendar year, that is, all suspected abuse which was investigated and recorded. When suspicions of child abuse were noted in the files of more than one agency they only featured once in our data. Thus, the notes of 168 police cases, 98 health visitors cases, 274 social worker cases and 43 probation cases were examined, giving a study population of 583 children.

As one would expect, records varied in quality between and among different professional groups. Social services' records were usually the most comprehensive; tracing the background of a single family frequently involved the scrutiny of three or four lengthy files. Police information, by contrast, was often confined to a single record sheet and to the timing and nature of reports and alleged offences.

From this data, we were able to identify administrative factors that might contribute towards outcome over and above any influence on the progress of an investigation which might be attributed to parents' perceptions. Before beginning the intensive study it was important to understand, for example, that an accusation against a father led to sterner action being taken than when the mother was suspected. The extensive scrutiny also demonstrated the sheer volume of child protection work being undertaken – more than 160,000 cases a year. Plainly, the way child protection professionals handled a suspicion of abuse had to be judged in this context.

The intensive study

The intensive study relates to 30 families in which 61 children were believed to be at risk of abuse. At the outset, to help us identify those issues parents saw as important, we conducted a pilot study, which explored retrospectively the experiences of four families who had experienced investigation. The results of this preliminary examination were nevertheless sufficient to inform our ideas and help us formulate relevant hypotheses. We also interviewed several mothers and fathers involved with the pressure group Parents Against

Injustice (PAIN), who described the sense of helplessness parents experience when confronted with suspicion.

An immediate problem, once we had begun the intensive study proper, was deciding the composition of the sample. On the basis of the extensive study we knew the range of cases investigated and the relative frequency with which they occurred, but gaining access to families sufficiently early in an investigation required great sensitivity. It was agreed that in order to be certain of their co-operation at the outset we should allow parents to select themselves. All cases in the two selected areas were alerted to our research but freedom of choice whether to participate – or to withdraw – at any stage was considered of paramount importance.

Our groundwork suggested that a number of problems would be encountered. There was anxiety that families accused of physical abuse would be more likely to respond to our request than those suspected of sexual abuse, and that families in which children were chronically neglected, though possibly willing to participate, would be difficult to contact (Lynch and colleagues, 1993). Thus, the self-selection process would be complex and the composition of the group we assembled would be governed by a variety of personal and social factors.

Selecting the families

The procedures we adopted to identify possible families, make contact with them and establish our credentials as independent observers had three stages:

1 After they had been interviewed by a social worker, health visitor, head-teacher, doctor or a police officer, a pre-printed notification card was given to parents by the agency worker. This informed them of our study, gave assurances as to its independence and sought their willingness to participate. Parents could agree to help or instruct the agency to withdraw their names from the research study.

2 The names of those parents who did not withdraw were referred to us. We next sent a letter which explained who we were, declared the object of the research and requested family co-operation. It also sought to arrange a first interview and, in the process, to allay fears about what might be involved.

3 If the response was favourable, we visited parents at home. During the first interview their potential contribution was outlined and the confidentiality and anonymity of the work stressed. Parents were also assured that their consent would be necessary before professionals involved with their case were interviewed or access was sought to confidential files; but they were warned that we were bound by an agreement with the Area Protection Committee to report any additional concerns about the children that might arise.

Finding a representative sample

By these means all 44 families confronted with a suspicion during a specified period received a card requesting help with the study. Thirty eight indicated a willingness to take part. After the explanatory interviews two families withdrew. Hence, despite the initial anxiety that we would not find any

Table 3.1 **Characteristics of families included and excluded in the intensive study**

Family characteristics*	Included	Excluded
Family composition		
Single parent	16	5
Both natural parents	7	5
Reconstituted family	7	4
Ethnic group		
White	23	11
Other+	7	3
Social class		
Middle-class	6	2
Working class	24	12
Parent/s employed	12	3
Known to Agency		
Social Services	20	7
Police	14	4
Not known	5	3
	N=30	**N=14**
Number of children in families	83	38
Considered 'at risk'	61	22
Type of abuse suspected		
Sexual	21	5
Physical	27	13
Emotional	6	0
Neglect	7	4
	N=61	**N=22**

* Not all categories are mutually exclusive.
+ The ethnic origin of families included in the study are described later. Of those excluded; one family was described as mixed race; one was of Vietnamese origin; one was Bengali; and the remainder were white.

parents willing to discuss their predicament, there were 36 cases from which to make a random selection of 30 families for study (the number agreed with the agencies).

To see whether the selected 30 cases and the 61 children considered to be at risk in those families were representative of the range of abuse situations dealt with by child protection agencies, we asked social workers to provide group data on the families who did not wish to participate. The selected 30 were then compared with the 14 exclusions. Table 3.1 compares family composition, race and social class as well as the type of abuse suspected. As can be seen, there is little to distinguish the two groups.

We drew additionally on the findings of the extensive sweep of 583 suspected abuse cases. This had indicated that several types of family were investigated by protection agencies, including some with multiple problems of which abuse was just one aspect. Such cases contrasted with those involving families whose only major difficulty was considered to be the maltreatment of children and others who became the victims of outside perpetrators of child abuse. The group selected for the intensive study reflected this classification.

Other characteristics of the families included in the intensive study

We were surprised by the diversity of the problems participating families faced. The incidence of marital violence (12 cases) and drug or alcohol abuse (8) was high. Eleven mothers had themselves been victims of relatively serious abuse as a child. Health problems were frequent among both parents and children: three mothers had recently suffered a miscarriage, two had cancer, five parents had physical disabilities and seven children had severe learning difficulties. Clearly, any assessment of the influence of parental perceptions on the outcome of the case would have to be made in the context of the severe and multiple problems faced by many families.

Seven families eventually included in the intensive study were from a minority ethnic group: one was Bengali, one was Turkish, one was from Nigeria, two were of Caribbean origin and there were two of mixed race. Understanding cultural influences on the perspectives of parents from ethnic minority groups posed problems which we explore in later chapters. We also encountered communication difficulties in that the Bengali and Turkish families had limited English. The use of interpreters enabled us to conduct interviews but we had to ensure that the views expressed were those of the parent and not of the translator. In certain cases such complication hampered our interpretation of the family situation.

One of our aims was to talk to the children. However, some were simply not old enough to participate; in any case, it would have been unwise to raise the possibility of intra-familial abuse with a five year old. Twenty four of the 61 children thought to be at risk of abuse were below school age; 23 were aged five to nine. We did not stipulate an age below which we would not interview, since the pace of children's cognitive development varies and the passing remarks of a four year old can be very illuminating. Nevertheless, we did not formally interview any child under seven.

It will be seen, therefore, problems of access and relationship notwith-standing, that the intensive study amounted to a prospective scrutiny of a cross-section of families involved in a child abuse investigation. By charting the progress of each case, we were able to examine how parental perspectives were established, how they developed and how they affected case outcome. By examining family history prior to the initial intervention, we were able to assemble and incorporate retrospective data.

Research began at the point when an agency first suspected that child abuse was occurring and made its suspicions known to the family. Many studies in the Department of Health's programme focus on the first case conference; but, as we demonstrate, this important formal stage in the investigation is preceded by much informal interaction which can be a source of great unease among parents.

Interviews

We conducted interviews with key figures in each investigation at various moments in the two year follow-up period. For reasons to be elaborated in Chapter Six they tended to take place near the time of an agency's first investigative interview, the registration of a child or the removal or departure of a family member. In addition to members of the family concerned in each case, we spoke to social workers, teachers, health visitors, doctors, police and mental health workers, similarly at regular intervals. We also attended all the relevant case meetings to explore the nature and consequences of the decisions made. Because factors such as experience, training and support will affect a professional's attitude to child abuse and his or her handling of a case, we sought information on the background, training and general attitudes to child-care of agency workers, before exploring their role as they became involved with families under suspicion. Interviews with agency workers were undertaken with the permission of the family.

Family members were encouraged as much as possible to talk freely during interviews. For example, we invited parents' reactions to the initial accu-sation, how they felt the agency had treated them, how they regarded their circumstances in terms of health and housing, what intra-family support or conflict existed and how they felt about the professionals and other agencies drawn into their lives. Interview schedules included a series of general questions and others very specific to the situations we wished to explore.

We tried to make interviews informal so that they would pass for ordinary social interaction (Hammersley and Atkinson 1983; Woods, 1986). Any other approach would have been very likely to fail, since a number of parents needed considerable encouragement and reassurance before they would talk openly about an incident they felt to be deeply violating and embarrassing. Some were very articulate, some never stopped talking, others were verbally and emotionally inhibited.

Care was taken to prevent distortion (Glaser and Strauss, 1967). Thus, cases were distributed between different researchers and a point was made of declaring their independence from social services and all other statutory authorities – a useful claim to be able to make, especially in contentious cases. Wherever practical, the work of interviewing the different participants in a case, for example, the parents and the agency staff, was also shared among researchers, so providing an additional cross-check on the material, but for consistency each individual participant was always interviewed by the same researcher.

We were concerned that the research process itself might markedly affect the ways professionals, parents and agencies interacted (Hammersley and Atkinson, 1983). There was danger that as a rapport developed between the interviewer and parent, qualitative data could be distorted. It is always the case that the veracity and credibility of data relies on the quality of the interaction between participant and researcher, and that a relationship may develop in which the researcher is perceived as an ally or friend. However, it is likely that this effect diminishes as participants become more familiar with the researcher's role (Bottoms and McClintock, 1973). Our work at Dartington has also shown that the impact of events, such as the removal of a child or the disappearance of the perpetrator of abuse, may well generate trauma sufficient to minimise the impact of any research pressure.

We obtained the permission of family members to tape-record all interviews, and a number consented to the use of videotape. Once transcribed, each interview was discussed by the research team before a decision was made about what information was relevant. The information produced by the interviews was used in assembling a profile of each family and assessing the changes that occurred over the follow-up period and it contributed to a review of the theoretical perspectives described in the previous chapter.

Observations of family life

Some of the most incisive social research has resulted from an investigator living the life of those under investigation (Becker, 1958). Alas, it is extremely difficult to be a participant observer in the life of a family, let alone of one in which child abuse is suspected. The principles and aims of the participant method have obvious attractions nevertheless, and in non-participant observation there exists a viable alternative procedure (Woods, 1986). This can be defined as 'observation, where the people under scrutiny are aware of the researcher's role and as participants become acquainted with and feel at ease with the researcher'. During our research, considerable time was spent with the families, especially in the aftermath of the initial accusation. On these occasions, interaction between family members was carefully noted, generating material that proved invaluable in its own right and provided a further means of checking interview findings.

In our observations of family life we were anxious to gather data on the condition of the child's home. For example, we were interested in circumstances that might make children more vulnerable to parental abuse, such as overcrowding, extreme poverty or the lack of adequate and easily accessible play areas. We assessed the quality of interaction between family members, for instance by scrutinising parental responsiveness to the child at bath-times and meals, and the quality of communication within the family. Of particular interest to us was how the suspicion of child abuse affected the way members of the family interacted with the suspected perpetrator and the supposed victim.

Managing the qualitative data

At the outset, certain referees doubted the viability of the proposal as submitted to the Department of Health, feeling that parental perspectives in the context of suspicion, by definition defied empirical investigation. But since so very little was known on the subject, it was felt that a qualitative investigation must yield something of value.

To have placed too great an emphasis on the qualitative aspects of the intensive study would in any case have been misleading because there are many quantitative components embedded in it. For example, in our scrutiny of reactions to social services' investigation among the 30 families, we identified five commonly-held perspectives on the work of the agencies involved, which were modified and aggregated over time. These we have analysed statistically. As in previous Dartington studies, the quantitative data creates a basis on which to judge the reliability of evidence collected from the 30 families we studied intensively (Bullock, Little and Millham, 1993). Thus, we have developed concepts, typologies and theories from both the quantitative and qualitative data sets and sought to check the validity of the data by cross checking interpretations of the results.

As would be the case in any scrutiny of research data, this analysis of the qualitative material begins with a general review of the evidence. In this initial stage, we were interested to understand the processes and sequences of events affecting parents under suspicion. Gradually, we developed more general concepts and constructed definitions to be used throughout the study.

Some were suggested directly by respondents, others resulted from our qualitative and quantitative interpretation of the data; all evolved as the study progressed. Our procedure then followed the sequence described by Lofland (1971) who suggests that researchers should consider how a problem is dealt with by the subject under study, next construct typologies, then modify the final categories in the light of deviations. Thus, we first considered the social context of the concepts and typologies advanced, asking whether they would hold good in a different situation. Second, we explored the temporal dimensions of these proposals in order to test how far they might be generalised, for example by asking whether the typology made sense later on in the investigative process. Finally we asked those involved in the study how they would refine the concepts and typologies we had produced.

Once we had some confidence in the concepts and typologies developed from the data, we sought to explain why such concepts and typologies were fruitful. To do this, we needed to advance ideas which related the various findings to one another. In this we were helped by the writings of Denzin (1978) who proposed six steps in the development of coherent theory from qualitative research data. First a rough formulation of the phenomenon being scrutinised is advanced, then a more specific hypothesis which explains the phenomenon. Each case is subsequently tested against the hypothesis, which is in turn modified. A theory is fashioned and again revised in the light of exceptional cases.

When examining the experiences of participants in a child abuse investigation, we found families entered the system at different points, could leapfrog or oscillate between various levels of suspicion and exit at one of a number of points. What became clear was that particular events were critical to all parties and could be used as a tool to extract meaning from the abundance of qualitative data. Three moments – the initial confrontation of the parent by the child protection professional, any subsequent gathering of professionals and situations when new information or changed circumstances alters the way a case proceeds, were key in the formation of parental perspectives, and we have written part of the study around these events.

By contrasting parents' perceptions of these events we were able to demonstrate how misunderstanding may arise. For example, following an anonymous phone call alleging rough parental handling, social workers told us they carried out a sympathetic and 'low-key' exploratory interview with the mother. The mother however, felt deeply violated, 'I told him I never hit the children but he wouldn't believe me. He had no right to question Amy, she's only five years old. Not only did he ask her if I ever laid a hand on her, but also if she gets anything to eat and whether I go out a lot. What's that got to do with it?' In contrast, the general practitioner involved in the case was far more concerned about the mother's health. 'When I arrived she was in bed bleeding heavily because of her recent abortion, she was my main worry.

Before I went, I discussed the case with my colleague, and knowing the family, we both felt the abuse business was utter rubbish.' A model by which to explore the contrasting, sometimes contradicting, perceptions of parents and child-care professionals is described in Chapter Six.

One further methodological issue needed to be resolved. How valid was the material collected and by what reckoning might it be said to be true? In a study concerning actions that may be concealed or denied and consequently the suspicions that they arouse, both are difficult questions. However, veracity is easier to demonstrate if established methodological procedures are followed. We therefore took the advice of Quinton and Rutter (1988), interviewed participants as near to critical events as possible, and used 'the reconstructive nature of memory to locate events within a coherent life-history framework'. Further, we adhered to Hammersley and Atkinson's (1983) argument that researchers' interpretations of events should be checked with their respondents and put to outside assessors before being analysed in the light of research questions.

The definition of truth poses problems of a different order altogether. In a situation where an occurrence is suspected, where some facts may be 'harder' than others, where participants may have contrasting views and where perceptions are predisposed to change, a positivist view of the existence of any absolute truth may be too limiting. What participants consider true in such circumstances may indeed be true for them. It was therefore necessary to develop a model which accommodated these mobile elements, and so, as described in Chapter Six, we arrived at the concept of an *operational perspective*. A method was then developed for assessing by what criteria and to what extent an operational perspective might be said to change as an abuse inquiry proceeded and for judging the effect the process had on case outcome as far as the children were concerned.

Conclusions

The methodology for this study of parental perspectives in cases of suspected child abuse is complex because it is to be applied to a field of study where very little is known and in which all participants are likely to experience feelings of anxiety and fear.

In devising our approach we therefore examined a range of research techniques in the belief that certain methods would be more appropriate than others in the exploration of different aspects of the material. Thus, the extensive work, which focuses on the incidence of suspected child abuse by examining the records of social workers, health visitors, police and probation, charts how suspicion comes to light and assesses where the burden of work falls. However, because this method reveals little about individual attitudes to the process or whether style of investigation affects the outcome of a case, an intensive study was designed to explore more fully the experiences of all those involved in an investigation. Aggregating the data from a series of in-depth interviews and from observations of interaction within each family enabled us to develop a number of concepts, themes and typologies, which are examined in detail in later Chapters in the context of specific events. The most important is the *operational perspective*. By this rather elaborate route it is possible to begin to understand the relationship between an individual's experience of a sequence of events that occur during an investigation and the immediate and long term outcomes of the case in which he or she is a participant.

Summary points

1 This study explores the ways in which parents react to and manage accusations that they have abused their children. It considers how parents perceive the interventions and motives of child protection agencies.

2 The study has extensive and intensive dimensions. The extensive study follows the progress of 583 children referred to and seriously considered by child protection agencies in one local authority. The intensive study traces the progress of 30 families and their 61 children who, at the point of first suspicion, were considered 'at risk' of abuse. A two year follow-up has been undertaken.

3 Not all families approached agreed to take part in the intensive study. However, the group studied was representative in that it reflected the range of abuse situations dealt with by child protection agencies. The sample included a proportion of middle-class families, those from a variety of minority ethnic groups as well as the disadvantaged well known to social and other welfare services.

4 The qualitative data has been analysed using a rigorous theoretical framework and applying the concept of an operational perspective. The study focuses upon events in the investigation especially significant to parents.

Chapter 5

The Extensive Study: Who is caught up by suspicion?

Systematic information concerning children placed on Child Protection Registers has been collected by the Department of Health since 1988, but we know relatively little about suspected abuse or what negotiations occur before a suspicion is considered sufficiently serious to warrant registration. In this Chapter we map the early stages of an investigation, the different roles agencies play in identifying and investigating cases and the relationship between the course of the suspicion and its likely outcome. We demonstrate, for example, how important is the discreet role of the school as a place in which confidences are received and cases of possible child abuse identified. We also discuss the characteristics of the suspected victim and whether there is any correlation between them and the type of abuse suffered. As little previous research has focused on the alleged perpetrators, we examine who they are and their relationship to their victims.

We analyse all incidents of suspected child abuse seriously considered by agencies in a single geographical area during one calendar year. 'Seriously considered' means some form of investigation was undertaken and records kept. Parents did not always know that an inquiry had taken place. We scrutinised files from five different agencies; social services, hospitals, probation, police and the health visiting service. A sixth, the NSPCC, which nationally makes a large contribution to the identification and care of abused children, was not active in the area where we were working, but relevant cases reported to local offices were referred to social services for investigation and so are included. Because of the difficulties in gaining access to the files of general practitioners, schools and child psychologists, the small number of minor abuse cases exclusively dealt with by them have been omitted.

The size of the problem

In all we examined 583 cases. We found 274 in social service files, 98 came from health visitors, 43 from the probation service and 168 from the police files. Suspicions of abuse recorded in the files of more than one agency were treated as one case.

Not all cases of suspected abuse resulted in children's names being registered; in our study of 583 reports the figure was only 29%. The ages and gender of the children in our registered group were similar to those of children registered nationally, as identified in contemporary Department of Health statistics and the NSPCC Annual Report. When combined with contemporary Department of Health figures, which show that in England during the year ending 31st March 1991, 28,200 children were added to the Child Protection Register, this evidence would suggest that nationally 97,000 cases of suspected abuse a year are investigated seriously – sufficiently so for a case file to be opened.

Even this high figure is likely to be a considerable under-estimate because as many minor suspicions frequently go unrecorded and do not feature in this analysis. Gibbons, Conroy and Bell's (1993) prospective study of all referrals, which includes minor cases, shows that as few as one in seven eventually leads to registration. This finding suggests that there are 160,000 abuse suspicions each year in England. However, a quarter of them are so insignificant they are quickly dropped, and another two-thirds do not proceed as far as a case conference. Some cases in which abuse is but one aspect of a wider problem may be dealt with by a committal to care rather than child protection procedures. We would emphasise that not only does this investigative work occupy much social work time – its contribution to child welfare is largely unacknowledged.

Characteristics of suspected victims

Suspicion of child abuse extends to children of all ages, although as the following Diagram illustrates, the majority in our study were under 10 and a third were infants. This trend in reporting suspicions almost certainly reflected general anxiety about the vulnerability of the very young. Such concerns are understandable, in the light of Home Office evidence (1990) that infants under one year old are at greater risk of murder than any other group in the population. They are also the age group most prone to entry into care.

However, this pattern did not apply in all types of suspicion. For cases of suspected sexual abuse, there was a more even distribution across age groups; indeed, the majority of suspicions involving adolescent victims were of a sexual nature. This may be because very young children are unable to speak of their experience and long histories of childhood abuse are often disclosed for the first time during adolescence. Smaller numbers did not signify that the problems faced by the children were any less grave or that resolving them required any less professional skill.

Below the age of 14, gender accounted for few differences between victims, but as the age of the children increased, girls predominated to the extent that four fifths of older suspected victims were female. The gender of the child was also important when the type of suspicion was considered: there was no significant difference between boys and girls with regard to physical abuse, neglect or emotional abuse but as many as 72% of the sex abuse cases involved girls. In fact, suspicions of sexual abuse accounted for half (49%) of all reports involving girls but only a quarter involving boys. This pattern does not altogether support the general belief that females are in greater need of protection from sexual exploitation than males since, as Finklehor and Baron (1986) suggest, there is a greater reluctance among boys to report their own victimisation. There are also increasing grounds for thinking that the extremes to which paedophiles go in order to conceal their activity may be a factor.

Diagram 5.1   **The age of children seriously suspected as having been abused**

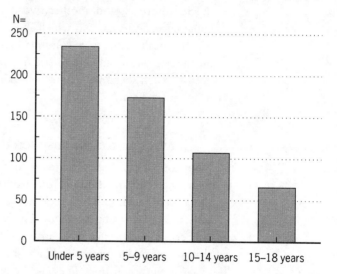

Children's physical and psychological health

The research literature has explored the possibility that certain groups are more at risk of abuse than others, and that children who are unloved and unwanted may be particularly vulnerable. However, it is also argued that abuse is an interactive process between child and adult and that the way children behave is part of the equation, so that hyperactive, misbehaving or overly clinging children, because they are more likely to make life difficult for parents, are more prone to parental abuse (Gil, 1971; de Lissovoy, 1979). Lynch (1975) suggests that babies are at greater risk when the birth has been prolonged or difficult, or when children are brain damaged or congenitally deformed.

Our sample confirmed the view that some groups of children are more likely to arouse suspicions. We have already indicated that young children were more likely to be investigated, but even within this group, children with chronic physical illness were over-represented. For example, 11% of these young children had been diagnosed as having a serious chronic physical illness or disability compared with 2.3% of young children in the general population (Wadsworth, 1991). In our sample, physical problems included fundamental difficulties such as a club foot or a missing kidney, as well as debilitating conditions, such as severe eczema or chronic asthma.

Among older children, unacceptable and bizarre behaviour was more likely to arouse concern. A third of children of both sexes aged between five and nine years showed behavioural difficulties, such as unaccountable swings of mood, destructive or violent outbursts or regressive behaviour. This proportion increased further with age; three quarters of the children over 10 displayed psychological problems.

It is clear from this evidence that the physical injury or neglect of children are rarely isolated phenomena. They occur in the context of other problems in the continuing relationship between adults and children and between siblings. They are influenced by the idiosyncrasies of individual personalities and events peculiar to the circumstances. No single factor can be said to be a predictor of child abuse, but, for any given factor, children and families tend to exhibit a higher than average incidence or concatenation of inauspicious circumstances and characteristics. Moreover, whereas some children in a family may be said to be at greater risk of abuse than others, once it is suspected that abuse has occurred, professional anxiety extends to all the other children in the family. So the suspicion itself increases the ramifications of any problems.

Household composition

It has been shown that many children who come into care have experienced severe family dislocation (Bebbington and Miles, 1989). We were interested to discover whether families coming under suspicion for child abuse demonstrated the same characteristic. It emerged that at the time of the suspected abuse, family units in which children lived with both natural parents were the minority (43%). Moreover, 40% were the only child in the household, although many were living apart from siblings. Thus, abuse could be said to be occurring in a range of family situations; the scenario in which a lone mother struggles to provide for a large family was but one among several possibilities. However, few families had children in care, and the ones we studied more closely resembled those identified by Packman, Randall and Jacques (1986) as highly vulnerable but likely to remain on the margins of care. Nevertheless, as our qualitative study shows, many families under suspicion struggle with housing and finance as well as with a multitude of personal and child-care problems.

The majority of children in our sample lived with a single mother (25%) or in a reconstituted family, usually with the mother and a step-father or male cohabitee. It was rare to find children living apart from their natural mothers: of the few that did, 10 lived with a lone father and 23 in a household comprising the natural father and his partner. Suspicions of abuse which involve children from dislocated families are likely to extend as far as members of the wider family, so that estranged fathers and their new families, or grandparents who share the care of the child, will frequently fall under the shadow of inquiry. Thus, an investigation for suspected abuse can severely disrupt care arrangements and the degree of mutual support offered by the extended family. Similarly, the trauma of the suspicion lingers and can have adverse long-term consequences for individuals well outside the nuclear group.

Some authorities maintain that very young parents, particularly teenage mothers, have poorer parenting skills than adults (Roberts, 1988; Hudson and Ineichen, 1991). Thus, teenage mothers might more readily be labelled as possible child abusers and so figure with disproportionate frequency among mothers falling under suspicion. However, we found a wide and even age distribution: such mothers had a mean average age of 28, a finding similar to Hyman's (1978) in a study of mothers who injured their children. Only one in sixty of those in our group were under 20 at the time of the alleged abuse.

However, a relationship between a mother's age and the abuse of her child can be measured in different ways (Connelly and Strauss, 1992). Thus, it emerged that a third of the mothers in our sample were teenagers at the time of the birth of the indexed child, which suggests that when judging the likelihood of abuse, professionals are taking into account the compounding stresses of early pregnancy and motherhood.

The suspected perpetrator

The relationship between the suspected abuser, the type of abuse perpetrated and the victim is very varied. The bulk of suspicion was laid at the door of the child's parents; they were the prime suspects in 70% of all incidents. However, within certain abuse categories, such as sexual abuse, outside perpetrators were also likely to come under suspicion. There was also a close correlation between who was suspected of sexual abuse and the gender of the supposed victim. Where the suspicion involved a girl, a member of the family was three times more likely to come under suspicion.

Although people other than parents come under suspicion in many cases of reported sexual abuse, there is little to suggest that there is a significant risk to a child of abuse by strangers. Data on outside perpetrators show that in only 9% of the incidents was the suspect a complete stranger to the child. Thus, most suspicions involving outsiders arose from behaviour within close friendships, such as under-age sexual intercourse, exploratory behaviour among schoolchildren or serious misbehaviour by babysitters or boyfriends of single parents. There was a small group of outsider suspects who were people in authority not necessarily known to the family, for example, scoutmasters, swimming instructors, teachers and employers of children doing Saturday jobs. All these perpetrators were male and boys were twice as likely as girls to be their alleged victims. We came across a few accusations of sexual abuse by teachers involving especially vulnerable children, such as those with special needs or attending boarding school. Finally, in six instances, a parent was suspected of abusing the friends of his children when they were staying overnight at his house, situations that reflect a pattern similar to that shown by Margolin (1991), in which the majority of such children were abused in the context of bedtime preparation or when in bed.

A classification of families and abuse situations

Once having explored the characteristics and circumstances of the children and the perpetrators of abuse, it is possible to suggest a classification of abused and/or abusing families Several groups emerged from the analysis but there was some overlap between them in terms of their characteristics and the type of abuse which they were alleged to have inflicted. Thus the classification is more theoretical than empirical and needs to be refined in future research by cluster analyses on different data sets.

Multi-problem families

Multi-problem families formed a sizeable proportion (43%) of the cases we studied. They are families well known to the welfare and control agencies who present an array of problems, including chronic ill-health, poor housing, long-term unemployment and financial and social incompetence. Role boundaries within the family may be blurred; petty crime and violence are common and substance abuse or other addictions can be an aggravating factor where financial difficulties are concerned. There is a high likelihood that in addition to their current disadvantages, parents will have suffered abuse as children, a circumstance which increases the probability of continuing parenting difficulties (Quinton and Rutter, 1988). Abuse in these families is multiform, including physical abuse and neglect, incest and inter-generational sexual abuse and emotional abuse. Multi-problem families may be stigmatised within their own communities, thus increasing the vul-nerability to organised abuse involving other families who share their norms and values (Wahler and Hahn, 1984). The object of community rejection and ostracism, they tend to be thrown together in sub-standard council flats reserved for rent defaulters or bad tenants.

Specific problem families

Specific problem families formed the second largest group (21%) of families in our sample. They come to the attention of the agencies because of a particular suspicion, such as intra-familial sexual abuse or physical abuse by a parent against a particular child within the household. The suspicion tends to remain hidden until a member of the family breaks the secret. Such families are not confined to any social class and their lives may seem to be the antithesis of those multi-problem families just described: they are generally quite well educated; they are in employment; quite unlike the multi-problem families just described they have not had previous contact with any statutory agency. However, investigation prises open a Pandora's box of guilty secrets, which, by various strategies – perhaps ostentatious exhibitions of harmony or else contrived social isolation – they will have striven to keep tight shut.

Acutely distressed families

Among those families we called acutely distressed (13%) problems accumulate, but are dealt with until one overwhelming incident precipitates child abuse. Such families tend to be composed of single or poorly-supported immature parents or others who are physically ill or disabled. The child abuse usually takes the form of physical aggression or neglect when parents cease to be able to cope. Triggers include the birth of a child, worsening financial difficulties, unemployment or the departure of a parent. The suspicion of abuse may reach the attention of the authorities because concerned neighbours report their anxiety, but most investigations are the result of the vigilance of health visitors, school teachers and social workers.

Infiltrating perpetrator families

The behaviour of someone, usually male, who infiltrates a family in the guise of a new caring partner or friend in order to abuse children is highly calculating. Frequently a man will manipulate the susceptibilities of a single mother by counterfeiting the behaviour of a loving new father, who promises a normal family life, but, once he is inside the family, the children become vulnerable. Suspicion is aroused in cases where the infiltrator has a record of child abuse and is consequently known to probation services or the police. Alternatively, agencies such as schools or health visitors may notice a deterioration in children's behaviour attendant upon the change in family circumstances. The safety of the children is compromised by the degree of collusion and denial by some mothers involved in such liaisons; indeed, mothers may occasionally sacrifice the safety of their children in an attempt to hold on to a new partner. Such an individual was thought to have been involved in 9% of the cases we examined.

Outside perpetrator families

The final group of families function normally until the children become the suspected victims of an outside abuser. Thirteen per cent of the cases studied were of this type. As we have already shown, the perpetrators are rarely strangers: they may be school friends, boyfriends of teenage girls or adult friends and teachers. The suspected abuse appears to have an opportunistic component, but once initiated, frequently becomes routine. Families are seldom aware of anything untoward until the child speaks of the abuse or, by his or her changed behaviour, betrays the situation. Families may themselves report their concerns to a statutory agency, but schools and health visitors are also key figures in alerting suspicion.

Although child abuse covers a range of behaviour and circumstances, some pattern is discernible in the relationship between family structures, family functioning, and the extent of economic and social deprivation, and the type of abuse and the characteristics of the victims and the perpetrators. While certain aspects of these findings are wholly unpredictable, relying on chance and personal idiosyncracy and as such could never form the basis of a child protection policy, clear indications emerge as to who is most at risk from whom and which circumstances are most likely to aggravate the situation.

Which agencies are involved when abuse comes to light

Having begun to understand how the suspicion of child abuse comes to the attention of agencies, one can consider whether the different ways in which abuse is discovered lead to investigations along different administrative paths. An allegation of child abuse will surface in one of three ways. A member of the family or an outsider may talk directly to a professional of their concern; a professional already working with a family or child may become suspicious, or certain behaviour or an event may precipitate scrutiny of the family and lead to or bring forth the suspicion of child abuse. This last route is referred to as an 'unrelated' event: for example, an accusation made by mothers engaged in a noisy argument at the school gates aroused the head teacher's suspicion; the police subsequently conducted a home visit during which evidence to justify suspected neglect of the children was uncovered. Because the same case may come to light simultaneously in more than one professional context – for example, a mother may disclose abuse to social services at the same time as a teacher identifies home problems – in some cases several routes are combined. The categories in the following discussions are not mutually exclusive therefore.

Suspicion arising from disclosures

In 397 cases, agencies were alerted because someone decided to speak out; this was the commonest way suspicions of a sexual nature came to light. We were interested to discover whether those reporting the abuse selected an agency to whom to reveal their concern and what determined their choice. Did teachers refer to social services? Were neighbours more inclined to telephone the police? Disclosures from parents, relatives and neighbours showed a consistent pattern as all approached social services or the police. Despite their considerable investigative powers, police and social services were viewed as shields and defenders when individuals felt distressed or considered children to be in danger. Children also used this channel, but 15% had talked to teachers first. There was also a link between the type of abuse suspected and the relationship of the person drawing attention to it: members of the family were more likely to raise suspicions about sexual abuse, neighbours and anonymous callers were more concerned with potential physical abuse and neglect.

Research in North America has found that as few as 15% of anonymous allegations are substantiated (Besharov, 1987). As a result, concern is increasing that families could be subjected to unwarranted harassment and that social workers may become preoccupied with time-wasting investigations. Although very few cases (N=17) in our study came to agencies' attention through anonymous calls, they nevertheless raised similar concerns, since none warranted placement on the Child Protection Register. Only one was referred for further investigation, but all took a long time to investigate. There is also anxiety in Britain and America about the number of estranged spouses who make false allegations of child abuse in their fight for custody of children or access to children (Thoennes and Tjaden, 1990; Bentovim, 1987; Jones and McGraw, 1987). We found few such cases among our study group.

Child protection agencies discover abuse

Another 303 cases were identified by professionals without any external prompting. Abuse suggested by behaviour encountered during work with children follows a well-trodden route to investigation, often beginning when children start school. Changes in children's pattern of play may be a sign of difficulties at home, hidden physical injuries may be uncovered when children change their clothes for games, or drawing and written work may hint at distressing secrets (Dale, 1991). Frequently, the infants concerned are from the 'multi-problem' families previously identified.

The agencies involved in the identification of suspected child abuse tend to be different from those approached by people seeking help. Social services, health visitors and schools have an important part to play in both processes, but the role of the schools as a place in which behaviour can be carefully but unobtrusively monitored frequently goes unacknowledged.

Suspicions which emerge through the investigation of unrelated incidents

In 80 cases some incident not related to the abuse of children triggered an investigation. In many cases, law-breaking or unorthodox family behaviour attracted professional attention. Often one misdemeanour exposed another, so that, for example, a suspicion of abuse came in the wake of criminal activity or drug abuse, or the deviant behaviour of the child acted as a signal, such as when an education welfare officer's anxieties about poor school attendance brought forth a suspicion of neglect. Likewise, the hospitalisation of a family member often led to more general scrutiny of home conditions. Though few suspicions emerged through such unrelated incidents, the police increasingly stress that all routine investigations should include an assessment of the possibility of child abuse.

To summarise these patterns, Table 5.2 lists the sources of the cases we scrutinised and distinguishes the route taken by the suspicion. Because cases come to light in a number of different ways, the categories are not mutually exclusive

Table 5.2 **The agency receiving referrals and the routes taken by suspicions**

	Disclosed %	Identified %	Unrelated Event %
Police	33	7	52
Health Visitor	10	16	0
School	5	27	16
Doctors	5	25	16
Social Services	39	25	16
NSPCC	8	0	0
	N=397	N=303	N=80

This evidence on the way suspicions emerge highlights the different roles agencies play in the investigation process. As the preceding table shows, the police and social services are most commonly used by those who disclose or report suspected abuse. On the other hand, irrespective of any external catalyst, many cases are identified among current clients especially by social services, schools, health visitors, and doctors. Finally, agencies, especially the police, are likely to uncover child abuse while investigating other events.

The short term outcome of a suspected child abuse investigation

All serious suspicions of child abuse examined in this survey led to investigation and assessment. As Table 5.3, shows, some children were placed on the Child Protection Register (29%) and some not registered were monitored by an agency (34%). Other cases were referred for further investigation (21%); with respect to the remainder no action was taken (16%). This evidence suggests that although only a third of cases are registered, most of the remainder are considered to warrant some continuing agency involvement. Thus, in most cases, irrespective of whether the child is registered, the suspicion lingers.

In a number of cases the outcome was more complicated. For example, 23 of the children were also removed from home under emergency proceedings and 28 of another 29 for whom care orders were sought were also separated from their families. Eight young children among this 51 were quickly placed for adoption. As for the suspected perpetrators, criminal proceedings were taken in 68 cases.

Diagram 5.3 **Administrative outcome for cases of suspected child abuse**

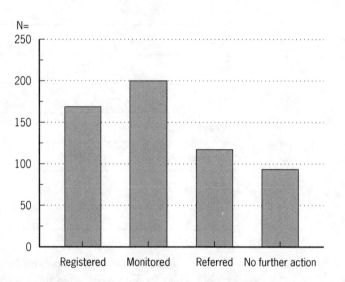

Factors associated with administrative outcomes

In an attempt to determine why certain cases result in registration we explored the association between the decisions made and: (a) the agencies involved in the investigation, (b) the identity of the victim, (c) the suspected perpetrator, (d) the type of abuse and (e) the family background.

a) Agencies involved in the investigation

We have shown that separately or in combination a number of agencies can be involved in the early stages of an investigation. Registration was more likely if social services, the police, hospitals or the probation service rather than health visitors or general practitioners were involved. Health visitors and doctors work closely together and some suspicions of minor abuse may be contained within the profession rather than automatically referred to social services. This suggests that two routes exist into the identification and registration process and that the consequences of opening the door to a health visitor or to a social worker can be different, at least for cases of minor maltreatment.

b) The characteristics of the victim

The gender of the victim was not an important determinant of registration but there were some indications that age was significant, since greater proportions of children below the age of five and young people over the age of 14 were likely to be registered. However differences are small and statistically insignificant.

c) The suspected perpetrator

As the following Diagram illustrates, when the male parent or an 'outsider' is the suspected abuser, children are more likely to be placed on the Child Protection Register.

Diagram 5.4 **The relationship between the proportion of cases registered and the suspected perpetrator**

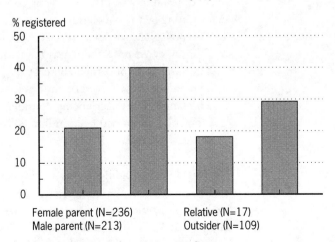

% registered

Female parent (N=236)
Male parent (N=213)
Relative (N=17)
Outsider (N=109)

In eight cases the suspected perpetrator was unknown

d) The type of abuse

When types of abuse were explored, it emerged that investigations related to suspicions of sexual abuse (35%) and those in the category of grave concern (32%) were more likely to result in the child's being registered. Official practice does not suggest that certain types of abuse are considered to be more serious than others, but, as following Chapters describe, social workers use informal criteria for judging seriousness. Thus, sexual abuse involving family members aroused great concern and – more so than with any other type of familial abuse – the victims were likely to be registered.

e) Family history

We also considered whether there was any connection between a family's previous history and the frequency of registration, by examining three factors; (a) families' previous record of child abuse, (b) their criminal history and (c) their previous involvement with social services. All three indicators were positively associated with a decision to place the child's name on the register: of all cases registered 68% of the families concerned had a history of child abuse, 69% were well known to social services and 48% had a criminal record, figures all twice those found for the non-registered group.

Finally, we considered whether children in any of the five categories of family we identified and described earlier in the Chapter were more likely to be registered. The proportion was highest where the family was suspected of having been infiltrated by an abuser (48%); next came multi-problem families (33%); outside perpetrator (24%) and specific problem and acutely distressed families (18%).

From this reckoning it emerged that certain types of investigation into certain situations where child abuse was suspected were significantly more likely to result in a child's name being added to the Protection Register. The determining factors were as follows:

1 The police and/or social service were involved in the investigation;
2 The suspected perpetrator was the father or a male outsider.
3 The suspicion concerned abuse of a sexual nature.
4 The family had a record of child abuse or other criminal behaviour.
5 The family was experiencing considerable and varied difficulties (multi-problem) and/or had been infiltrated by someone with a record of child abuse or violence.

How do these findings from a single geographical area compare with other available evidence? We have referred to the research of Gibbons, Conroy and Bell (1993) who examined the investigative process for children under 16 in eight local authorities. Their study included every referral for abuse, no matter how minor, and so identified cases at an earlier stage, but, interestingly, many of our findings supported theirs. For example, both surveys indicated a high proportion of parents as perpetrators (89% in Gibbon's study, 70% in ours) but infrequent identification of mothers in incidents of sexual abuse. The role of non-family members was also highlighted. Certain family characteristics were comparable, such as the proportion of children living with both natural parents (30% and 40%). From both surveys schools emerged as a significant source of referrals.

More illuminating were the results of independent predictive exercises designed to identify cases where referral would commonly lead to a case conference and registration. Although Gibbons looked at conferencing and we at registration, many similar predictive factors emerge.

Factors associated with referrals leading to conferences and registration

Gibbons et al	Dartington
Sexual and physical abuse	Sexual abuse
Perpetrator in the home	Multi-problem family or infiltrated by perpetrator
Family previously investigated	Police or social services involved at time abuse surfaced
Family history of criminality, mental illness, violence or abuse	Family history of child abuse or criminality
Mixed siblings or only boys in the family	—
Relatively severe abuse	—
—	Perpetrator a male parent or outsider

It will be seen from both studies that the factors associated with making decisions about children at risk are complex and disparate. The type and severity of abuse has to be seen in the context of the history of the family and its composition. Decisions whether to proceed with child protection strategies depend on an equation which must attempt to assess the amount of substantiated evidence and the perceived degree of continuing risk.

In order to disentangle these factors, we carried out a further, multi-variate analysis which indicated that three aspects of a child abuse inquiry influenced, independently and in combination, the likelihood of a child being registered. This followed the procedure usual for such exercises. Initially we looked at those factors statistically associated with the outcome which concerned us. We then considered the correlation between the dependent variables and subsequently excluded certain items. Three sets of factors were considered: the characteristics of the child and the circumstances which led to the referral; the type of family from which the child came, and the way in which the abuse came to light. Logit analysis indicates that investigation of a suspicion of child abuse is most likely to lead to registration or even stronger action if:

1 The family is multi-problem or endangered by an infiltrating perpetrator.
2 Social services are involved in the case at the time abuse comes to light.
3 Professional scrutiny leads to the discovery of abuse.

Although fewer than a third of the 583 children whose cases we scrutinised were eventually placed on the Child Protection Register, we found that four-fifths of children from families described as multi-problem *and* who had long been known to social services *and* who had also failed to disclose the abuse of their offspring were eventually registered. Indeed, children in these circumstances were nearly four (3.8) times more likely to have their names added to the register. Similarly, 86% of children in families where a new cohabitee had a known history of child abuse and where social workers had not been informed of the change of family composition were registered. These cases were four and a half times more likely to lead to registration than those relating to other children suspected of having suffered abuse.

Thus, families who were new to the system and sought help with their problems were likely to experience a less severe intervention. They were the same families described earlier as needing help with a specific issue, acutely distressed or unknowingly exposed to an outside perpetrator. Such circumstances were usually less fraught and the likelihood of registration was reduced by as much as three (2.7) times.

That said, placement on the register was not as serious an event as parents supposed at the outset. Nearly all (91%) of the children whose cases we scrutinised stayed at home, including many of those identified as having been victims of sexual abuse. Social workers and other professionals working with the family were able to use this evidence to allay parental concern over their child's possible removal. Anxiety over such loss and the public humiliation it might involve was sufficient to overwhelm parental perception of much else that occurred.

Conclusions

This scrutiny of the 583 cases of suspected child abuse demonstrates that suspicion may follow any one of several routes, but that ultimately social services become involved in nearly every investigation. However, less than one in seven investigations and one in three cases seriously considered result in a child's name being added to the Child Protection Register. In the majority of cases, suspicion lingers unsubstantiated or the child is considered to be no longer at risk.

Local authorities deal with several types of family, each of which poses different problems, and this variation calls for different investigation and support strategies. A variety of routes leads to the point at which investigation normally begins. We have shown that two-thirds are the result of disclosures by the child, his or her family or a neighbour, while other suspicions may surface during a regular visit by an agency or as the result of an unrelated, even accidental, event.

A decision to register is more likely for some children than for others. Previous contact between the family and the statutory agencies, for example with social services or by way of a criminal conviction, seems to increase the likelihood of registration. Not surprisingly, the type of abuse is important: 35% of cases referred for suspected sexual abuse were eventually registered. The involvement of particular agencies is also influential: social services, police, hospitals and probation were significantly more likely to have taken a key role in cases that led to registration.

The findings laid out in this Chapter provide a useful background to the intensive study of parental perspectives. The data show that many children in families caught up in an abuse investigation are old enough to be able to express their feelings with some clarity. Over half of the suspected victims were over the age of ten and a fifth had reached adolescence. It is also clear that parents' perspectives will be influenced by the domestic circumstances from which an abuse allegation emerges. Because *multi-problem* families and social services departments tend to be well-known to each other, parents' attitudes to the work of child protection agencies are likely to be ingrained before any investigation begins; but in the case of *specific problem* families, who are probably experiencing agency intrusion for the first time, perceptions will be in a more fluid state. Different again are those families who fall prey to an *outside perpetrator;* parents' perceptions are much more likely to accord with those of the professionals by whom the intruder is unmasked.

As the majority of suspected abuses occur within the family, we are bound to ask what impact does the investigation itself have on the dynamics of intimate relationships? Since the majority of those surveyed in this Chapter are relatively poor and many are living in recently-formed or reconstituted family groups, there is surely a danger that the attentions of child protection workers, no matter how sensitively pursued, may exacerbate existing problems. It is worth considering that were the intimate behaviour of even the most competent parent and the house-rules of even the most conventionally successful marriage to become the object of independent examination, it would not be long before parents and children began to see each another as if with 'new eyes'.

Summary points

1 In one local authority, we examined all incidents of suspected child abuse seriously considered by agencies in a single year. We identified 583 cases where suspicions were sufficiently strong to merit recording. Of these, fewer than one third of the children eventually had their names placed on the protection register. Since about 28,000 children are added to registers in England in any one year, this would suggest that nationally 97,000 serious investigations are conducted annually. In addition, it is likely that as many less pressing cases are dealt with but not recorded.

2 Child abuse investigations extend to children of all ages, although the frequency of reports declines as children get older. Younger children are more at risk of neglect and physical abuse than adolescents who predominate in sexual abuse investigations. Sexual abuse accounts for half of referrals involving girls but for only a quarter of those involving boys.

3 Some children are more prone to abuse than others, and the abuse is often discovered as a result of physical illness or behaviour problems at school. A third of the children whose cases were investigated aged five to nine and three-quarters of those aged ten were in this general category.

4 Abuse is suspected in several types of family. Some form of family reconstitution is likely and suspicion most commonly falls upon close family members, particularly those recently recruited. Mothers and fathers equally come under the spotlight for physical abuse but in neglect and emotional abuse cases mothers predominate and in sexual abuse investigations fathers, cohabitees and males outside of the family are likely to be the chief suspects. Abuse by strangers, however, is not frequent; the perpetrator is usually known to both child and family.

5 The data lead to classification of abusing families and have proved useful in understanding information from the intensive study which follows. We identified:

   a) Multi-problem families (43%) are well known to social services and display multiple difficulty. In addition, the adults in these families are highly likely to have suffered abuse themselves as children.

   b) Specific problem families (21%) came to notice because of a particular suspicion. Such families have rarely been the recipients of welfare interventions or police concern. Ostensibly, they live well ordered lives and cross class boundaries.

   c) Acutely distressed families (13%) share many of the characteristics of the first group but are distinct in the degree and frequency of accidents, misfortune and trauma they experience. Parents cannot cope, a breakdown occurs which results in abuse, usually physical maltreatment or neglect.

    d) Infiltrating perpetrators (9%) affect a minority of cases. Here, a new arrival with a history of offences against children joins vulnerable, often single parent, families.

    e) Outside perpetrators (13%) often known to the family are also relatively infrequent among the case files of child protection professionals.

6 Child abuse surfaces in different ways.

    a) someone may decide to talk to a professional

    b) an agency working with the family may become suspicious

    c) an unrelated incident, such as an accident or police investigation arouses concern.

7 Of the 583 suspicions investigated, 29% were registered, 34% were not registered but their progress was monitored, 21% were investigated further and in 16% of cases no further action was necessary. Of those registered, just under a third were also removed from home.

8 The likelihood of a child's name being placed on the Child Protection Register increases if social services, police, hospitals or probation, as opposed to health visitors and G.Ps are involved, if the abuse is sexual rather than physical or emotional, if a male parent or infiltrator is the suspected abuser and if the child's family has a previous record of child abuse, criminality and previous involvement with social services.

Chapter 6

Parents' perceptions and operational perspectives

In the previous Chapter we examined the case files of social workers, health visitors, the probation services and the police in order to identify the range of factors associated with the outcome of child protection procedures. Such an approach is useful, but only partially satisfactory: it does not tell us very much about how parents come to terms with the sudden involvement of professional investigators in intimate aspects of their lives. What does it feel like to be suspected of abuse? Do parents feel violated? Can they be reassured? Can relationships distorted by mutual antagonism and mistrust at one moment, such as when abuse is first suspected, later improve?

An individual's view of the world at any given moment has physical, psychological and sociological components. Try to understand the negotiations that accompany even the most mundane aspects of domestic life, such as the transitory rituals associated with washing up or lawnmowing, and the problems soon become apparent. When the quality of a person's relations with his or her children is investigated by those who come to help but who can greatly interfere, the complexity of the interaction between participants is extreme.

At the outset, we thought an orthodox psychological approach might be sufficient. It might have been argued that in order to gain insights into their respective understanding of parenting and child abuse, we needed only to ask parents how they perceived their social workers and social workers how they perceived parents. But, because our underlying interest was in the developing impact on parents of suspicion and investigation, and free-standing perceptions were plainly only one aspect of that multi-faceted process, we needed to develop a more flexible strategy. For guidance, therefore, we turned to the work of psychologists interested in the social context and to those sociologists whose primary concern has been the behaviour of the individual.

Understanding perspectives

Try to lay hands on a workable definition of 'perception' and one quickly finds oneself on the side of the eclectic scholar J.R. Smythies who in his *Analysis of Perception* (1956) regretted that,

> in order to construct a comprehensive theory of perception it would be necessary to have at least a good working knowledge of epistemology and the philosophy of sense perception, neurology, neuro-anatomy and neurophysiology, psychiatry and psycho-pathology (with particular

reference to the effects produced by the hallucinogenic drugs), anthro-pology, physics and experimental psychology.

Sociologists and social psychologists have in more recent years become preoccupied with the social aspects of perception. Ideas about self perception have become more amenable to external cultural influences. For example, theories of interaction, self presentation and power exchange in ordinary relationships have been developed, many of which are relevant to this study.

Most notably Rom Harré and others have introduced a social psychology of actions. They contend that it is futile to try to understand the mind in isolation from the social context in which the individual operates. They argue that the key to understanding interaction lies with the rules that underpin and guide our action. Understand the rules that govern any particular social situation and one will begin to understand the mind, its motivations and intentions.

Harré identifies different levels of social interaction. Some behaviour, he explains, is an automatic response to stimulus, such as a mother's involuntary tearfulness on opening the door to find a social worker on the step. But in most circumstances conduct is more considered. Consciously or not, we plot a course of action from several permutations available to us, and, since there is a tendency to choose what seemed to work the time before, interaction at this level tends to become routine. It would not take much fieldwork to become expert in predicting the way an accused person will respond under cross-examination; likewise, there is something dispiritingly predictable about the reactions of parents suspected of abusing their children.

When a social worker calls to see a client, the interaction between them is shaped by the knowledge of similar encounters that has been assimilated into the culture. Even recent disturbing events will play a part. At the beginning of an inquiry, a parent may well think 'Cleveland! - Will my child be taken away?' while at the back of the social worker's mind lurks the ghost of Jasmine Beckford.

Rom Harré's insights into the structure of social interaction helped us to assess parents' perspectives, but it did not entirely answer our needs. The study raises issues about the relationship between the State and the individual which are exposed during the examination of a parent by a social worker. We turned for further help to those philosophers and social scientists, such as Foucault, Berger and Luckmann, who have come to regard truth, normality and deviance as socially constructed notions. Were such writers to focus on child abuse, they would draw attention to the historical legacy of child rescue and the intrusion of the State into the intimacies of family life.

Developments of these ideas have further relevance for this study. What might once have been considered to be the language of ignorance, prejudice or simple misconception is increasingly regarded by social psychologists as very significant in behaviour. For example Potter and Wetherell (1987) argue that because everyday versions of events can be much varied without their becoming entirely wrong, the way different versions are produced and the intentions behind them are important. *Discourse analysis* suggests that many descriptions of events are designed to discredit alternative accounts as well as to justify one's action. To remember a social worker as someone insensitive to the needs of young children helps construct a version of events that the rememberer considers will best serve his or her interests at a given moment. A mother's explanation of her partner's enthusiastic kissing and cuddling of their daughter as 'horseplay' will keep the spectre of sexual abuse at a distance and control her suspicions by reinforcing the image of the partner as a caring father. Different memories of the same set of circumstances may serve different functions at different times.

Our pilot interviews indicated that it was too simple to focus solely on how participants in an investigation classify each other, because, as was quickly demonstrated, all may hold, simultaneously and serially, a variety of perceptions on what is happening. Some perceptions appear to conflict, but all may be valid according to their function. Faced with an accusation of child abuse, whether welcome or unfamiliar, as he or she struggles to form a coherent picture, an individual may 'forget' or ignore what does not fit. As discourse analysts would argue, a person may construct a script to meet the circumstances – and, very commonly, will accommodate simultaneously several different perspectives on what is happening, any of which may prove interchangeable. Thus discourse analysts have helped to create conditions in which the significance of different perspectives on the same set of circum-stances – and the significance of the fact that such discrepancies exist – can be acknowledged and better understood.

This study has involved interpreting alternative renderings of the same event – the reading and re-reading of scripts. As Goffman and others have found, it has been akin to dealing with theatre texts. This dramaturgical model for the study of social interaction is well grounded in Goffman's work, well documented in Harré's and useful to ours because, since the approach is ironic and detached, role becomes as important as the aims and outcome of social activity. It also appeals to commonsense: those entangled in the legal process frequently speak of the experience in terms of theatre, of being trapped at the centre of a rehearsed performance, unable to intervene.

As one of Pirandello's *Six Characters in Search of An Author* complains:

> My drama lies entirely in this one thing... in my being conscious that each one of us believes himself to be a single person. But it's not true... each one of us is many persons... many persons... according to all the possibilities of being that are within us... with some people we are one

person... with others we are somebody quite different... and all the time we are under the illusion of always being one and the same person for everybody. But it's not true... it's not true. And we see this very clearly when by some tragic chance we are, as it were, caught up whilst in the middle of doing something and find ourselves suspended in mid-air. And then we perceive that all of us was not in what we were doing, and that it would, therefore, be an atrocious injustice to judge us by that action alone. To keep us suspended like that... to keep us in a pillory, throughout all existence... as if our whole life were completely summed up in that one deed.

Thus, by one or other of a variety of routes we arrived at the notion of an investigation as a process subject to and determined by the perceptions of its participants. At the simplest level W.I. Thomas's famous theorem had to be accepted, 'if men define a situation as real, it is real in its consequences'. But the consequences of certain perceptions become institutionalised; they are organised into a more general and enduring view of a situation, object or phenomenon, a social construct Merton (1957) defined as a 'perspective'.

Consider three short parallel extracts from the unfolding story of the Clayton family, which will be referred to in more detail in Chapter Eight. A teenager who has attempted suicide says:

> *When we got to the hospital it was 'What did you take? How many?' I was like 'I dunno'. They said to my mum 'Did you bring the packet in or anything?' Mum said she was in such a hurry to get me down here. Mum panicked. Sarah was crying as well and you know I just remember being sick and because I was still conscious, they didn't have to pump my stomach, but I was sleepy. It was not very nice. Then I flaked out . . .*
>
> *One of the nurses, when they were moving me to the ward -um- one of the nurses asked me why I did it. Um, I was just, like babbling - it was like talking to someone on a train - you don't know them and you don't think you'll ever see them again so you just tell them and um, I got transferred up to the ward and when I woke up in the morning, one of the nurses came in and said she would like me to talk to a social worker and a psychiatrist - so I padded off down to talk to these two women. I was worried. I was in such a state. It was like somebody had put an axe through my head; it was like the worst hangover I'd ever had... I sat down - I mean the psychiatrist didn't say anything really - I sat talking to the hospital social worker. I was so relieved to have somebody to talk to and I remembered that I'd told somebody and I thought this is my opportunity to get something done about it.*

Her father says:

> *At that point – when they'd been to see Margaret at hospital and she'd started screaming sexual abuse, they came, well they were waiting here for me when I got home from work and I'd got half an hour to get out of the house or else be arrested. I wasn't even given a choice in it - well I was given a choice. I could either refuse to leave, in which case they would arrest me and put me in the cells or I could go and find somewhere else to stay for an indefinite period until they'd completed what investigations they wanted to complete...*
>
> *Not only was I treated like a criminal - I was tried and convicted and found guilty, without even being given a chance to explain what has happened in our family over the years. They've just taken this little bit out of context and said sexual abuse. He's admitted it. He's guilty. You know . . .*

Her mother says:

> *I felt devastated. When this was going on I got to the hospital, it was like pounce. It was pounce we want to see you, we want to talk to you, and then what they said to me at the hospital was yes, you're free to go home if you wish, but should you do that, we have to interpret that as you are not putting the welfare of your child at the forefront of your mind, because Margaret 18 coming up to 19 – she's an adult. She doesn't come into it, but Sarah does. So they said, if you leave here, we have to interpret that you're not putting her welfare first, and then, maybe, we will have to take Elizabeth away from you, for her protection. So they weren't wrapping a ball and chain round me physically, but they were . . .*

The number of players in such a case is endless, but even inside a family distinct points of view have an integrity and an underpinning rationale. We have chosen to call the composite view held at any moment by a participant in an investigation, whether child, family or professional, and articulated in his or her account of a particular event or sequence of events an *operational perspective*.

Operational perspectives

We define an *operational perspective* as that collection of socially-oriented perceptions which people hold, use and have the power to modify in order to make sense of their daily lives and help them cope with an abuse accusation. While all participants will need to make sense of new situations, certain individuals will rely more heavily than others on coping mechanisms. In the case of Yvonne Oomah which follows, it will be seen that her operational perspective was as much an expression of her efforts to adapt to an accusation as of her need to understand her predicament; as far as the social worker who wrote the letter was concerned, it was a routine investigation – for her, coping was not an issue at all.

There are certain fixed points when parents and professionals confront each other – the most obvious is the child protection meeting – and when operational perspectives are most likely to be negotiated and modified. Charting the evolution of operational perspectives at such moments and relating their development to the outcome of the cases under scrutiny – how and to what extent they alter, whether or not they become entrenched or cast off – forms a central aspect of this study. Our hypothesis is that the closer become the operational perspectives of parents and professionals, the more satisfactory is the outcome on a range of criteria.

Our interest in concordance or conflict in this context demanded that we should be systematic in our approach. We needed to identify specific indicators of a participants' viewpoint at successive moments in an investigation.

We found it useful to concentrate on five dimensions of an operational perspective, which we attributed to two categories – first those *psychological* perspectives, internal to individuals, including those derived from past experience and aspects of personality, second *social* perspectives, externally-driven, concerning, for example, the power of social services and the procedures an investigation must follow.

Thus the *psychological* dimensions of operational perspectives concern:
1 Interpretations of situations, events and phenomena.
2 Self perception and emotional responses of participants.
3 Experience and expectations.

And the social dimensions of operational perspectives concern:
1 Power relations with others.
2 The way private information becomes public.

By this means it proved possible throughout our involvement with families to expose significant discrepancies between the attitudes of parents and professionals and to examine the extent to which they tended over time to converge. For example, at the outset, irrespective of whether suspicions are well founded, to be under investigation for child abuse is highly threatening. The intrusion is perceived by most parents as a traumatic event; normal family life is disrupted; it affects the most intimate of relationships. But for social workers an abuse investigation is frequently routine: its procedures are well-established; the alternatives are clear; seldom need it interfere with lunch. The contrast in operational perspectives at the outset could hardly be more extreme.

Psychological dimensions of operational perspectives

As we have seen, much psychological writing on perception explores how information is sorted, prioritised and given meaning. This process is influenced by personality, belief and previous experience, all of which vary between individuals, producing different responses. Certain other factors may also impinge, such as those highlighted by Argyle (1964), namely the quality of the interaction between participants, whether one or other individual may be considered dominant, and questions of motivation. He writes,

> it is not realised how far our perceptions of others are the result of categorising people into carefully learned private categories, and how they are distorted by motivation.

In the early stages in an investigation it is easy to see how the operational perspectives of parents and professionals can be poles apart. Professionals sense the vulnerability of parents, but even compensating gestures, such as offering to entertain a tearful toddler while the mother changes her baby's nappy, may be interpreted by her as a judgement against her competence as a parent. Parents will also dwell on their own emotions and motivations. For example, in the Clayton case, the mother may be inclined to talk about sexual abuse for a combination of reasons: she may be concerned about the child's sexualised behaviour and be seeking advice; she may want to rid herself of an unwanted partner or, alternatively, seek the child's removal in order to regain her partner's affections; she may be concerned about her daughter's health. Reasons for disclosure are seldom discrete and may prompt a variety of strategies.

However, as an inquiry proceeds operational perspectives may gradually converge. Parents often begin to recognise the advantages of welfare involvement and so overcome their earlier sense of hurt and violation. While the intrusion may be unwanted, it can bring welfare benefits in its wake, such as a family aide or a nursery placement. As a result, families have to weigh the advantages of keeping the agency worker at a distance against the need for continued help.

In recording their reactions to an abuse accusation parents felt frightened, ashamed, guilty or powerless, but some experienced less predictable emotions, such as excitement, jealousy and the desire for revenge. As we shall see in the coming chapters, responses are difficult to forecast in circumstances of extreme duress. Does a mother's vehement defence of her partner indicate affection, collusion, repudiation or a coping strategy? And what will be the long-term impact on the progress of the inquiry of having, at the outset, interpreted her behaviour to mean one thing and not another?

Perceptions are coloured by past experience. Parents who were themselves raised in families known to welfare services are familiar with social work practices. Three quarters of our families had been previously involved with social services, while others understood the role of social workers from television programmes. Those who were grateful for past support were often shocked when they encountered the same professionals in an unfamiliar investigative role. One parent bemoaned the complicity of her local primary school, 'We all know that school is full of Nosy Parkers paid to interfere, but teachers should teach, not listen to lies and gossip.'

Expectations also help to shape parents' perceptions. What they imagined might happen in future months influenced their attitude to their current predicament. One mother said:

> *Sue (the social worker) hasn't been back since the first visit. I'm sort of hoping that she's forgotten about it. They must have lots of difficult families and they probably can do without me. I hope so. If that happens we can all get back to normal as if nothing has happened.*

Quite commonly, parents drawn into an investigation sought to maximise benefit from the inquiry, but the enduring psychological reaction to investigation was guilt and self-blame. What more dirty linen lies among the videos and thumbed magazines at home to dent more deeply the self image of a parent under suspicion? Small wonder that short-term perspectives based on denial, anger and paranoia typify the early stages of suspicion.

Social dimensions of operational perspectives

Many social negotiations highlight differences in power. They may be long and well established, such as in interaction between father and son, boss and worker, or they may be sudden and unanticipated, such as between speeding motorist and police. The powerful remind the powerless of the differences in power by their behaviour: fathers by occupying the most comfy chair and clasping the TV remote control, others by the use of crested notepaper, portable phones and Filofax diaries. Any interaction is a vehicle for these messages. 'Robes and furr'd gowns hide all' muses King Lear. Thus, parents visited by a social worker at home felt more confident than those summoned to the social work office. To enter a busy, unfamiliar, possibly hostile office deepens the anxiety generated by the spectre of child abuse, and parents' sense of control swiftly disappears. In the hospital and the police station, the inviolability of the Clayton family evaporates. Operational perspectives are influenced not only by the quality of human interaction but by the conditions in which it occurs – the shape of the room, the design of the furniture, the colour of the paintwork. Just as social workers believe they discover meaning in the domestic surroundings of the families they visit, so do parents in the severe aesthetics of a social services department.

Other aspects of the context are important. Some parents are sensitive to issues of gender or race; some men resent the challenge to their role as protector. Poor and shattered families, who make up the majority of those suspected of child abuse, are reminded of their vulnerability. In the case of middle class families, who may be more keenly aware of their rights and more competent in their dealings with authority, the hackles rise and a battle may ensue. One of the problems in such situations is that the investigating professionals have little to offer. Seen in terms of Blau's (1964) exchange theory, the situation is one in which parents discover that the rewards for co-operation and reciprocation are low and the costs high. As a result, much-needed support may be rejected.

The way in which suspected abuse comes to light is another important factor affecting parents' and professionals' operational perspectives. Situations in which a parent discloses possible maltreatment are constructed and experienced differently from those in which parents have an investigation thrust upon them. Broaching a suspicion of child abuse gives a measure of control, witness the attention given in hospital to Margaret Clayton; she retained the power to decide when to talk, whom to talk to and what to reveal. There is seldom any cathartic revelation: information is likely to be disclosed gradually and grudgingly and in order to test professional responses. Nor are the professionals the only witnesses to the unpicking of private lives, other family members sense what is happening and bring their anxieties to bear. A strong sense of betrayal was a common perspective among those compelled to acknowledge that abuse existed in their family life.

Situations in which a social worker or health visitor confronts parents with a suspicion of abuse are quite different. The challenge to parents' shortcomings undermines their sense of reality and control. It is as if the door has been opened to a room in which everything said and done assumes sinister significance. At the end of the investigation the door stays ajar; the contents still spill out. Irrespective of the outcome, parents must struggle to integrate what happened into their normal understanding of the world – to form a revised operational perspective of their situation.

Conclusions

In the light of the work of social psychologists, in particular the writing of Harré and contemporary discourse analysts, we have described how perceptions, some conflicting and contradictory, come together to form an operational perspective. In a context dominated by suspicion, we have suggested that the operational perspectives of those involved in a child abuse investigation are rarely congruent and have indicated several areas in which the perceptions of parents and professionals are highly likely to be at odds. Further, we have shown that even within families the social and psychological dimensions of a perspective will differ: the cohabitee may have a concealed past, the adolescent may fear revelations that will compromise peer relationships, a mother may have been made to fear a loss of sexual allure. We hypothesise that the more closely in accordance are the operational perspectives of each participant, the better will be the outcome for the child. This possibility we explore in later chapters.

But an operational perspective is modified by new information and changed circumstances. The process is gradual, continuous, and at certain key moments, the scale and significance of change is greater; indeed, so memorable are these moments to parents under suspicion, we have called them *events* and made them the focus of our qualitative study. In interviews these events are recollected vividly and are used to account for subsequent action.

The first is the initial *confrontation* when social workers or other professionals tell parents of their suspicions of child abuse. The second is *the gathering* of professionals to discuss the case. Finally, there are *moments* when perceptions are revised in the light of new information or changed circumstances.

In the following Chapters we explore these events applying the analysis of participants' operational perspectives described above. We consider why, when and to what extent there are dissimilarities between the operational perspectives of professionals and parents, whether or not such differences can be said to be damaging, and, more important, to what extent the degree of correspondence between operational perspectives can be shown to affect the outcome of a case. In addition, we consider what changes to policy and practice may be warranted.

Summary points

1 The focus of this study is the way parents perceive their situation when under suspicion for abusing their children, and the effects these perceptions have on case outcome.

2 Although definitions of perception have long preoccupied social scientists, particularly psychologists, the concept resists clear and adequate definition. In this study, we use a synthetic approach; we understand perception as the process of selecting, interpreting and organising information; one that gives coherence and meaning to situations.

3 Faced with an accusation of child abuse, irrespective of its gravity or the weight of the evidence, parents devise coping strategies, which, as far as possible, will accommodate the accusation and its implications. This means of 'getting by' combined with the interpretation of events led us to develop the concept of an 'operational perspective'.

4 The behaviour of each of those involved in a child abuse investigation, parents and professionals alike, is governed by his or her 'operational perspective'. Parents and professionals are unlikely to share similar 'operational perspectives' at the outset. It is hypothesised that as time passes, in successful outcomes, the 'operational perspectives' of all parties converge.

5 Operational perspectives have psychological and social components.

6 At certain key moments in an investigation 'operational perspectives' are more likely to be modified. They occur at the initial confrontation, during meetings of professionals or when circumstances change or new information comes to light.

Chapter 7

The confrontation

We have described how the course of a child abuse investigation is influenced by the operational perspectives of all who participate in it and how these perspectives are moulded by social, cultural, emotional and intellectual forces. Further, we have argued that certain moments during an investigation are of enduring significance for parents, and that in the heat of such moments, under challenge from several professional quarters, operational perspectives are most likely to be adjusted. We have identified three such events as a basis from which to explore how operational perspectives evolve: the confrontation, when professionals gather and situations when new information and changed circumstances alter the way a case proceeds.

Here we focus on the first of the three events, *the confrontation*, when the issue of child abuse is broached with parents by a child protection agency. Because parents were asked to participate in the study after the confrontation had taken place, it was an experience shared by all 30 families in the study. In terms of the types of family described in Chapter Three, 14 had *multiple problems*, nine had *specific problems*, four were *acutely distressed* and three had been *infiltrated* by an abuser. No child was suspected of having been abused by someone outside the family.

Emerging suspicion

We have explained that a suspicion of child abuse most commonly comes to the attention of professionals by passing along one or other of three channels. Information may leak from the community to an agency, for example when someone other than a professional reveals or reports an anxiety; professionals may become aware of the possibility of child abuse in the course of routine work, or a particular occurrence may attract professional attention and, in the process, arouse suspicions. Generally speaking, suspicion gathers momentum slowly and is likely to be contained within a neighbourhood as an 'open secret' for some time. Some attempt at problem-solving may occur within the extended family system for fear that exposure to a statutory agency will bring shame and humiliation. In other circumstances, disclosure may be triggered by some seemingly trivial event which awakens latent anxieties. For example, the turning point for one mother was watching her husband and daughter sitting close together – normally the most ordinary of domestic events:

> *Suddenly, seeing them together like that watching the telly, turned my stomach. I knew it couldn't go on, I had to do something.*

We now consider confrontation from the point of view of participants in three investigations. One case concerns a family which we would describe as being acutely distressed, in another suspicion focused on a specific problem, the third is a multi-problem family. The suspicion of abuse is disclosed by a different route in each case. In the first, a mother speaks to a health visitor about her anxieties; in the second, a teacher notices sexualised behaviour in one of her pupils; in the third a drugs raid brings the neglect of a two-year-old girl to the notice of the police.

The Blake family (an acutely distressed family)

Lorraine Blake is 21 and lives with her husband Tom in a small cottage tied to Lorraine's part-time cleaning job at the local manor. She was brought up an anxious, unhappy child by parents who much of the time waged internecine war on one another. By her early teens Lorraine was depressed, overweight and suffering from bulimia. For long periods she shut herself away in her bedroom and made contact with the outside world only by Citizen Band radio.

By the time she was 18 her radio hobby had driven her into the arms of a fellow enthusiast. She soon became pregnant and decided to marry, seizing the opportunity to get away from home, but two births in quick succession were both difficult and she became subject to bouts of post-natal depression. To make matters worse, her eating disorder reappeared and increasingly she felt trapped, bored and isolated. She continued to be depressed and could not face returning to work. In those difficult circumstances her perspective on the confrontation was as follows.

> *It was my husband's attitude that really got me down. I know he's tired and that, what with Tina screaming every night, but he just seems to ignore her. It's not as if he doesn't like children. He was brilliant with our 'Chelle, but with Tina it was different; right from the word go he seemed to hate her. I know she's an ugly and whingey baby, different from our Michelle, but we've got her now and we'll have to look after her, won't we?*

> *I was really depressed that morning the health visitor called. I've always liked her, I think its because she's a nurse and that makes me trust her. Anyway, this time she made me a cup of tea and seemed understanding and kind. I just burst into tears and it all came out ...how it was all his fault because he wouldn't look at the baby or touch her, how withdrawn he was and how he hardly touched me any more. I even found myself suggesting it might be best if we had her adopted. I found it such a relief to talk to someone. You see sometimes I don't see anyone but Tom and the babies for days. She seemed so nice and I was really pleased when she stayed to have a word with him when he got home. I knew he'd be mad, but I was glad someone was going to give him a good talking to. But when she started on about social workers visiting us I began to wonder whether I shouldn't have just kept my mouth shut. I think she saw how worried we were, though, because she suggested that we both go and talk to the doctor. After she'd gone I was glad I'd said something, I felt better and maybe he'll get over whatever's wrong and help me a bit more.*

Lorraine is sinking under an avalanche of misfortune, acutely distressed in every sense. Her self esteem is low, she is ambivalent towards her children, she is dissatisfied and depressed She resents her husband's freedom but worries that he will reject the family for a quieter life.

On the other hand it is a relief for her to be able to give vent to some of her anxieties and she is pleased that someone with power is prepared to accept responsibility for doing something – 'giving him a good talking to'. In exchange for this support, she raises vague suspicions, but distances herself from any involvement in possible abuse. The suggestion is that Tom is having problems relating to the baby. She is prepared to seek the help of a professional whom she has learned to trust, but does not want anyone else to become involved, certainly not social services. At the end of the exchange, Lorraine feels someone has taken the trouble to listen to her story, has respected her wishes and is willing to help her, without questioning her competence as a wife and mother.

But what of Tom Blake, the suspected perpetrator, confronted with an abuse accusation? He, too, had an unfortunate childhood. His father brought scandal on the family by running away with a 16 year old girl, as a result of which Tom became over protective towards his mother, who eventually became seriously ill with cancer. She lived on for several years but on the two occasions when she went into hospital for surgery, Tom was fostered, and when she was home she was dependent on him for care and comfort. Tied to the house for different reasons, like Lorraine, Tom became interested in Citizen Band radio. After his mother died, Lorraine eventually moved in and the radio equipment was consigned to the loft.

> I saw the (health visitor's) car parked outside the house. I try to avoid seeing her, because somehow she always makes me feel I've done something wrong. When I walked in I could tell they'd been talking about me. It makes me mad when Lorraine does that; we're meant to be a family and a family sorts out its own problems. I'd only just got in the door when she starts asking me how I get on with my kiddies, and Lorraine looking on all the time to see what I'd say. It was as though she thought I hit them or something. It made me feel quite sick; I wouldn't do anything to hurt them. It wasn't fair. I got so angry that I found myself shouting at them, telling her how I leave the house while it's still dark to get the milking done and, except for coming home for me dinner, I work 'till eight every night. When I get back, half the time the place is like a pigsty, so I clear that up and on top of it all she expects me to find time to play with the baby. I'd worked myself into a right rage. But when she suggested she send in the social worker, all the wind went out of me. I just shut up after that, we don't want any social worker nosing round here. Lucky for us Lorraine decided it had all gone too far and she became as sweet as pie. She put a stop to it by telling the health visitor that we could manage really. In the end I felt the health visitor had some understanding of what we were going through and even offered to arrange some sort of home help.

From his account it is clear that Tom's operational perspective is influenced not only by the way the suspicion has come to light but by his current sense of betrayal and past feelings of guilt. The balance of power weighs against him; he has to justify his behaviour both to his wife and the health visitor. Nevertheless in the course of the interview, his attitude to the health visitor changes and, by the end, he feels she has understood his difficulties. We now turn to the third player, Mrs Bartlett the health visitor. She is very experienced, has a particular interest in preventative work and has been involved with the Blake family for three years since the birth of their daughter Michelle.

> I am a bit worried about this family. Every time I visit, Lorraine looks so overwhelmed by everything and I can see life must be difficult living so far from

anywhere. I know they've got money problems and this second baby is going to make it all the more difficult. When I arrived that morning she really did look quite done in and I wasn't at all surprised when she broke down and told me she wasn't sure she could manage any more. But I really began to worry when she talked about Tom's apparent hatred for the new baby. I've always thought that, although they are up against it at the moment, there's not really much wrong with the family. Little Michelle is very bonny and well up to her three year 'milestones'. I've really no worries about the baby either because when I undressed her for weighing she was clean and sweet smelling and just gurgled with delight. Although I don't have many worries about the children, Lorraine is still struggling with post-natal depression. I suggested another appointment with Dr. James and she seemed to calm down after that.

When Tom got back I tried to get him to discuss Lorraine and the baby, but he took it the wrong way and immediately flew off the handle. When I listened to his story, though, it was clear both of them were under a great deal of stress. In fact, I felt very sorry for both of them. I did wonder about getting social services in to help but, they seemed frightened at the suggestion so I let it drop. I think I'll just keep a close eye on everything for the time being. Perhaps Lorraine's outburst against Tom was a way of getting him to pull his socks up and help her more. I left feeling the visit had achieved quite a lot; Lorraine and Tom appeared much more reconciled and both little girls were well. I don't think it will be too long before the family is back onto 'an even keel.'

The health visitor's perspective on the situation is noticeably different from the Blake parents'. As in the majority of child protection investigations, initial abuse suspicions are quickly dampened. Mrs. Bartlett's examination of the children reveals no obvious signs of neglect or injury; Tom's outburst revives dormant anxiety but unwarranted intervention is forestalled by her experienced handling of the situation. By impressing on the parents that her chief concern is for the welfare and development of the two children, she feels she is able to assuage parental anxiety and preserve a good relationship with both parents. This strategy, she believes, will be in the best interest of the children.

Yvonne Oomah and her son Samuel (a specific problem family)

Yvonne Oomah is the child of well-educated, middle-class parents, who emigrated from West Africa to Scotland before she was born. Her father was a university lecturer, her mother became a hospital pharmacist and, because of the competing claims of their professional lives, when Yvonne was two she was sent back to Africa to live with her grandmother. When she was 13 she returned to Scotland for the sake of a British education and did well academically, although she had to put up with teasing and had few friends. She gained a place at University College, London to study law but, much to her family's anguish, abandoned her university career to marry a taxi driver. She became pregnant and for a time assumed the role of housewife, but the relationship quite soon deteriorated into acrimony and occasional violence, and, after the 'mother of all rows', in which the police had to mediate, she left her husband.

Yvonne's case begins when her son Samuel's nursery school reports suspicions of sexual abuse via an education welfare officer to social services who then write to her saying a social worker will visit her in the near future. The letter is otherwise unspecific, but, significantly, all this activity takes place at the time the Orkney child abuse case is being widely reported. How does she react to the intervention?

When I got the letter I was very shocked. I said 'Ah-ah... what's happening with the social worker! What have I done? Are they coming to take my child away?' I was scared. I hoped what happened to the Orkneys isn't going to happen to me now. I was just – 'O, God!, if anyone rings this bell, I hope – O, God! – it's not them!' Anyone who rings the bell, I look out of the window first – don't open the door – and I say 'Who is this?' From what I've heard from the telly, you know, I was very, very scared. And I phoned the social worker up. She wasn't in there! I phoned about three times and she wasn't actually in. And I left a message. But I didn't get a reply from her.

Circumstances seem to conspire against her

So I say, 'O.K., well, I'm going to sit down and wait for her to come.' Put my mind at rest, and, um, on the day she was supposed to come and see me she didn't turn up, and, you know, can you imagine how I feel? Because I'd made up my mind I would see her, and she didn't turn up, because they were on strike! – She shouldn't have made the appointment. I had to phone up again and say 'Why is Anne not here?' or something. And the next day she came – and I wasn't in! I'd already taken Samuel to nursery and I went round doing some shopping, so I came back a little later than usual, and when I got back I saw the note. And I went to her. She told me – she couldn't really express herself, you know – but I could see the point she was getting at and I was very angry.

Like Tom Blake's, Yvonne's anger is as much as anything to do with a sense of exposure and betrayal. Until this moment she has treated Claire, the head of Samuel's nursery school as a confidante. When Samuel was throwing tantrums and seemed to Yvonne to be eating too little Claire helped her to deal with both problems. 'Samuel was like fire, you know. He has really cooled down now,' she says. When she realises that the social services inquiry is the result of information passed on by the school, she is horrified. To make matters worse, Anne, the social worker, is also an acquaintance:

I knew Anne when she came in the neighbourhood office. I used to take Samuel down there at the mother and toddler group every week and she used to come, so I knew her – not that I had a problem or anything, but personally, socially...

It went round before I heard it. It wasn't the full thing I heard. Anne told me, 'Samuel's been exposing himself.' O.K. So I took it and I went to Claire. You know, she didn't tell me Samuel has done it just once or two times – you know; she just said 'Samuel has been exposing himself'. I was like, 'Are you sure? Are you sure Samuel is, because there's no man living here – just me and him.'

You know, I still couldn't take it in. It was like a dream, and I'm waking up out of a dream, and I was really angry, and I told her 'If I tell you I'm not upset or even angry I am lying.'

I went straight for Claire, and Claire saw me there and I was very angry. And she was, 'Calm down, cool down.' You know I'm very disappointed in her. You look at it – I'm the mother and I feel I should be told first. It's not that I can change anything about it...That's their role – you must get in touch with them – fair, I understand your part of it, but I feel I should have been told. And Claire was upset with Anne, that Anne didn't handle it properly and should actually have got back to her, and made a date to see me before the case was taken up. But this didn't happen. The way it happened – it just went bang, bang, bang – case conference – bang, bang, bang.

Beyond the sense of shock and betrayal there is great embarrassment

> *They said he's been exposing himself. When he goes to the toilet he wouldn't zip up his trousers and, you know, there was a little girl in the toilet and he went in with her, and, you know... So I say I find it very, very embarrassing. It's funny the way it happened, but still – I wasn't very pleased with it. You know, he must have seen something – that was the conclusion – so Claire was very concerned. He goes down to his dad every other weekend and he has come back telling me, 'I saw Daddy kissing Ruby' and he has said this not once – several times. You know, I have to protect myself as well, so now they concluded that Samuel must have been witnessing sexual intercourse or something like this. The teachers in the nursery, they were a bit concerned – he cuddles the teachers a lot. He cuddles them really tight. I said to them, he does it with me. I said maybe the weaning off the breast – the weaning process is still going on and cuddling – he's used to that.*

Yvonne is clearly distressed by the whole incident and her paranoia is fuelled by the social worker's delay in seeing her. During the confrontation, she veers between anger and fear as she struggles to establish her innocence; she fails to convince the social worker that there are no grounds for concern and is frightened at the prospect of Samuel being taken away. How does the social worker – herself the child of West African parents – view the same event?

> *There was a bit of a messy start in this case. I didn't know the family professionally and the first inkling I got was a rather vague telephone call from the educational welfare officer telling me of this little boy's sexualised play. I wasn't really very worried, but I did write to the mother. Then there was an office strike, not to mention a couple of cases which flared up, so, to cut a long story short, there was a bit of a delay in getting to see the mum. When I did talk to her she was very anxious; I think cancelling the first appointment didn't help, but the other cases were real emergencies and then there was the strike action. When I saw her I wasn't sure if anyone had already talked to her about Samuel, so I sort of 'felt my way'. I soon realised she had no idea what our concerns were and as I talked to her about his sexualised behaviour she became very agitated. I know from my own family African mothers never talk about sexual matters. When I tried to suggest he might be imitating what he has seen, she was horrified and adamantly denied ever allowing men in the house. Eventually she suggested he might have seen something when visiting his father. I felt it was all a bit vague, but if Claire Adams (the head mistress at the nursery) was concerned enough to refer him to us, I felt we had to conduct a thorough investigation. I found the interview quite difficult. It was clear she was not used to how social services worked and thought that she could persuade me not to call a protection meeting. In the end I think we parted on good terms and she started to trust me.*

This perspective is in sharp contrast to that of Mrs. Oomah. For social services it is a routine case of low priority. There has been little planning prior to the confrontation and we are given the impression of a rather confused interview. Looking back, the social worker feels confident that she has successfully reassured the mother and steered the meeting to a calmer conclusion.

Susan, Tony and baby Jane (a multi-problem family)

This case introduces a teenage couple, Susan and Tony, and their two year old daughter, Jane. Both parents grew up in families well known to the statutory agencies and allegations of one sort or another were commonplace. In this instance, a police drugs raid on Susan's bedsitter leads to renewed concerns about their baby's welfare. Let us explore how Susan, the 18 year old mother, interprets the visit.

It must have been about nine at night. We were just sitting watching telly and that. There was a knock at the door and loads of them come in – police dogs – everything. They were all mouthy and that. The coppers were all mouthing at us, and there was a piece of flex on the table – I remember that – no, on the floor, and Jane picked it up and started putting it in her mouth. So I took it off her, and put it on the table and said 'No!', and one of the coppers picked it up and put it back on the floor. So I went mad and said she could put it in her mouth and choke, or anything. There was about seven or eight – police dog, policewoman. Jane was crying her eyes out. I even had to take her to the police station with me.

Anyway, Tony's friends were smoking cannabis while the police were here, so I had to go to court last week and I got fined £70 for letting people smoke on my premises. There was nothing here, nothing found in the flat, nothing found on me or Tony. We just think it's because we got busted for drugs that Jane's got to be put on the High Risk list. I don't see the point of it. I mean, she's pretty fit.

It's going to be specially hard to get a decent place now, cos our names are in the paper and that... People have been a bit funny – definitely. Plus the landlord's giving us hassle all the time. Anything that goes wrong it's me. Like Tony moved out, and now he's moved back in. He's giving us hassle all the time.

An array of fears, insecurities, unhappy memories and misunderstandings influence Susan's reaction to the police raid and its aftermath. She was brought up by foster parents. Her pregnancy was the result of an under-age liaison with Tony and the couple lived together in a squat during part of her pregnancy. She explains:

Then our lease was up on there, so we moved into a bed and breakfast, and I didn't get on with the landlord, because basically he tried it on with me, and Tony went mad, so he kicked us out. So we were basically walking the streets with Jane with nowhere to go. A friend of Tony's put us up for a couple of days, then we went to Social Services. They said all they could do was get Jane with a foster parent at night time. So we done that, and, like, I had Jane during the day, and me and Tony were sleeping rough for about five weeks, anywhere we could find to sleep in.

The prospect of registration for child abuse is not fully understood, but her problems are so overwhelming that suspicions of abuse take a low priority. In retrospect, Susan is angry about the intrusion, but her anger speaks for older grievances. As the description of the characteristics of multi-problem families in Chapter Five illustrates, child abuse in these situations must be seen in the context of a welter of disadvantages. In this instance they include deprivation, poverty, the threat of homelessness and some history of drug abuse.

The police raid on Susan's flat reflects a different set of priorities. Since the officer responsible for it belongs to the drug squad, it is understandable that the action is conducted with such punitive efficiency, and, that despite the presence of a WPC, anxieties about child protection do not appear to be high on anyone's agenda. The officer is clearly distressed by the poverty of the household and the vulnerability of the child, but the circumstances do not permit him to explain himself. So he says subsequently:

This is the third time I've had to go into this family and, frankly, I feel this child is at considerable risk living in such squalor with parents who are clearly not fit to look after her. This time we became concerned because we'd been informed by a friend of Susan's that the baby was given drugs to keep it quiet. I know there are all sorts of unsavoury people visiting the house. The whole family is always in trouble and I suspect Susan is involved in her father's drugs business and young Tony is always getting into fights.

My first instinct was to get a WPC to remove the child but the least we should do is place her on the Child Protection Register. Her safety then depends on the social worker doing her job properly. Nevertheless, I feel fairly sure that either one, or both parents, will end up 'inside' and, as I stressed at the meeting, social services must be prepared once we arrest the parents to take the child into care.

Interpreting the data

Having considered parents' and professionals' accounts of the confrontation, let us explore how their operational perspectives are framed at the outset and modified as the investigation begins to unfold. As we indicated in the previous Chapter an operational perspective has several dimensions. Some may be described as *psychological* and internal, representing self image and emotional well-being or people's perceptions of one another, and there are also *social,* externally-driven dimensions, representing, for example, the power wielded by professionals and the sensitivity with which information private to the family is treated by outsiders. In terms of this classification of experience, then, how did families seek to get by?

Psychological dimensions of operational perspectives

Judgements concerning role and competence based on appearance are an obvious aspect of the action of an operational perspective. For Mrs Blake, the health visitor's uniform signifies matronly reassurance, but it is treated by her husband as a badge of authority which reminds him of past failings. Susan and Tony's angry reaction to the uniformed police raid, is, under the circumstances, a more predictable response to familiar intrusion of authority figures into their lives, and serves to bring to the surface a string of grievances, some justified, others not, but all *operational*.

Thus, while the confrontation may be regarded as giving those who participate in it an opportunity to revise pre-established attitudes, most people in such fraught circumstances instinctively rely on orthodox, familiar self-presentation in order to get by. However the police conducted themselves in Susan and Tony's company, even if they were extremely compassionate in their dealings with the mother and her child, it is unlikely that Susan and Tony's view of the police would have changed. Their experience determined what was likely to happen long before any interaction began. Nevertheless, hold in one hand the picture of a uniformed policeman with a dog invading the home of a semi-destitute teenage mother and threatening to take away her child, and in the other that of a helpless baby being rescued by an honourable guardian of the law from squalor, degradation and amphetamine poisoning and one can begin to grasp the significance of operational perspectives where child protection work is concerned.

A particular difficulty in the very early stages is that some professionals consider parents deceptive even when they are being honest (Bond and Fahey, 1987). In Yvonne Oomah's case, the social worker's suspicion about sexual abuse increases when faced with the mother's reluctance to discuss sexual behaviour. Yet had the mother rushed into discussion of intimate matters, that, too, could have been interpreted as lacking in propriety, if the social worker had chosen bring to bear her own racial perspective ('African mothers never talk about sexual matters.'). As for Yvonne, she attributes her keenly felt embarrassment to the fact that she knows the social worker and the nursery school teacher as friends:

Q *Does it make it easier for you to talk or more difficult?*

A Makes it difficult, because I've known her, and I was ashamed. I'd rather have someone I didn't know.

Parents often told us that during the initial confrontation they felt trapped because everything they did or said was given a hostile interpretation. They felt guilty until proved innocent. Just as most people have something to hide or find certain topics difficult to discuss and their anxieties will influence their behaviour during any form of inquisition, so other factors weighed on these confrontations, not least the Blakes' concern about their marriage, Yvonne Oomah's guilt at 'abandoning' Samuel to nursery school and Susan and Tony's use of cannabis.

A suspicion of child abuse profoundly affects people's perception of self and other family members. Naturally, parents attempt to manipulate the inquiry and to massage their bruised emotional well being. Lorraine Blake, for instance, fights off low self esteem by blaming others and casting herself in the role of 'hard done by'. Tom grapples with a history of failure and inadequacy and the suspicion of neglect and indifference forces him to reassess his self-image as a hard-working bread winner doing everything possible for his family. Yvonne Oomah is outraged. For professionals working daily with extreme distress, violence, illness and exploitation, it may be difficult to comprehend just how great an affront to one's self image as a parent suggestions of abuse can be.

In these situations, parents swiftly learn techniques of neutralisation (Matza and Sykes, 1957). Tom Blake recounts his busy day, implying that anyone so overwhelmed would behave as he did. Tony and Susan deny all and, with some justification, divert attention to their poor housing and lack of money, burdens under which the best of us would buckle.

Previous experience of the child protection system will also affect the quality of the interaction and may help parents to interpret the signals they receive during a confrontation; but it will not provide all the answers. For example, Susan and Tony view the violence of the police raid with a certain familiarity; it is just another example of what they regard as police harassment and unnecessary social work interference in their private lives. Both parents accept professionals with extreme caution, have little expectation that any intervention will be to their benefit and judge that the best way of dealing with authority is 'to keep your head well down'. Lorraine Blake, on the other hand, has developed a close and rewarding relationship with her health visitor. Although she would not normally reveal 'family troubles' to an outsider, she confides in 'a trusted friend' hoping that the response will be sympathetic and supportive. She senses little danger in implying that her husband may be guilty of abusing their child. Yvonne Oomah's case is different again. She has no previous experience of social workers (except through her acquaintance at the mother and toddler group) and is susceptible to the messages then current in the media that social workers can be over zealous in their desire to protect children.

The considerable burden of child protection work means that professionals can become less sensitive to the concerns and uncertainty of parents. We found that the more experienced staff thought false reports of abuse rare and that they could easily be identified. Evidence that did not accord with this professional view tended to be ignored or misinterpreted.

These case studies show that a confrontation about suspected child abuse is a far cry from the social interactions most parents normally encounter. Even for the most socially skilled, it is an extraordinary situation in which the rules governing effective behaviour are obscure. Participants are prevented by the roles in which they are cast from exploring each other's perspectives. Faced with a suspicion of child abuse, parents make rapid assumptions about professionals' likely behaviour. They are uncertain whether the suspicion is justified; they do not know who has started the process by saying or doing what; the consequences of adopting one strategy as opposed to another are unforseeable. Hence, defence and evasion are appropriate strategies. After all, what would hurling missiles at a departing social worker achieve – unless it is Winnicott's collected works or Freud's which fly down the garden path?

Social influences on operational perspectives

Twenty-two of the 30 parents participating in this intensive study were poor. They lived on the margins of society and they faced severe problems more extreme than the abuse allegations with which they were confronted. Their ability to interact with child protection professionals was diminished accordingly. Indeed, it is significant that Yvonne Oomah, who came from an educated middle-class background, was the only one here to stand her ground.

> *I told everyone, I actually wrote a letter to the director of social workers. You know, I don't want what happened to me to happen to somebody else. If the press hear things like this happen, they will take it up and it will get out of hand.*

In comparison with the others, she knew her rights. She was watchful and attentive; the rest sat and waited, because they had learned that their passivity was expected and might sometimes result in their misdemeanours being forgotten or something being done to relieve their problems. Effective belligerence is a professional skill professionally learned.

To most parents, it is apparent that professionals not only hold all the cards but control the rules of the game. The child protection system sets the style and pace of the investigation, makes judgements based on undisclosed criteria and decides on courses of action regardless of parents' views. Even the confident Yvonne Oomah held back in the knowledge that convincing the social worker of her parenting skills could influence her child's future. Interacting in her own world she is more secure:

> *I actually thought about going to see a sleeping expert because Samuel's sleeplessness was getting on top of me. I have to work and if I was tired, when I got to work, I had to tell them – 'Look, I don't sleep – if I do anything, just forgive me.' If I tell anybody off and I'm on the brink of quarrelling with everybody, I actually go to them and say, 'Please, this is my problem; I don't sleep very well because of my son – please forgive me.' When I explained to them and they saw Samuel as well, they said 'We can see what you mean!'.*

Professionals are in control but they bring different priorities to each case. The health visitor was primarily concerned with the health of the children and had no hesitation in undressing and physically examining the Blake baby. The policeman saw his prime function as law enforcement. The social work role, however, is less straightforward because social workers have to balance a requirement to protect the child with a need to support the family. As a result, when social services become involved in an investigation, parents receive ambiguous messages; as Yvonne Oomah said, 'I didn't know what she was trying to tell me'.

The way suspicions come to light influences the progress of the inquiry. Yvonne Oomah had to demand information from her social worker, a request which became muted as soon as the possibility of child sexual abuse was raised. Most people view sexual abuse as something 'outside' the family, so that at the moment of confrontation confident denial is difficult. In contrast, because she decides to seek advice and help from the health visitor, Lorraine Blake retains a measure of control and the confrontation, to some extent, takes place on her terms. Hardly surprising, since he is cast in the role of the perpetrator, Tom Blake views the experience slightly differently; he feels betrayed by his wife's decision to make public what he considers a private matter. In contrast again, Susan and Tony have lived most of their married life under the sideways gaze of one agency or another; the police raid is just another example of the extent to which privacy is denied them.

All that said, in reality, overworked professionals are not anxious to delve into every shadowy corner of private life, and, as a result, erring on the side of indifference, they may fail to recognise parents' anxiety. In the case of Yvonne Oomah, the social worker's insensitivity can be explained by burden of work; by her standards to let a week go by between writing a letter and seeking to deal with its consequences was an acceptable way to manage her caseload; for Yvonne Oomah the waiting was intolerable.

It is also important to remember that not all parents are determined to protect their privacy to quite the same extent: Lorraine Blake speaks of her relief that 'things are finally out in the open'. Nevertheless, there are some aspects of the family life that she is reluctant to share with professionals, no matter how close and supportive they may seem. By the same token, others in her position may find that to raise suspicions about a husband's attitude to the care of a child is to take a risk. Lorraine might well have been more wary had she known how other similar cases progressed.

How might the situation be improved?

We have considered the experience of three families in the early stages of a child protection investigation. From this evidence, we have extracted material relating to the psychological and social components of operational perspectives described in Chapter Six. We have found, perhaps predictably, that parents' operational perspectives of the confrontation are in various respects at odds with those of professionals. Is there anything that could be done to bring their perspectives into closer line with each other and by so doing improve the outcome of the case?

The child protection system tends to fall between two stools. There is a desire that it should be specialist, equipped to deal only with child abuse and to divert those families who have other difficulties towards more appropriate provision; at the same time it seeks to be general in its approach, wishing to place abuse in its wider context and to respond to the range of difficulties that beset families. Consequently, at the moment, the protection process is neither sufficiently focused nor sufficiently eclectic to deal with the issues child abuse raises and some professionals and many parents are perplexed by its multifarious functions, aims and objectives (Dobson, 1992).

Current arrangements have considerable strengths, nevertheless. As we saw in Chapter Four, a range of professionals is providing families with support in a variety of situations, but there seems little attempt to match the service provided with the particular situation of the families involved. When the suspicion of abuse is first raised with parents, the difficulty of the moment is such that the interaction needs to be handled with great sensitivity. Would it be possible to link certain professionals with the requirements of particular types of family? The evidence certainly points to a need for increased training to prepare those professionals who must articulate suspicions of child abuse.

The scope for influencing the psychological perspectives of those involved in the early stages of an investigation may be limited. However, simply by taking into account the enormous burden many parents already carry, by offering practical help and focusing on any strengths that may exist inside families, social workers can moderate parents' sense of invasion. The evidence offered by Gibbons and colleagues (1993) might also prompt child protection professionals to think twice before referring first suspicions to other agencies.

The social dimensions of operational perspectives are, by contrast, more amenable to change. Three improvements suggest themselves: (i) More information to help smooth the interaction of professional and parent; (ii) more encouragement to social workers to reflect upon the nature of their task; (iii) greater effort to safeguard the rights of individuals caught up in an inquiry.

Parents enter the child protection system unaware of the complexity of what is likely to be explored in their name. They are entitled to more information about the issues and why they have surfaced and about what is and what is not regarded as acceptable behaviour. They also have a right to know the most likely outcome of the case, which, almost invariably, will involve telling them that their child will *not* be taken away from them. In short, professionals need to be honest with parents, even when it may not entirely suit their strategy. There are circumstances in which most mothers and fathers find themselves suddenly bereft of effective 'parenting skills'; nevertheless, at that or any other moment they would rightly resent any general charge that they are *bad* parents. Therefore allegations should be expressed in specific terms and tempered with a clear admission that definitions of good parenting practice do not exist. It may help all involved in an investigation to bear in mind the limitations of the science.

The senior practitioners we interviewed felt that professionals might well reflect more deeply on their actions. One experienced social worker said, 'if you ask yourself, what are your motivations for doing this? at each point in an investigation, you make life easier for yourself in the long run'. Otherwise, in relation to parents attempting to cope with official scrutiny, they might ask themselves, 'how would I feel if I were in their situation?'

Finally, what of the rights of parents? In the absence of any legal representation, parents need guidance on what they ought to reveal during an interview and what information they are permitted – and may be well advised – to keep private. They could also be offered the option of a second professional opinion if they disagree with the official ruling in their case, or of a new social worker should they feel the relationship is hopeless. Needless to say, each of these suggestions has resource implications and might protract what is already a lengthy process; but, given the numbers of families experiencing this sort of intervention each year, paying attention to the needs and rights of consumers would seem to be a priority.

Helping particular types of family

We have talked generally about the ways in which child protection procedures might be improved, but might there also be strategies specific to the different types of families caught up in the process? In the case of acutely distressed families, such as the Blakes, the central question is whether the child protection system is the best servant of their needs. Section 17 of the *Children Act* offers the alternative avenue of family support and there are other possibilities such as recourse to the social fund or family therapy.

Specific problem families are rather different. Since the suspicion of child abuse is a new experience, the parents' view of the child protection process is more amenable; but, as in the case of Yvonne Oomah, things can go awry: swifter action would have allayed her fears; greater sensitivity, respect and honesty, together with a clear explanation of protection procedures might well have led to a more satisfactory outcome for all concerned.

At the other extreme, multi-problem families are well known to many welfare and control agencies, even to the same extent as Susan and Tony, who relied on social services' support during much of their childhood, and whose adult life was a continuous struggle with drug and alcohol-dependency, unemployment, homelessness and poverty as well as the miasma of domestic violence. On the brighter side it can be said that such cases would benefit greatly from a general service and from inter-agency intervention. In such cases, particular care could be given to deciding which professionals should initiate and which prosecute an abuse inquiry; certainly such an investigation should not be the by-product of a drugs search.

Conclusions

Parental perspectives in cases of suspected child abuse change over time, but there are key moments in the process when individuals take stock and a new operational perspective emerges. Here we have explored the first key event, the confrontation, when a professional meets a parent and attempts to communicate his or her concerns. But many of the issues are trivial. The Blakes' marital problems would have gone unnoticed a decade ago, when the terminology of emotional abuse was unknown. The case of Yvonne Oomah, a middle class parent of a possibly sexually-abused son, promises more drama, but her struggle to communicate with social services and her understandable sense of betrayal by friends turn out to be the only remarkable features of the case. The invasion of Susan and Tony's bedsitter by policemen and a police sniffer-dog is reminiscent of pedestrian TV dramas, but from the point of view of the child protection services its value is negligible.

It might be argued that all 30 families we scrutinised in the intensive part of this study had chronic problems which would have responded more readily to other types of intervention. However, regardless of parents' low opinion of the abuse investigation process, it seems that many subsequently benefit from contact with the child protection service.

Nevertheless procedures could be improved to close the gap between the perspectives of parents and professionals. It is important to get things right at the outset because many cases do not progress beyond the first confrontation. If the interrogation ends acrimoniously, a parent's jaundiced view of the system may well endure. The next time a social worker knocks on the door, parents may be uncooperative and reluctant to seek help, even in situations where child abuse is not the issue.

Summary points

1 Suspected child abuse comes to light (a) when someone in the family or in the neighbourhood reports a situation; (b) when abuse is noticed by professionals in the course of their duties; (c) when an event or aspects of the child's behaviour alert concern. Using the classification of families employed earlier in this study, we have explored parental, family and professional perspectives as suspicion emerges and an accusation is made.

2 In the majority of situations, those in which parents are ignorant of mounting suspicions of abuse, the impact of an investigation is very considerable. Parents feel angry, resentful and violated. They worry that the accusation may be a prelude to prosecution and the removal of the child. It is difficult in these early stages to distinguish the anxiety and anguish of the innocent from the fear and remorse of the guilty.

3 Social workers and others must display extreme sensitivity, tolerance and awareness at the point of confrontation because it is the moment when parents' operational perspectives crystallise in a form that may colour the case during subsequent months. Parents' coping strategies may include expressions of disbelief and denial, but their perceptions will differ from those of their offspring. Mothers may come to suspect the involvement of others in the family, their partners may resent those who seem prepared to

divulge family secrets, siblings are resentful of the publicity, the victims of abuse may retreat into denial that anything untoward ever occurred.

4   The professional, burdened with many abuse investigations and other problems, may lose sight of how violating to families are accusations of and investigations into child abuse. Child protection procedures have a momentum of their own, aggravating parents' feelings of powerlessness and vulnerability. Particularly important is the way suspicion surfaces and who deals with the accusation. Naturally, a cry for help from parents tends to incline all those involved to a more benign perspective than does suspicion aired by a stranger outside the family. Nevertheless, most cases generate feelings of trust betrayed.

5   Suspicions of sexual abuse are particularly difficult to manage both for families and caring professionals. There is great embarrassment and a reluctance to talk, the awareness of child and adolescent sexuality may be unwelcome, family members and close friends are regarded with unease. The integrity of the parental relationships and the loyalty and honesty of the victim and other siblings are called into question. Above all hangs the prospect of punishment and loss.

6   The scope for influencing the operational perspectives of those involved is varied. Psychological aspects are particularly difficult to influence. More can be done with regard to the provision of information, heightening social workers' awareness of their task and safeguarding the rights of individuals caught up in the process

Chapter 8

The professionals gather

Many child abuse investigations do not progress beyond the confrontation discussed in the previous Chapter, because there is agreement among professionals that no further action or involvement is warranted. However, in 22 of the 30 situations we studied, there was at least one subsequent meeting at which the case was formally reviewed. Such gatherings took the form of a case conference, a case review or a planning discussion. Thus, another opportunity for re-appraisal arises.

When this study was mounted, parental involvement in case conferences and reviews was unusual, and in both participating local authorities parents were excluded from child protection meetings. As the fieldwork was in progress, policy was brought more closely into line with the Government guidelines *Working Together*, but even at the time of preparing this report there were inconsistencies: it was not uncommon for parents to be permitted to attend only part of a meeting and in certain circumstances they were excluded altogether. Whatever the degree of parents' involvement, such set-pieces constitute a major event in their lives, and for good or ill can influence attitudes to those intervening in intimate aspects of their relationship with their children.

In examining how operational perspectives may be modified in the event of a case conference, we focus on three other families representative of the types described earlier: an acutely distressed family, a family with a specific problem and a multi-problem family.

The French family (an acutely distressed family)

Mary French, the youngest of four girls, had what she described at the outset as a happy childhood in a settled home, and she was still in fairly close contact with her parents. By her own assessment she had been consistently unfortunate in her choice of sexual partners. The father of her 11-year-old daughter Katrina and nine-year-old son Jason abandoned her to live with her best friend, and in the course of the investigation, having until then continued to support her and their children, he emigrated to Australia. Her second marriage was to a persistent offender from whom she was estranged and who, at the time of the investigation, was in prison for drugs dealing. The father of her younger daughter, twenty-two month-old Keri, had had a very unhappy childhood and been stabbed, near fatally, by a previous wife. She was jailed and their sons were taken into care. Mary came bitterly to regret her relationship with this man, but, because of the help given to his sons, developed a certain respect for the work of social services. She said of the marriage, 'I think what it was – I could never accept that I lived with a man and was married to him for six years and he never loved me. All these years I wanted him to love me, and he never could and it was really hard to accept. He was never close to me or anything, even when we slept together.' Their daughter, Keri, was the focus of the abuse investigation.

One evening Mary left the younger children in the care of Katrina to visit a woman friend; she stayed longer than she intended and when she returned found the street busy with firemen. An explosion in an electrical sub-station had made it necessary for police to evacuate nearby houses, and in the process they discovered Keri and Katrina asleep and alone (Jason was already outside playing on the green). Social services called a protection meeting. Simultaneously, criminal proceedings were begun against Mary French for the abandonment of Keri.

Mary was not permitted to attend the child protection meeting, but her attitude to what transpired there and to the account of it given to her afterwards by the social worker was coloured strongly by her impression that she was considered guilty by association with a criminal husband.

> *The police were like dead anti-me straight away, although they could see I was in a terrible state about the fire. They dragged me off down the police station, made me make a statement about what had happened and reported it to social services.*

The operational perspective of the policeman responsible for the inquiry was at that juncture not far adrift from her jaundiced assessment. There were indeed suspicions that she was continuing to deal in drugs while her husband was in custody, that her absence from the house was connected to that trade and that there was some unspecified connection between drugs use and the 'waif-like' appearance of Keri. Concern about the child's failure to thrive was of long standing and had been fuelled by neighbourhood gossip.

The social worker assigned to the case was also familiar with the atmosphere of suspicion in the neighbourhood concerning Mary French's behaviour and, following the imprisonment of her husband, of her relationships with other, younger men. Similarly, the health visitor was already aware of Keri's frailty, suspected that there might be drugs in the house – but had no anxiety about the possibility of abuse until she received an anonymous telephone call. Thus, in the enforced absence of the mother, the child protection meeting absorbed and intermixed these preconceptions and uncertainties. Keri was registered as the object of grave concern, and, somewhat unusually, a family aide was assigned to the case on the advice of the social worker, who visited Mary French to tell her what had transpired:

> *The social worker came to the door as bold as brass and said 'By the way two of the children aren't registered, but Keri is'. I'd been sweating all day about it and the social worker walked in like it was buying a loaf of bread. Nobody would tell me exactly what was said. It was bits and pieces. All I could get was neglect. I had neglected Keri. If they had wanted to visit me – weekly, monthly – I would have been willing to accept that, but they called in doctors, teachers – so many people were involved. As soon as you say Protection Register, it could be anything.*
>
> *I don't like it. I feel I've failed as a mother. I've gone over and over it and I'm afraid to move or do anything. She said I could get done if I walk three houses to the phone box, or if I went to a neighbour and left the children. Two days ago Keri slipped in the garden and grazed her eyebrow. I was in a terrible state thinking, they'll think I've done it. She said Keri was at risk, which, fair enough, I had put her at risk, but I wasn't likely to do it again. I feel it escalated from me going out for half an hour to being a complete idiot in what I was doing.*

Mary French's case was one of only two in our intensive study in which the investigation resulted in criminal proceedings. Two months after the child protection meeting the abandonment case was heard at the Crown Court, as she had elected for trial. Somewhat paradoxically, it was during the weeks leading up to the court hearing that Mary French began to regain a measure of control over the events that had overtaken her and so to adjust her perception of the power of the system with which she was dealing. She went to a solicitor who urged her to deny the allegation, regarding it as having been vindictive. The only witness available to her was her other daughter, 11-year-old Katrina, whose presence in court was demanded by the prosecution and who was consequently involved in a curiously theatrical episode in which she gave her evidence in full view of the bench, with an aunt – one of Mary's sisters – at her side, but separated from her mother by a curtain. The confidence with which Katrina conducted herself – the extent to which her presence spoke for the solidarity of her family – became a factor in the argument, and the case was dismissed.

As Mary French began to demonstrate a degree of skill in dealing with the formal process, so the operational perspectives of the social worker, the health visitor and the family aide were conditioned by a mixture of admiration and wariness. Thus the health visitor described her graciously as an 'intelligent, agonised, survivor' but added, 'it was difficult to be straight with her; I don't feel she is being totally open – but it's just a hunch.' Likewise, the family aide remarked on the ease of dealing with her, but described her as 'a bit too clever'.

> Nothing will come of it, but things will always be a bit iffy... She's no angel but there will be nothing she can be tripped up with... She is only complying to get social services off her back. She wants us all to piss off and leave her alone.

The social worker spoke of a mutual lack of trust, extending to her own relationship with the police. At the outset the police inspector had described Mary French merely as an appendage of Keri's imprisoned father 'she's 'Mad Mike's' girl'. Because Mary had refused to name the friend she visited on the night of the fire they had assumed she must have been up to no good and so were determined to pursue the court case against her. Nevertheless, the social worker herself said:

> My gut feeling is that there is more under the surface. She is sexually very active. She is still buying new things all the time. Her standard of living is better than you would expect for anyone living in a council house on income support.

All these professionals were bound to concede that general intuitions and anxieties about Mary French's lifestyle did not necessarily have any bearing on her ability to care for Keri, whose feeding problems were meanwhile being diagnosed and remedied. Fortified by the outcome of the court case, Mary began to assert herself by seeking a review meeting, dismissing her family aide and more openly criticising her social worker:

> I don't want to be rude, but I'm getting tired of all these visits, because I'm not gaining nothing. Barbara (the social worker) doesn't bother to visit me, and when she does she walks in and picks fault, walks out and upsets me. In the beginning they thought I was a neurotic mum who couldn't cope with my children and they were going to come in here, I was going to be in pieces, and I was going to say 'have Keri, I'm going out for the day' like most other people.

Two weeks after the court case, partly as a result of her pressure, which included going over the head of her social worker, the review meeting was convened. By Mary French's own account the experience was traumatic:

> *Like, I was there, and there were all these people staring at me. Really, I'm a shy person. All I kept saying to myself was I'm fighting for my children, and that pushed me on to do it, like when I was in court. They were sat there dictating my life. They didn't know me from Adam. I could have been a trampy, scruffy woman, but I said what I wanted to say, and if I hadn't said what I said, the social worker would have made me sound like a prostitute, who didn't care about the children.*

But by then the social worker's attitude to her was more charitable – and resigned – than Mary was prepared to acknowledge:

> *I knew I hadn't a hope of retaining the child on the register. I was anxious only that the meeting didn't get sucked up with Mary's feelings or with her denials that there was anything at all the matter. I tried not to totally alienate her, and to keep hold of an entrée to the home. She was terribly polite at the meeting. She conducted herself beautifully and got exactly the result she wanted.*

Rather curiously, considering how important the latter's contribution had been to the outcome of the Crown Court hearing, the social worker expressed worries about Katrina's well-being and the burden of responsibility for looking after Keri she seemed to be prepared to shoulder: 'She is too grown-up, too ready to talk, for an 11-year-old too ready to comply with adult demands,' she said. In the same fluid atmosphere, Mary found that her former family aide was prepared to help her fend off the concern about Katrina's compliance and come to her rescue when the social worker insinuated that she might be involved in prostitution. By chance the family aide had come into contact with the 'friend' Mary visited on the night of the fire, 'a young, scruffy, chaotic, swearing mother of four'. Mary had always maintained she had been on a mercy mission, delivering nappies to a housebound friend; possibly the family aide was more inclined than previously to see the world through her eyes.

The upshot of the meeting was that such anxiety as there continued to be about the welfare of the children was directed away from the child protection system. The meeting concluded that voluntarily accepted support services available under the *Children Act* were the most appropriate form of action. Nevertheless, as far as Mary was concerned, she bore the scars:

> *I don't feel we're going along in our own sweet way like most families – just living our lives – I do feel we are labelled, for example, I can't be a child-minder any more because of what happened, it will never go away.*

And her underlying insecurities, brought to the surface during the investigation, were undiminished:

> *I'm always striving for a man to love me. I relate to men like they were my father; I tend to give in. I feel sorry for the kids. They've been through ordeals in their lives. I want to protect them, to spoil them. My dad was very hard with me. Both my parents were never loving.*

The Clayton family (a specific problem family)

Our second cameo, already referred to in Chapter Six concerns Brian and Betty Clayton and two daughters, Margaret, by Betty's previous marriage, and Elizabeth. They are the sort of family who normally do not come to the attention of social services: Brian is a College graduate; Betty was a nurse before she gave up work to look after her children and has an interest in reflexology. For the Claytons, disclosure by their elder daughter insinuating sexual abuse of herself and her sister by her stepfather left the family thunderstruck, while hospital doctors, police and social workers were meanwhile plummeted into a round of interviewing and consultation which culminated in a child protection conference. The suspected abuser bitterly resented his exclusion from what he regarded as a trial by lynch-mob:

> First they tell me I'm sexually abusing my own daughters and then they won't allow me to defend myself. We were excluded out. We were told definitely we couldn't go; all we were allowed was to make a submission in our defence. We tried to pre-empt what questions they would be asking or what subjects they would be talking about and to try to submit something, but if you don't know what they are talking about... how can you?

> All social services say is... we have a situation where sexual abuse is alleged. It was either get out of the house or spend the weekend in a cell. They didn't want to hear 'justifications' which is what they called them. Every action has got a justification. Even if it is only making a cup of tea, there's a reason why you put the milk in it or the sugar and you've got to be able to justify that... They were not prepared to listen. They want to look at a little bit and not the whole thing.

> All the social workers I've met – there was at least three at college studying psychology and so forth, but they were there as a result of advice from psychiatrists that they needed therapy. They were all there because they needed social workers, and this is what I've found out about social workers – that nobody needs a social worker more than a social worker. The ones that I've met are all screwed up in their own way and instead of dealing with their own problems they are out there messing about in other people's lives.

Betty Clayton was just as scathing in her judgement of the secrecy of the child protection conference. Their relationship was fraught and the sexuality of the family extremely complex, but, at the outset, under what they saw as unprovoked assault by strangers, husband and wife were united:

> At the end of the day, they are discussing us. The family should be represented, with a member of the family – because they're talking about us, but all they say is well, you should have written a letter in your defence. They've taken a piece of our lives and they've labelled us as whatever they've labelled us as. In the whole context they don't know any of us, and they are not prepared to listen even. Without all the added information, you don't get the full picture; you don't get the complete puzzle.

In circumstances when the quality of the relationship between family members is obscured by a shared sense of outrage, the work of professionals becomes extremely difficult. In specific problem cases like the Claytons' when the individuals involved were barely known to social services and so information was lacking, the hindrance to mutual understanding was apparently insurmountable. The evidence of severe distress was nevertheless persuasive and cogent: after swallowing too many sleeping pills in a 'suicide performance', Margaret came round in hospital and shared her secret of sexual abuse by her stepfather with a sympathetic nurse. By the time of the case conference, Margaret was back with her family:

> After the whole event I just isolated myself totally and just put a wall round myself and wouldn't talk to dad; I didn't want to go anywhere near him, but then what happened was, one night, it came up – can't remember how – I was sitting watching the TV and just blocked myself off so I'd got my back to everyone. Dad switched the telly off and said 'Look, we've got to talk about

*this, because the situation can't go on'. I was just like, 'Leave me alone –
fuck off! I don't want to know'. Everybody else started crying and there was
like 'Can't you see what you're doing to us!' ... and I thought 'It's not my fault!'
and luckily, because I'd been to the social worker and everybody, I knew it
wasn't my fault. When all this was going on dad just got really angry; he was
downing the scotch like nobody's business and he just threw the glass at the
wall. It was just like shock. I'm more violent than he is. But, you know, that
just broke it – not only the glass but the situation.*

*Liz (her sister) started backing off. She was saying, 'I think about it now, and
it wasn't abuse or anything' but she was trying to protect her dad, whereas
I've always felt a certain isolation from him anyway because he's not my dad,
and I could never tell him that. The sad thing is I like him a lot, but I don't love
him like I love Lizzie and mum. Mum was saying, 'Don't you love your dad,
don't you love him?' and I could turn round and say 'No! I don't.' But it's really
difficult.*

For Margaret, dealing with the consequences of having disclosed her abuse was obviously the priority and the issue of whether or not her step father or anyone else should
have attended the meeting was unimportant. Her behaviour, the consistency of her
accounts and the urgency of her appeal for help made her a formidable witness. From
Elizabeth, the younger daughter, however, we get a different perspective.

*I feel that everything we've said as a family has basically been seen as us try-
ing to protect ourselves. I feel that what we have said has just been twisted
round to be put against us. It just isn't like that at all. I feel that Margaret puts
herself outside the family. She does, but then to anyone like the social worker
or people like that, she just says 'they don't love me', but she puts herself in
that position where she goes outside the family. Nobody's pushed her out
there, or helped her out there. She's done it herself, but she blames us for
her own fault...*

*One of the teachers, she was asked to talk to the case conference or what-
ever it was, and the difficulty for me is – I don't know whether they did it on
purpose, but they actually said it was the nurse. And the nurse has not actually liked me since I went to that school and I actually hate her. She's bitchy
to the kids and more towards me – and she's the one that went to this conference! I'm not surprised they put my name on the register if she was there,
she's always had it in for me. I can't go back to school now. The social
worker said no one would know, but I don't trust them. You can bet everyone
will know'.*

In the general mêlée of a child protection meeting, it is possible to overlook the specific
concerns of children. Elizabeth dreaded that the suspicion would become public knowledge, especially in school. Against this practicality the truth or otherwise of her half-
sister's allegations against her father paled into insignificance. The social worker, John
Langtree, who is also a psychotherapist, gives his version of events.

*This case came up at the hospital and we investigated the allegations jointly
with the police. Our policy is to try to keep families together wherever possible, although at the time the police were keen on prosecution and wanted
the father out of the home. They seemed convinced by the evidence.*

*Suspected sexual abuse cases can be very difficult and this one is particu-
larly demanding because the girls are telling us different stories. As I said at
the meeting, a thorough assessment needs to be done to explore the family
pathology.*

One of the first things that will have to be addressed is to discover what really happened and who is telling the truth. Brian is adamant that Margaret is lying and his behaviour was an expression of love. I'm convinced the only way to sort out these sorts of issues is through family therapy. After all, adolescent girls don't make these sorts of allegations in well functioning families.

Things didn't look too good at first. When I called to tell the family about the girls being registered, Brian was badly shaken by the whole affair. On the other hand, I felt that the mother responded well and appeared open to the idea of family work. The girls showed different problems. Elizabeth was obsessed that her school friends would find out and kept insisting she was never going back to school. But Margaret really worried me. When I arrived she was closeted in her bedroom and wouldn't talk to anyone.

The social worker's concerns were again different from those of the family members. John Langtree did not want the parents to attend the meeting because a consensus needed to be fashioned and the police were reluctant to discuss their evidence so openly. Neither did he think prosecution would help. He did not know whether the allegations of abuse could be substantiated but he believed any allegation indicated something must be wrong, and that family therapy was required. Placing the children's names on the Child Protection Register was regarded as a means to that end. Unfortunately, Elizabeth's school problem, rather mundane in the context of such extraordinary events but all the same likely to have long-term consequences, seemed to be little considered.

The Jackson family (a multi-problem family)

Finally, we introduce Irene Jackson, a young mother suspected of physically abusing her eight year old daughter, Tracy. Irene lives alone with four children whose ages range from two to ten; each has a different father, all of them Afro-Caribbean. The family was well known to health and social services – among her other problems Irene had a serious hearing difficulty – but abuse had never previously been suspected. Nevertheless, Tracy's teacher became concerned about Tracy's development, and the appearance of a bruise over the eye led to a school medical examination at the end of which Irene was informed that a protection conference would have to be held. Irene was permitted to attend the second part of the Child Protection meeting, but, by her own account, the flurry of interest in her affairs left her in a state of disempowered bewilderment.

I don't really know what they are doing or what they are trying to do, but I just let it bypass me now. If I really sat down and thought about it I think I would crack up. I just try to ignore them. I mean when I was sat in the room, I really did not want to voice my opinion 'cos to me it wasn't really worth anything. Because you could see they had all made their mind up. They are putting their opinion to me and they think it is right, and I can't put mine to them 'cos they would think that it is so wrong.

I mean there was not one person in there out of the bunch of them that really believed me. That's why I couldn't really say much. You know, when they say I don't go to the school as often – well I do go to the school, I've always gone to the school. She said I don't go to the school, that I don't take an interest in my kids' work, but I've always gone to the school on parents' meetings; I've only missed Tracy's and that's because this happened.

Irene's attitude to the Child Protection meeting and her operational perspective on what transpired there was influenced by much that had happened to her during the previous weeks, but in particular by what she regarded as her own and her children's humiliation during the medical examination at school:

> The social worker and the senior came to see me and I met them over at the school, and the doctor was there and the head teacher. It was embarrassing, I really felt very embarrassed. I would have felt embarrassed if I had done it, but to be sat in front of the doctor, the social worker, the senior social worker and the headteacher... I never really spoke to any of them. When the doctor examined the children – the full strip and everything! – I couldn't really believe that they had me sat there, thinking I beat my children up.

> I was really quiet and sat listening to everything they were saying. I didn't really question any of it. I did say to the doctor, 'I never did anything to her face'. And he said, 'I've still got to do the full body examination.' I said 'it's all unnecessary'. And I said to the doctor, 'this is going to cause a problem.' I can understand that you have to do your job and everybody else has to do their job, but I think they could have done it in a more discreet way. When I walked home I just felt like taking my children to my mother to bring up. Even though I knew I hadn't done anything, it just made me feel so... that I wasn't a fit mother or something.

Many parents who attend child protection conferences express satisfaction, but Irene's experience of the process was clearly very unhappy. The taciturnity of her own behaviour – possibly attributable to her hearing disability – would not have helped, but she had good grounds for feeling humiliated by her treatment during the school medical examination and her sense of inadequacy was, if anything, reinforced by her experience at the subsequent Child Protection meeting. Lacking family aide or solicitor's advice, both valuable in Mary French's case, she was left feeling abandoned and alone.

Irene's neighbour, Maddy, had a lifestyle similar to Irene's. A young white woman with a black boyfriend and two mixed race children, she was present during part of the research interview. She said:

> I don't understand why they are picking on Irene; there are other families who should be looked at. I look after her children; I know they're O.K. Alice is the one; she's only 12 and always hanging round with old men. We don't let our girls play with her. But Irene gets all these meetings just because Tracy told her teacher her mother smacked her one time. It's really stupid.

Maddy, like many of the frequently disadvantaged parents we spoke to complained that social services misdirected their energies. There was indeed widespread concern on the estate for the child, Alice, and Irene had previously told her social worker, Andy, about the gossip and suspicion. Parental discipline was not generally regarded as a justifiable cause for intervention.

The social worker, Andy was recently qualified and a little unsure of himself. He consequently found Irene Jackson's uncooperative stance threatening. His superior was aware of his problems but had little time for supervision. Andy said:

> I've only been working with this case for a few months and from what I see all the children are showing signs of insecurity. Irene Jackson has particular difficulties managing Tracy and told me that if she was taken into care all her problems would be solved. I've been trying to work with her by encouraging her to talk about her own relationship with her parents, but she's very resistant. All she seems to want is financial help.

> The protection meeting wasn't easy. I talked to my senior beforehand and, what with the negative medical report and Irene's attitude to social work,

> we'd decided that registering Tracy would only make my job more difficult. Unfortunately, we had a fight on our hands because most of the other agencies wanted her registered. I think they wanted the case neatly wrapped up, with social services taking all the responsibility.

> I was glad we'd agreed to invite Irene to the meeting because I think having parents in makes them realise that child abuse must be taken seriously. By the end the message was clear, unless she took greater responsibility for Tracy, and that meant co-operating with social services, then we'd have to think again about registration.

Far from being the united group of adversaries perceived by Irene, the professionals at the conference were deeply divided over the decision not to register Tracy and in the degree to which they were confident that Irene understood that more care must be taken. Furthermore, Tracy's head teacher was concerned about an altogether different problem, barely aired at the meeting. She explained:

> Tracy's behaviour has regressed quite dramatically since the summer. She's always been a forlorn little thing but now she has taken to wandering off on her own and we find her in a quiet corner masturbating. I am really worried she may have been sexually abused. Nobody was surprised when she asked if she could tell me something privately, but the story of her mother punching her in the eye was hardly what I had expected.

> I was disappointed that the Chair decided against registering Tracy; registration would have ensured that the family and particularly Tracy were monitored. As it is, because Irene Jackson won't speak to her social worker, I'm not sure if anyone besides us, will be keeping an eye on things.

Let us consider how the operational perspectives of participants were influenced by the meeting, recalling that operational perspectives are determined by psychological factors, such as peoples' perceptions of one another, the roles they are expected to play and the emotions aroused during the meeting, and also by social forces, such as the power professionals wield.

Psychological dimensions of operational perspectives

Parents bring to the meeting the distress and unhappiness caused by the accusation. The degree of pain they feel should not be underestimated; they will have spent days brooding on the event. Such dredging of emotions colours parents' expectations. Mary French came to the protection meeting emboldened by a successful, but nevertheless traumatic Crown Court appearance; in contrast, Irene Jackson arrived feeling helpless, having endured the medical examination of her children: 'I felt there was no point in me saying anything'. She was probably right.

For those overwhelmed by an accusation, a sympathetic presence at the meeting can help. The importance of a companion to banish fear hardly requires substantiation and, in scientific terms, is well documented (Bowlby, 1973). Mary French's experience was particularly significant in this respect: in the formal – and, as it turned out, highly theatrical – context of the court hearing as she defended herself against neighbourhood gossip and police suspicion, she was able to rely on the help of a solicitor, a sister and her own daughter. Paradoxically perhaps, the criminal proceedings not only reinforced her belief in herself, but influenced the professionals' view of her behaviour. Social workers encourage advocates to be present at meetings, but many parents feel too embarrassed and humiliated by the suspicion to confide in anyone and, therefore, go alone. In the same vein, one wonders to what extent lack of general understanding of the nature and legal status of a child protection meeting is an inhibiting factor where the use of advocates is concerned.

Regardless of who goes to the meeting, the occasion does offer an opportunity for participants to appraise earlier impressions. Mary French's situation demonstrated the extent to which even polarised positions can change and perceptions converge. The professionals' view of an inadequate woman who neglected her children in order to cavort with younger men and deal in drugs was considerably modified. Mary, who had regarded her social worker and family aide rather as different organs of the same official antagonist, witnessed the defence of her reputation by one against assault from the other.

The interdisciplinary nature of child protection work is now well established; different agency workers share common value systems, behaviour patterns and professional vocabularies, and certain informal procedures have become institutionalised. For example, in one area office we studied, professionals met for coffee ten minutes before meetings to discuss contentious issues. A consensus was fashioned before the formal discussion began. Unfortunately, all such codes, signals and tacit understandings, taken for granted in middle-class professional life, are aspects of behaviour alien to many parents. They come to the meeting like castaways to a foreign shore.

The atmosphere of the room in which the meetings take place, the arrangement of the furniture, the way in which parents are introduced to strangers and professional acquaintances, as well as the language, dress and demeanour of the professionals all influence parents' perceptions. Having to wait outside in a corridor while the team discussed her case deepened Irene Jackson's sense of alienation, and is a plight more normally associated with criminal proceedings – as Mary French discovered: 'I sat in a corridor with two policemen I saw on the night of the fire, with them staring at me all the time, but nobody speaking. Then a WPC and another policeman turned up. I thought they were there to take me and Keri away.' It is difficult for a closely-knit group of professionals to make anxious parents feel that they have a role, are welcome and are essential to the satisfactory resolution of an investigation in an atmosphere commonly associated with that of televised courtroom melodrama.

Social dimensions of operational perspectives

Attending a child protection meeting is an uncommon experience for any parent, even those with children in care. Some attempt to anticipate what will happen but few have any idea of what to expect. Most sense that they are standing trial; most, like Mary French and the Claytons tend to regard professional attitudes as uniform and uniformly antagonistic to their predicament until someone visibly breaks ranks. Almost without exception, parents regarded the outcome of the meeting as a legal and moral adjudication. Thus, Mary French saw the decision not to register her daughter Keri as a victory, when all the time her social worker regarded that outcome as inevitable.

Parents frequently complained about the way decisions that intimately affected them were reached. As well as imagining that professionals were united against them, those not party to the proceedings feared decisions were based on false or inaccurate information or that certain behaviours had been analysed out of context. As Betty Clayton put it, 'They've put things together like bits of a jigsaw puzzle and come up with the wrong answer'. One might easily counter her argument with the weight of our evidence that demonstrated painstaking and considerate interventions by social workers and health visitors often in difficult circumstances over very long periods; nevertheless, it is invariably the case that professionals direct the pace of the proceedings and decide what is important and what to tell parents. The power they wield over families is undeniably great.

Alas, only articulate parents are better able to prove their competence. Mary French was socially skilled enough to secure medical support for her case; she demonstrated she was capable of acting independently on behalf of her family, her reputation was buoyed by good school reports on her two older children and, in the eyes of a social worker whom she believed disliked her, she conducted herself 'beautifully' during the case review. However, manipulating the system to the extent of being able to make use of the relative status of participants, requires extraordinary composure. Most parents accused of abuse have had no opportunity to acquire the social skills relevant to an abuse inquiry; indeed that they lack them is an aspect of their larger predicament. For shattered, tearful and inarticulate people, such as Irene Jackson, it can be a vicious circle of disadvantage and incompetence.

Two of the families so far described help us assess the significance of race and culture in determining operational perspectives. Naturally, a person's social and cultural background will shape their view of the world and key events, such as an abuse investigation; but our case studies suggest that this may be overstated. Race may be very important, as in the case of social workers' perspectives on the character of Irene Jackson whose children had black fathers, but we should not let it obscure other aspects, such as social class and economic status. In extreme situations, such as those addressed in this study, social and cultural factors may be irrelevant.

This is illustrated in the case of Yvonne Oomah, whose experience we described in the previous Chapter. She is black, a factor which inevitably played a part in the social worker's operational perspective on the family situation, as it did ours; but the social worker quickly learned, as did we, that more important was Mrs Oomah's middle-class capacity to take on state agencies, and her socio-economic status as a single parent. Since Yvonne's social worker was also black, one might have expected a certain concordance in operational perspectives, but Yvonne was African-born whereas the social worker was British-born; she understood her client's reluctance to talk about sexual matters, but it was hardly part of her cultural background. Generally speaking, these social and cultural factors lose their significance in the context of the enormous upheaval that follows a child abuse investigation. We should not let our preoccupation with a person's racial and ethnic background blind us to other aspects of their identity.

How might the situation be improved?

Probably not much can be done to alleviate the fears of those parents whose case is reviewed at a Child Protection conference, but it ought to be possible to remedy certain unhelpful, social influences on their view of proceedings. Respect for parents can be demonstrated most simply by inviting them to attend the meeting but, unless their contribution is valued and carefully considered, participation may be counter productive. It is also important to allay parental fears that the meeting is crudely judicial – that they are on trial and the ultimate punishment is the loss of their children or criminal prosecution.

How much do parents have a right to know? Meetings are routine for professionals but they are alien to parents. To those whose lives are spent at meetings, the fact that most people are fortunate enough never to have to attend one may come as a surprise. They can be daunting to the uninitiated; the combination of formal procedure and informal conversation, of famil-iarity and artificial politeness can be very disconcerting. Failing to inform parents fully about the purposes of a child protection meeting will make the event more difficult still to cope with comfortably. Social workers, in particular, need to set aside sufficient time to explain carefully and clearly what the meeting is designed to decide, who is likely to attend and why. For example, we have found that the presence of some agencies took parents and particularly children entirely by surprise. The younger Clayton daughter's hostile reaction to her school's involvement is a good example.

Any skilled social worker can assess the most likely outcome of the meeting and prepare the ground. It is particularly important to stress confidentiality, the overwhelming likelihood of the child's remaining at home and the opportunity the meeting provides for airing other concerns, for example to do with health and housing. Although a social worker's crystal ball is sometimes clouded, likely outcomes, perhaps in the language of best and worst scenarios, can normally be described. Parents who are to attend the meeting need warning of the procedure and, perhaps most important, to know that their views will be sought and carefully considered. In order for this to happen, preparation time needs to be set aside or someone briefed to act on parents' behalf.

It could also help if parents know what the meeting room looks like, how it is arranged, where they will sit and what people will wear. They themselves deserve guidance on what to wear and how to conduct themselves. Normally families must compose themselves in a public reception area, while professionals gather in the meeting room, where they may be overheard chattering. A private room where distressed parents and children might retreat before and after meetings would be a civilising influence.

Although some parents were reluctant to attend meetings, the majority were all the same anxious to participate. However, as Thoburn and colleagues (1993) are finding, the notion of attendance is open to interpretation and, depending on how it is defined, has different consequences. Thus, if parents were called in half way through proceedings or sent out when the police wanted to speak or when decisions were taken, they reacted with dismay; they felt they had been singled out and that the process was a humiliating charade.

Consideration could also be given to the moment when parents actually enter the arena of the meeting (Burns, 1992). Should all the professionals be sitting in wait? Should the parents be the first into the room or is a steady trickle of arrivals and a series of careful introductions more helpful? The entirely benevolent purpose of the meeting is to ensure that children are protected, but the considerable rights of parents must not be lost sight of. For example they have the right to honesty, though professionals may prefer to shy away from hurtful or embarrassing subjects. Even when the information is unpleasant, parents want and need to know the extent of what is being alleged. They resent the piecemeal way that facts and suspicions are some-times presented and later reconstructed.

Confronting a group of strangers who suspect that your child has been abused is a threatening experience; to face accusers alone is almost unbear-able. Parents need an advocate conversant with the system who will represent their side of the case. Social workers should talk to parents about their right to contact specialist solicitors or support groups, such as PAIN or the Family Rights Group.

It may be necessary to bear in mind that families are not homogeneous and that different individuals need individual representation. Senior practitioners we spoke to were aware that meetings could be dominated by an opinionated or articulate parent at the expense of other relatives. Furthermore, if parents feel powerless at a meeting, it must be far worse for the child, many of whom must endure interrogation by professionals in the presence of an abusing or beleaguered parent.

Delays and parents' operational perspectives

Although many investigations concern relatively minor incidents of abuse, the time taken by professionals to decide what action is appropriate can be considerable. Delays are stressful for family members and may become an irritation which adversely affects their perception of the value of any help they may be offered. After the first referral, protection agencies usually respond quickly. For 50 of the 61 children in our study the confrontation with parents occurred within a week of the suspicion surfacing although in one exceptional case it was eight weeks and, in another, 16 before parents knew there was a problem. It is generally in the later stages of an investigation that there is a danger of the process slowing down. For 46 of the 61 children we monitored, further action was considered necessary, usually taking the form of a consultation between professionals. These 'planning meetings' frequently took place without parents' knowledge, although many told us they suspected that something unusual was happening. As in any busy office, the 'in tray' can be slow to empty, so that while 22 cases were dealt with inside a fortnight, the remaining 24 included 12 in which six weeks or more separated the initial inquiry from some sort of formal discussion between professionals. For a proportion, the investigation continued, so that eventually 29 children were placed on the protection register. As we can see from the following Table, in all but two cases several weeks elapsed between the first meeting of professionals and the point of registration.

Table 8.1 Time between first meeting of professionals and the final decision to place the child's name on the Child Protection Register

less than one week	2
1–2 weeks	11
3–5 weeks	13
6 or more weeks	3

As in the case of Yvonne Oomah, the interval between confrontation and further action tended to prolong parents' anxieties, so that the root cause of their deepening distress might in reality be undermanning in the neighbourhood social services department or bureaucratic inertia. Since *Working Together* now stipulates that parents should be included in deliberations, their notion of an acceptable time-scale, which in a crisis can be very short, needs to be taken into account. It is an area in which the proper requirements of the individual and the system can be brought closer together to the mutual good.

Helping particular families

We have discussed in general how the informal and formal procedures of meetings could be improved. We now consider more specifically the ways that different types of families could be helped to cope with the experience. We have suggested that the child protection system may not be the most appropriate route for acutely distressed families and that they might be better dealt with under Section 17 of the 1989 *Children Act*. Professionals frequently come to a common understanding with parents from such families on the nature of the problem and what needs to be done. Most acutely distressed families work happily with social services and the use of child protection strategies are unhelpful.

Families with a specific problem, however, are a different matter. Parents often come from groups not normally drawn into the welfare net. Some are themselves professionals. At the confrontation stage, these families feel they are being judged by their peers and see themselves as relegated into the 'client group' of outsiders in need of help. Issues of self esteem, status and visibility suddenly surface. Careers and social life can be at risk. Exclusion from the child protection meeting is especially violating because they feel sufficiently articulate and skilful to defend themselves against accusation. The inclusion of specific problem families in meetings, clearly informing them of their rights and assuring them of absolute confidentiality can go some way to allowing these families to retain their dignity and work co-operatively with agencies.

Since multi-problem families present chronic difficulties, when a suspicion of child abuse surfaces, an inter-agency meeting could usefully be arranged to co-ordinate help from a number of different sources. Indeed, it is this group of families that benefits most from abuse procedures. Care must be taken if parents are not to feel violated, for, after all, they have few resources to call upon. A more flexible social services' approach to Irene Jackson, which offered a change of social worker, may have resulted in her accepting social work intervention more readily. It is unlikely that the majority of parents suspected of child abuse will come voluntarily to social services, indeed much research has demonstrated that 'once bitten by the welfare', one is twice shy of seeking subsequent help; but some parents have no option and reluctance to involve agencies can make the problem much worse when it ultimately surfaces.

Conclusions

In this chapter we have explored the meeting, the second major event for parents caught up in a child abuse investigation. There are costs to a Child Protection meeting. They are expensive in terms of the time and resources needed to bring professionals together and the high levels of stress they generate for families. Are such case conferences always the most appropriate means of early intervention?

We would suggest that the value of those meetings is variable. Mary French's sufferings might, arguably, have been avoided altogether if the police had not pressurised social services. Social work assessment might have led to the case being filtered out of the system prior to any meeting. Several other families could well have been dealt with in this way. But, for some, the case conference is clearly a necessity and, for others, it can prove beneficial. It is an opportunity for participants to reflect on what has happened and to work with others for the child's safety. It can marshal resources, particularly if the child is registered, although parents tend to regard such an outcome as a punishment. Professionals seem to thrive on meetings, but the value of many is questionable and others do not serve their stated purpose. Considering that so few children are actually registered and given the minor nature of the violations under consideration, more economical use of conferences would seem wise.

Although parental attendance at meetings is now commonplace, genuine participation is difficult to achieve. The distribution of power is inevitably uneven, but it is eminently possible to inform parents of their rights, to direct them to support groups and to be open and honest. The precise function of registration must always be borne in mind. Are we registering a child because we honestly feel it is in his or her best interests? Is it a way of laying hands on an otherwise scarce and inaccessible resource? Is it primarily to protect professional integrity against the threat of scandal and the fear of unwitting negligence?

Because it brings together professionals and parents, the meeting provides an opportunity to modify operational perspectives formulated during the confrontation. Perceptions can change for all manner of reasons, some simple – for example because it occurred to someone to ask parents how they felt – some complex, perhaps as a result in changes in professional practice. But the process continues, circumstances change, new information emerges and plans go astray. As we now explore, there are moments in the weeks and months after the meeting when perceptions change and new operational perspectives form.

Summary points

1 After the initial confrontation many child abuse investigations cease and professionals decide to take no further action. Of all suspicions, a quarter are so minor that cases are dropped almost immediately. Nevertheless in the cases we considered which proceeded as far as a case conference or similar meeting, the impact on parental perspectives of such gatherings could be considerable.

2 During the study, the involvement of parents and, where appropriate, children in case conferences became widespread. However, several families in our study were excluded from all or part of the case conference and were indignant that a 'trial without representation' had taken place.

3 Parents vary considerably in the operational perspectives they adopt when faced with a case conference. All fear some public humiliation and the likelihood they will lose their children. Some lone mothers passively accept the stress as inevitable, but many more parents mount strategies of denial, non-co-operation and marshal external support. Most parents accept that suspected abuse should be investigated, but view the incident as minor and the accusation as malicious. Trust has been violated, professional intervention is threatening and parents shrink from voluntary co-operation.

4 Professionals, as they intervene, are unsure and distressed. They retreat into orthodox, guarded role performance, aware that any case could haunt them for dereliction and incompetence. Instead of being rewarded with a client's smiles of gratitude for what they consider real practical assistance, they endure hostility and silence. Neither are their anxieties soothed by colleagues, the views of professionals conflict and their guiding ideologies are at variance. Consensus is difficult to achieve, is often fragile and can swiftly disintegrate. This adds to parental confusion and unease as they pick up a variety of messages.

5 While it is difficult to allay the fears of parents whose case is reviewed at a Child Protection Conference, the information provided for them in advance, on the manner in which meetings are conducted and the ambience in which discussions take place can do much to increase the respect accorded to them and boost their confidence. Strategies need to vary for different types of family.

6 Child protection procedures are sometimes delayed. Child protection professionals moved swiftly in confronting parents about suspicions, but planning meetings and eventual registration can be long in coming.

Chapter 9

New information or changed circumstances alter the way a case proceeds

At the start of a child abuse investigation parents' perspectives seldom accord with those of child protection professionals – not surprisingly, since few of us would relish the prospect of being told that we or someone we know is suspected of abusing children. Indeed, in the early stages of an investigation there is probably a limit to what can be done to improve parents' operational perspectives; there is a natural tendency to recoil from scrutiny and as far as possible to limit the intrusion into private behaviour. Yet when one comes to look at the families in our intensive study two years on, a much altered picture emerges: in two-thirds of cases significant changes in operational perspectives have occurred and in most instances there can be said to have been some improvement.

Here, we return to two of the families whose experiences are described in the previous Chapter in order to discuss contrasting fortunes: in the first case an extraordinary event occurs which, although exceptional, illustrates how a review of operational perspectives leads to a more favourable outcome than that expected; in the other, the situation deteriorates.

Any number of considerations can play a part in the development of operational perspectives. Change may be triggered by several factors: a new allegation of abuse; new evidence about the family; remarriage, death or birth; changes in living situation, or the arrival of a new social worker. These influences are discernible in the experiences of the two families whose cases we now re-examine.

Operational perspectives change for the better

It will be recalled that the suspicion that she had assaulted her eight-year-old daughter left Irene Jackson feeling humiliated, alienated and unco-operative. Social work visits declined, rather as the professionals themselves feared, following the decision not to register the child, and the family received little support. The case lay dormant for five months until a tearful eight-year-old from the same estate telephoned the police to expose the alleged sexual antics of a male driver employed by the same social services department.

Extensive police interviews followed and Irene's daughter, Tracy, was identified as having been among the girls the man allegedly lured to his flat, as was Alice, whose sexualised behaviour Irene had complained of when her own treatment of Tracy was being investigated. It was, by any standards, an extraordinary turn of events. The discovery that one's child has been sexually abused is devastating; when the alleged perpetrator turns out to be an employee of an organisation which previously, and apparently groundlessly, challenged the propriety of one's own intimate behaviour – what then?

Irene went to the social services department:

> *I said, I blame you social workers for everything that has happened to Tracy. Because before you came and got involved she was a quiet, normal happy-go-lucky child, but when you got involved she changed. I mean, I'm not saying she wasn't difficult, she'd always been difficult, but not difficult in a way that I couldn't handle her.*

> *The woman I saw said, how come it happened because of that? I said because, let's put it this way, for one she stripped off in front of a male doctor who she'd never seen before in her life – right full strip from head to toe, him looking at the private parts of her body, examining her – and then she had that male social worker who sat and gave her confidence. So that when she went down to another male, who pretends he's a social worker, what do you expect? And that's why I'm blaming you, because you made men towards her seem trustworthy, and they wasn't. Even the doctor and the social worker, none of them should be trustworthy.*

> *And I said to them, if a child's got confidence to strip off in front of a doctor, why shouldn't she have the confidence to strip off in front of somebody she didn't know!*

In the context of assessing a parent's operational perspective on the behaviour and competence of her social worker, no statement could be darker or bleaker in its implications. At that juncture Irene would not let a social worker into her house. She and her daughter were happier to confide in the local CID.

For their part, the police had next to try unravel the significance of the behaviour of Tracy's classmates at school. There were the allegations of sexual abuse to be reckoned with, but also talk of a subculture involving certain pre-pubescent girls. Tracy's drawn and written work contained unmistakable sexual overtones, but in the circumstances it was extremely difficult to determine how much was a reaction to real experience. In more normal conditions social services might have been expected to play an important role as subtle and caring enquirers, but so great were the secondary problems attributable to the unsatisfactory outcome of the earlier investigation, they were forced to withdraw from Tracy's case altogether. A case conference was called to discuss the alleged attempted assault of Tracy by the home carer, but it was in large part preoccupied with the misfortune that had befallen the social services neighbourhood office. As the minutes of the meeting recorded:

The neighbourhood officer explained that the alleged abuser had been charged with attempted assault. She also stated that Social Services understood that there might be strong feelings about the office on the estate. She reminded Irene Jackson that she, the neighbourhood officer, was ultimately responsible for the home care organiser who was the accused worker's line manager, and she was also responsible for trying to help victims of abuse and their families. She also informed Irene that she understood that people on the estate were aware of friendships within the office and explained that the decision had been taken by senior management to remove friends connected with the accused man to other offices, so that the public could come to the neighbourhood office to use all the services with complete safety. She wanted residents in the area to know that management felt that people should regard the office as a safe place to come

The record ends with the rather poignant reminder: 'N.B. It should be noted that Irene Jackson has a severe hearing problem and that, during the time she was in the conference, several statements had to be repeated.'

By that time Irene had decided it would be better to send Tracy to her own mother's home in Cuttleton, to arrange for her to attend school there and, on her mother's behalf, make contact with the local social services department. The home social services department contributed towards the cost of the expedition, agreeing with her that it would be a good idea for her and all her children to get away from the estate temporarily. Thus her rejection of social work intervention was not general, and one might observe that, thankfully, she was able to distinguish between the value of an organisation and the possible frailty of one person within it. Irene used to live in Cuttleton with a former husband and spoke of it in rosy terms:

> *Social workers were social workers. They were different; they were friendly. They was concerned, you know, wanted to know your whole life. Or they didn't interfere or keep knocking at your door. And so I said to them, 'I don't know what you lot are doing, like here, but the only reason I'm having you as a social worker is to protect my mother.' To protect her, because if Tracy goes to school down there and says something or something happens, at least I have let the social worker be involved from the day she goes.*

By another reading, in the context of a researcher's own changing operational perspective, it needs to be added that the possibility of moving Tracy to Cuttleton may from the beginning have been in Irene's mind. A year previously, long before any sexual abuse allegation surfaced, she explained:

My mum was going to have Tracy for me. She said, 'If you really think that it's really bad, and you really think she is a difficult child I'll look after her', cos my mum is still young... But at the same time, my mum wouldn't really let her get away with anything; she would find it so different, 'cos it would be in from school, in - finished.

Certainly Irene was always desperate to escape from the estate, and came to refer to sexual abuse as a metaphor for its awfulness, as if it was an endemic disease in the neighbourhood:

Like, the kids that live over that road, they've been sexually abused. I mean the whole estate has been sexually abused as far as I'm concerned. A lot of these kids have been sexually abused by their fathers. Even the police said this area is one of the number one areas for child abuse. I mean, I went to see the housing to ask about moving. I told her why I wanted to move and - do you know what? - she turned round and said to me, she said, 'don't think I'm being unhelpful, but when I was as young as you I had a big problem. I was living in this house and I wanted to get out. I would have done anything to get out, but I stayed there. Now, when I look at it, I'm glad.'

But I said, Yeah you can say that now because your problems are gone, but my problem may be different from yours, in that my child, forget about me - I can cope with life, but it's different when I'm talking about a child who gets abused, and the actual child who took her to where it happened walks the street like nothing's happened, and the other kids are teasing them.

Did social services' views about the Jackson family change as a result of the abuse scandal? Once Tracy had moved in with her grandmother and the tension had eased, the senior social worker was able to reflect on the case.

There is no denying we got off to a very bad start with Irene and, looking back, I realise we could have done things better. The social worker allocated to the case, Andy, was out of his depth. When the police reported their suspicions about the home carer, Andy had given up visiting altogether. I felt that we had to do something for Irene and so I went round to see her myself.

She was very angry with the way she'd been treated, and I do sympathise with her. One of the skills in social work is to help those who don't want you to approach. She couldn't be expected to be welcoming. Not only did she resent male social workers and Andy in particular, she had had her daughter abused by someone who works for us and calls himself a social worker. When I went to see her she was very tearful and it was clear she needed someone to talk to.

She reminds me of the struggling young mothers I used to work with and I have to admit I liked her. The house was clean and tidy and when we settled down she was so grateful to have someone to listen to her, I don't think I have ever been offered so many cups of tea. She struck me as resourceful and very concerned about her daughter. In taking Tracy to live with her mother she solved a lot of problems not only for herself but also, quite frankly, for us as well. Nevertheless, she'll return home and we need to work with this family. In recent weeks Irene's rung me twice to chat about various things and I'm delighted she feels she can.

We should recall that at the outset, Irene was seen as the abuser. Later events could not have changed the attitude of the neighbourhood social services department more radically, even to the extent that she came to be regarded as a victim of its own unfortunate choice of personnel. Taken together, the circumstances were in the end quite exceptional, but the constituents of the case were typical of much that we have sought to suggest about the construction of operational perspectives and the workings of suspicion: neighbourhood rumour, hidden agendas driven by poverty and deprivation, confusion concerning the definition of physical, emotional and sexual abuse, and the relationship between the private, imaginative world of a developing child and the realities of shattered family life all played a part. It is against that background that one can view the belated improvement in operational perspectives held by Irene Jackson, her daughter's school and the social services as having been significant. The result of the sexual abuse investigation was all the same ominously inconclusive: Tracy's alleged attacker was found not guilty; Tracy said she was terrified that during the trial the man would leap out of the dock and 'get her'.

Perspectives change leading to a poor outcome

It will be recalled that Margaret Clayton claimed to have been sexually abused by her stepfather. After the case conference, members of the family harboured quite different perspectives on the investigation. The parents, Betty and Brian Clayton, were united in their indignation and loudly protested their innocence. The younger daughter, Elizabeth, hostile and distrustful of authority, and, for her age, extremely articulate, complained bitterly about her sister's behaviour, arguing that she had sought to alienate herself from the rest of the family. Margaret, whose overdose was the indirect cause of the investigation, found some benefit in the concern shown for her following her disclosures.

The names of both girls were placed on the Child Protection Register and plans for a programme of family therapy were put in place. Parents and children went to one session and, for once, were of one mind: it had been a disaster. Margaret said:

> *The guy was just a berk. It was like, . . . he'd sit there and say Mr So-and-so and Miss So-and-so, and we thought, how can you expect us to talk in this situation? There were cameras all over the place and a microphone in the middle of the room. And he kept on disappearing off and there were like people sitting behind this two-way mirror which I could see into because I was at a certain angle and they'd got the lights funny so I saw straight through.*

> *There was a point when I got very upset because the guy said to Dad, 'Why did you do it?' and Dad said, 'I thought she wanted me to,' and I just burst out crying. Then he said, 'Why do you think Margaret got upset when you said that, Mr Clayton?' Dad said, 'I don't think she got upset when I said that.' I sat there and didn't say anything and thought 'How can he be so blind?'*

The younger daughter Lizzie's view of the subtleties of the clinic's approach was as ungenerous:

> *I refused to say anything. Then he said to mum or dad, 'Do you know what's wrong with Elizabeth?' I said, 'I know what's wrong with me. This is such an awkward situation. You've got a big mirror, three cameras in the room and a microphone, and it isn't right. It's such an awkward atmosphere.' He said, 'Yes, that's part of it.'*

As a result of their unanimous dislike of the group interrogation, Brian Clayton was able to re-assert himself – in language curiously reminiscent of a trade union negotiator:

> *The therapist said he would be prepared to work with us further, but as a family we are not convinced that we want to go any more. It's due to come under discussion; I mean, I only just got in from work. But as a family we are yet to discuss whether we are yet to go back for any more sessions at all.*

By that time a change had occurred in the relationship between Brian Clayton and the social worker in the case. Previously, of the four he had been the most dismissive of his support. Now he was saying:

> *Unfortunately John cops the flack from me a little bit. We don't see eye to eye. The reason is not necessarily because of him, it's because of what he represents and what he represents is what's been done to our family. I've lumped him together with a lot of other social workers. Now I know that John himself has come to social work by a strange route . . .*

Brian Clayton's perspective had been much altered by the social worker's disclosure that he, like Brian, had family problems and had recently separated from his wife and children, so confirming Brian's prejudices against the profession 'nobody needs a social worker more than a social worker!' and restoring his sense of control over his family. But there was a new problem:

> *Any moment he is going to be pulled off the case, because he wants to move out of social work. So somebody is just going to get a heap of papers on their table from him, and we'll become somebody else's problem. I think that is totally unacceptable.*

From Margaret's point-of-view the slackening of the investigative process was disappointing:

> *Nothing seemed to be happening. I was never sure John Langtree really believed me, I think I was stupid to trust him. He's obviously not going to help us, he doesn't bother to talk to me now. It's really depressing when I think that perhaps he's (Father) got away with it again. I'm not worried for me because it isn't me he's after now. But Elizabeth, she believes anything Dad tells her. While we were having this big argument he made a 'I won't do it again, I promise' speech. I said, 'You're fucking right you won't; you've run out of daughters, haven't you?'*

Within two months of the Child Protection meeting, support plans had crumbled. Not only was the family therapy sabotaged but Elizabeth, to the dismay of the social work team, started to be educated at home and the family became insular to the extent that only Brian had much contact with the world outside. The social worker, John Langtree, left the scene as predicted and for several months the case remained unallocated. Then came another important change, two women social workers were assigned to the Claytons. Jean Fox's assessment was much different from John Langtree's and that of the investigating police officer, whom she described as 'macho'.

> *The intervention clearly had a dramatic effect. It has blown open a family secret and challenged the father's power base. It's also freed up a lot of anger between Margaret and her father, who had managed to set up a 'bad' person, 'troublemaker' image for her, and it's exposed differences between how Margaret and Elizabeth are treated. More important, it's challenged the myth they created for themselves that they were a family which communicated openly and freely and that there was a balance of power between the four of them.*
>
> *There were features about the case which really worried me. For a start, I suspected the family were blaming Margaret for making the accusations. The women were being offered no basis for an alliance - a female worker*

could have helped to correct the level of denial, and Margaret most certainly should have been allocated an independent worker. No one has seen the children on a regular basis for some time and no one knows what's happening. We begin by asking serious questions such as have these girls been sexually abused, then we put them on the register and forget all about it.

I felt we needed to do something quickly otherwise we could find that either we had a scandal on our hands or we'd lost them altogether. I knew it wasn't going to be easy and I needed help. My supervisor called a team meeting to discuss the case and I found this very helpful. We worked out a careful plan of action which included the original aim of systematic family therapy. I don't think we should underestimate the extent to which Brian Clayton may be a threat. I find him manipulative and self-consciously seductive in his dealings with women.

For Brian Clayton in particular, the resumption of family therapy was a rude awakening. 'I wonder how qualified they are to talk about sexual matters, it struck me they are probably lesbians,' he said. Neither was Betty Clayton very pleased initially:

For ages it felt as if we were living in a state of limbo. When we didn't hear anything I'd convince myself it was all over, but then I'd remember that the girls were still on the register. When the new social workers came round I started to panic all over again. But we seemed to get an awful lot said in the sessions and I was able to talk to them about things I was never really sure about, like Brian insisting on massaging the girls after bath time.

Nevertheless there was still evidence that she was enthralled by her husband's behaviour:

The family massage doesn't happen any more; there's no more open nudity around the house and we can define the difference between sexual abuse and massaging, but we aren't convinced there is agreement out in the world. What happened between Margaret and Brian, the touching of sexual organs, was very different to what happens between Elizabeth and him. Margaret is not his daughter, so it's different; with Lizzie it was playing. Lizzie became uncomfortable about the playing at the onset of puberty and it has stopped. Brian should have been more careful.

The Clayton family's experience illustrates how certain key events can change the perceptions of participants in a child protection inquiry. After a brief hiatus, a change in social worker brings new insights to the scrutiny of family relationships. Suspected of having abused his daughters, the father is understandably a reluctant participant but his wife, initially reticent, warms to the social workers and provides information which appears to lend credence to her daughter's earlier disclosure. The children also have cause to welcome the family therapy sessions, in as much as the father's abusive behaviour ceases.

Nevertheless, at the heart of the Clayton case, there was a cold hard stone of significance which none of the child protection strategies used was able to prise out. It came to be generally accepted that some form of sexual conduct which would not be expected in a normal father-child relationship had taken place between Brian Clayton and both girls. Social workers did not over-react, the police were not heavy-handed, an attempt was made to deal with the family's problems holistically, but the outcome was not encouraging. A follow-up interview with the Clayton family several months later exposed the transience of social services' interventions in child abuse cases. The family therapy came to a natural end after five months with Brian protesting a desire to acknowledge his daughters' changing needs as they moved into ado-lescence and adulthood. Whether any real insight was gained into the aetiology of the abuse is doubtful and the children remained at risk. Moreover, the relationships between family members and particularly between the sisters were severely shaken, indicating damage that was a feature of many of the cases we looked at.

Interpreting the data

These two case studies illustrate the fluidity of the perspectives of the participants in child abuse inquiries: views however strongly held at one point may not last. We have also noted the complexity of abuse situations: not only are perceptions malleable but change favourable for one participant can have disruptive consequences for another. Even so there are limits to the mobility of perceptions: none of the families we studied took pleasure in being on the receiving end of an abuse investigation, and hostility to and mistrust of official procedures was general.

The implications for social work practice of this crude assessment are more encouraging than might be thought at first hearing. No-one wants to be investigated for child abuse, but even if the relationship between investigators and recoiling parents begins badly, as is frequently the case, it is possible to work constructively with families. The evidence discussed in this Chapter shows in what quarter the opportunities for beneficial change arise if the conditions for change are reasonably propitious, that is to say if parents feel the conduct of the investigation is fair, if they are clear about why it is taking place and what the procedures are, if they are given an opportunity to speak their mind, if they have been directed to sources of support and if they consider the balance of power to be manageable.

However, there is much to suggest that an investigation can irretrievably damage family dynamics. Mothers and fathers never view each other in the same way again and the quality of the relationship between parents and children, as well as between siblings, is all too frequently damaged. Parents also complained that their relations with the outside world were affected: some felt 'less free', others feared gossip from neighbours, children were taunted by classmates. Many were left with a lingering mistrust of professionals, so that a routine school medical or any consultation with a doctor became a source of great anxiety. In short, parents never felt 'off the hook' and social workers were reluctant to close the file. Cases were moved on to the back burner and the suspicion that some abuse might have occurred or would be uncovered at some point in the future remained. In this respect, operational perspectives prove all too intransigent.

The case studies show how common it is for the consequences of an investigation to have an unforseeable impact on emotional behaviour. Elizabeth Clayton stopped going to school. Other children shied from being examined by their doctor or were intimidated by inquisitive classmates. Irene Jackson's claim that her daughter had been sexualised by the very people who suspected she was a victim of physical abuse was extreme, but nonetheless to be reckoned with. Minor insensitivities can do sensitive children lasting harm.

Whenever it occurred, a key moment in an abuse inquiry was a change of social worker. The families we studied drew clear and significant distinctions between the attitudes, demeanour and perceived prejudices of the individuals they dealt with. There was little neutrality, they liked them or they didn't like them, and they liked them better if they could relate to them as struggling parents like themselves, as survivors of a difficult childhood or as fellow travellers on a rocky road. 'She was older than I'd expected, but nice; she reminded me of Mum', was how Irene Jackson, previously one of the fiercest critics of social services, described her last social worker. Beyond appearances and perspectives, it is worth considering the degree to which each of us is a different person depending on the company we keep. The social worker, John Langtree, eventually permitted Brian Clayton to regard himself as one motivated by a manly desire for sexual liberty and free expression; by the analysis of the two women who took over the case after John Langtree had ridden into the sunset in search of his own freedom, Brian became a manipulative seducer – 'potential rapist' their file notes said. Thus, respondents were very concerned about the gender of the social worker. Mothers frequently expressed a preference for a woman; in the Clayton family, though the gender dynamic was more complicated, it was clearly an important factor.

Regardless of the gender of social workers, parents seek to correct the imbalance of power in their relationships with professionals. Some evaded social work scrutiny by moving away from home; intentionally or not, Irene Jackson brought about a wholesale reconstruction of her case by sending Tracy to live with her grandmother. Other parents used cruder avoidance strategies: some greeted social workers with open aggression, in one case, two enormous, unrestrained snarling dogs were kept on patrol.

There are moments when opportunities for change present themselves to the child protection services. For example, should they receive a new report of suspected abuse involving a family they know well, their decision will be influenced by the previous history of parents' operational perspectives. If parents have been unco-operative and secretive, the removal of the child is high on the agenda. But dealing with suspicion is frequently a frustrating and unrewarding task for social workers. The truth eludes them – the sexual dynamics of the family may simply prove unfathomable – and the attempt to effect any significant change in families' situations or their perspectives ends in frustration.

What is to be done? Although social workers may feel isolated, they are, in theory, members of a team. The desire to share frustrations and anxieties with colleagues should not be regarded as a sign of weakness. Discussions with a supervisor, at a group session or during a planning meeting can have a number of benefits, and the occasional brainstorming session may help to shake meaning from the behaviour of a family with whose idiosyncrasies a particular social worker has become over-familiar.

In all service industries, dissatisfied customers have a right to complain. In health and education, they can also demand a change of worker. Where custodial agencies are concerned the conventions are very different: people clearly have no choice, for example, with respect to which police officer will arrest them, and generally in the case of social services, which sit somewhere between the two extremes, if parents are dissatisfied with their relationship with their social worker, change is difficult. There would inevitably be resource implications, but a policy permitting some choice would be beneficial. In some of the area offices we studied, an intake system operated and a different worker was assigned to each case following the initial investigation and case appraisal. It seemed to us to create a valuable opportunity for careful judgement.

Social workers face the problem of constructing a satisfactory basis for working with families where children are at risk, and where, by definition, relationships of any kind are established only with difficulty. Here, the introduction of a family aide, a family centre worker or a child guidance specialist is one way of involving a greater diversity of professional skills. Parents may view these individuals in a different light from the social worker, creating a route by which parents' prejudices can be overcome and the operational perspectives of professionals and parents drawn together.

But, it must be stressed that our study demonstrates that families are not cohesive and the interests of individual members will very likely conflict. A lone professional working with a large family can easily be drawn into the complex dynamics and become partisan. One solution, neglected in the Clayton case, is joint working, a practice successfully employed in much marital therapy. The family pathology may then be transmitted to and replicated by the paired workers, a process which, if carefully managed and evaluated, can do much to illuminate the parents' world. The involvement of more than one worker can have very practical advantages: it can ensure there is someone to comfort the baby, listen to a tearful teenager or pay attention to a neglected father. Joint working also reduces the risks associated with approaching angry and aggressive individuals. Sceptics might argue that hunting in pairs will only serve to heighten parents' paranoia; suffice it to say, we could find no evidence of this.

Conclusions

At a general level the weight of evidence points to the trite-sounding conclusion that the closer are the perspectives of all concerned in an investigation of suspected child abuse, the happier will be the outcome of a case (a finding actually more subtle in its implications than first acquaintance may suggest).

However our studies have also uncovered the complexity of the process by which operational perspectives are negotiated and adjusted according to changing circumstances. At the moment a suspicion begins to be investigated, there is clearly a diversity of viewpoints within the family. Parents rarely agree with each other, individual children respond differently to interrogation and the role of the extended family varies. Much depends on the type of family and on the nature and context of the abuse, but, whatever the circumstances, the intrusion into normally private behaviour acts as a catalyst which alters family relations for ever. These changes may reflect wider problems – an abuse investigation may well hammer the last nail in the coffin of a disintegrating marriage – but, whatever the domestic climate, suspicion and accusation are potent forces. This is especially so in cases of suspected sexual abuse, which are more likely than those of physical abuse to be followed by family breakdown or changed membership and have a profound effect on subsequent dynamics. Outsider perpetrators are also likely to disrupt established family structures.

Gradually families adapt and manage to re-establish some semblance of equilibrium. As children are often empowered by abuse disclosures, and may indeed use disclosure as a way of establishing greater power, parent/child relations will be different from those that prevailed previously and there may be a surprising degree of deterioration in peer and sibling relations. Each family dyad has its own history, its own emotional temperature, very possibly its own secrets. As a result of the investigation process some relationships will be strengthened at the expense of others.

In the realm of perception and operational perspectives, much depends on the meaning attributed to 'abuse' in different situations and by different families. In a *multi-problem* family, physical abuse may be but one symptomatic feature of a generally turbulent and violent lifestyle. Hence, suspicion is unlikely seriously to affect relations between the mother and father. In a middle-class family, however, a physical assault might mean something quite different: as we have said it is perceived as a *specific problem*. But, as with the events we have described, the significance of the type of family is only important up to a point; beyond it the extent of abuse, especially sexual abuse, the quality of interpersonal relations in the family and the intentionality of the act will override all else.

In looking at the meanings of abuse in different contexts, we come to identify a major source of discrepancy in participants' perceptions. Social workers have to apply clear standards when deciding whether or not abuse has occurred and considerable tension exists between the use of absolute and relative criteria. On the one hand, there are clear definitions of abuse, such as touching private parts or causing injury; on the other, behaviour has to be interpreted in context. For example, possible neglect arising from the use of alternative medicines by travelling families was a major issue in the Shire county we studied. The extent to which hurt is felt and the degree of underlying 'intentionality' are the two variables that determine the meaning of abuse, and they in turn will affect the development, consistency and durability of operational perspectives.

Summary points

1 The discrepancies between the perspectives of parents and professionals at the outset of a case need not endure. When families are scrutinised two years after the initial confrontation, significant changes are found to have occurred in their circumstances and attitudes, most for the better.

2 Changes in perspective are not confined to parents, professional perspectives on families may also change. There is frequently renewed anxiety over abuse; in some cases concern simmers, in others the professionals warm to the needs of families and the efforts made by mothers to overcome hardships are recognised.

3 The perspectives of parents may become less extreme, but a lingering wariness of social services and other professionals can be a legacy of the initial suspicion and accusation. This is of concern since many families continue to need support in relation to problems quite distinct from abuse-related issues.

4   While not the focus of this study, the raising of suspicion and the anxiety generated by an abuse investigation have considerable repercussions among siblings and members of the wider family. The accusation acts as a detonator to the volatile mixture of hate, love and calculated indifference that, undisturbed, binds families together.

5   Changes in the operational perspectives of parents may result from the arrival or departure of close family members, by geographical movement, by improvements in health or material circumstance. Particularly significant is a change in social worker, the arrival bringing new perspectives, the departed carrying away the incubus of guilt, betrayal and anger.

Chapter 10

Parental perceptions over time

Having reviewed the evidence from the qualitative study of 30 families, we will now present the main findings from the accumulated evidence. It will be recalled that in order to understand the complex dynamics of investigations into suspicions of child abuse we sought to develop an appropriate methodology derived from several theoretical approaches. Our focus has been the *operational perspectives* of parents and professionals and, in particular, the degree of correspondence between them at certain key moments in an inquiry. This approach has proved fruitful, because it has drawn attention to the continuous process by which parents receive and generate information which they and others must accommodate in all their subsequent negotiations. Significant events in child-care interventions have to be viewed in this larger fluid context.

But so complex are the workings of perception that even though we have confined ourselves to the early events in a child protection investigation, we have encountered a wide range of viewpoints. Indeed, we have been constantly reminded that parents' perspectives do not necessarily coincide with those of their children and that the perspectives of one parent seldom mirror those of the other. In some families, particularly those where child sexual abuse is suspected, we found that a change in the perspective of a mother and her daughter led to shift in the perspectives of other family members. This was evident in the Clayton case.

In this Chapter, we demonstrate the degree of correspondence between parents' and professionals' operational perspectives at the start of an investigation and the nature of the shift that subsequently takes place. In the following Chapter we seek to show that operational perspectives are important not only in their own right as a key to understanding how people behave under duress – but as an influence on the outcome of child abuse investigations.

Intention and meaning

Many of the 30 families in the qualitative study were struggling to cope with multiple problems and so, on those grounds alone, it was not surprising that social workers should have been dissatisfied with standards of child-care. The professionals responsible for investigating abuse were also taxed by difficulties of various kinds, and, on occasion might have failed to acknowledge the sensitivities of parents, but it would be churlish to chastise them, since in the majority of cases they behaved with great care, understanding and tact.

Generally speaking, then, we can say that *all* those involved in the abuse inquiries we studied meant well, including the child's family. This is not to say that dangerous and sadistic abusers do not exist, clearly they do, but in none of the cases we scrutinised did we find parents acting with the *sole* intention of doing harm. Neither did we find any parent who failed to condemn child abusers; the problem was more that they did not believe the label applied to them.

In the same way, although we identified shortcomings in the investigation of child abuse, in every case we studied, social workers and other professionals intervened with the clear intention of protecting the child. They may have been driven by other motives too, not least the need to protect themselves and to ensure that they did not become the next *cause célèbre* of the social work press, but child protection was always the highest priority.

Nevertheless, hard-pressed professionals can easily misinterpret the intentions of errant – probably frightened – mothers and fathers, whose motives may be numerous, conflicting and inconsistent. How parents themselves perceive a particular situation at the outset is therefore important. We recall Lorraine Blake at the end of her tether unburdening her anxieties to Mrs. Bartlett, the sympathetic health visitor. Janet revealed her husband's emotional abuse of their daughter with the expressed intention of getting the health visitor to 'talk to him'. Her behaviour was also influenced by a belief that Mrs. Bartlett would deal with her disclosures sensitively and not take them out of context. In other cases, we found that intention was governed by beliefs about what was good for children attributable to fashion, sub-culture, neighbourhood wisdom or to ideas inherited from parents: some minor physical abuse and questionable health practices and choice of diet were explained by parents in this way.

Since the influences on intention underlying acts viewed as abusive are so varied and, since, for the most part, parents behave benevolently towards their children, abusive acts must, on occasion, be well-intentioned. Consequently, child protection professionals frequently have the daunting task of interpreting ambiguous behaviour. Smith and colleagues (1993) found that nearly all parents hit their children *sometimes*, by implication compelling social workers to view all such violent outbursts in context. Many of the families we talked to simply did not regard minor physical abuse as anything to warrant special attention and managed to differentiate between smacking or shaking and assault. We continually heard variations on the old adage, 'a clip round the ear didn't do me any harm'.

Particularly difficult for parents to comprehend is the concern that professionals reserve for 'neglect', especially if it is a bruise that tips the balance on scales that weigh 'abused' to the left and 'in need' to the right. All the allegedly neglectful parents we interviewed professed to love their children, although it was love rarely expressed in terms of providing clean clothes or a balanced diet or helping with schoolwork. Professionals are thus left with no alternative but to try to reconcile competing perspectives when seeking to unravel the intention and meaning which underlie suspected abuse – and it is precisely this which makes child protection work so problematic. (It is worth reminding ourselves that among the 160,000 annual investigations are the case files of 100 children who die each year as a result of neglect or injury.)

The professionals' task is made all the harder because their analysis, like our own, must distinguish between what is actually happening, what might be happening and what could happen. The evidence presented in the last three Chapters clearly demonstrates that parents' perceptions are a mixture of the actual and the possible. Sometimes they will speak of what has occurred, on other occasions they will describe what may happen at some later date. Depending on the changing circumstances, during an investigation different temporal dimensions of a parent's perspective will be successively advanced or retracted. One general practitioner summed up the dilemma thus,

> *When a patient comes to me with a health problem he is inclined to tell me the truth. But in an abuse case, the truth encapsulates a dozen and one possibilities; in fact, I would go so far to say that the (child protection) system is currently organised so that parents are very unlikely to tell me what is actually happening.*

Nevertheless, precisely because of these complexities, parents' perceptions must be regarded as important. As we have tried to show, an individual's point of view not only gives some clue to the intention and meaning to be attributed to his or her behaviour during an investigation, it influences the subsequent behaviour of all those associated with it. Furthermore, at any particular moment, how parents perceive their predicament is of great private significance to them. As anyone who has faced a crisis will testify, life glimpsed darkly from the perspective of two o'clock in the morning is very different from that viewed at midday, but both versions are convincing and, moreover, seem reasonable at the time.

Operational perspectives during the events of a child abuse inquiry

Unlike the professionals who often have to make swift judgements in awkward circumstances, we were able to talk at length with parents and to make a careful assessment of their perceptions. In order to evaluate the mass of interview material collected, we used the model of operational perspectives described in Chapter Six, focusing on three characteristic events. First was *the confrontation* when a professional raised the question of suspected abuse with parents; second was *the gathering of professionals* when the participants in an inquiry assembled to discuss what should be done; third were those moments – rather more loosely defined – when, for better or worse, new information or changed circumstances altered the course of an inquiry. In using this approach, we took account of the intention and meaning participants ascribed to situations as they developed.

It will be recalled that five components of an operational perspective were identified and explored. These we combined to make a template of common factors which enabled us to simplify and so to analyse the progress of situations which by more ordinary reckoning might be said to be chaotic, unpredictable and highly emotional. First we considered certain *psychological* aspects of participants' operational perspectives, which encompassed their interpretation of situations, events and phenomena, their perception of self, their emotional behaviour and the extent to which their current predicament was cast in the image of experience and expectations. We next scrutinised the *social* components of an operational perspective, including the power dimension embodied in the relationship between professionals and parents and the way in which private information became public. Because we wanted to know whether at those moments to which we have just referred the operational perspectives of parents and professionals were more or less congruent, we were primarily interested in tracking fluctuating levels of agreement. The rights and wrongs of professional practice or parenting behaviour did not concern us. Thus, if a social worker exerted pressure upon parents during the confrontation, we needed to know if family members regarded the use of power as acceptable; whether or not the practice was beneficial was a secondary consideration.

Wherever possible, the development of operational perspectives on all five dimensions for each participant in each family was mapped. This analysis exposed the degree of discord and in certain cases open conflict between members of the same family. Additionally, in some circumstances, disagreement among professionals was uncovered: despite the promise of inter-agency co-operation, in the early stages of an investigation police and social workers did not always see eye to eye, and, as the Jackson and Clayton case studies show, it was not unknown for social workers to criticise each other.

For the sake of clarity we have to limit the data presented, and so we focus initially on the relationship between the operational perspectives of the child's mother and the key professional involved in the investigation. Information was successfully gathered in all cases except two of our 30: in one case we were unable to maintain adequate contact with the mother, in another we were unsure that the translation of interviews with a Turkish woman told us enough about her operational perspectives.

It will be recalled from Chapter Five that a five-fold classification of families was developed, but that the 28 families studied intensively fell into one or other of only four, there being no case of abuse by an outsider. If, for the sake of brevity, the three families which had been infiltrated are assigned to one of the three larger groups that best matches their characteristics, we find that 14 of the 28 mothers were from multi-problem families, nine were being investigated because of a specific problem and five were acutely distressed in that they were experiencing a temporary breakdown in the normal pattern of family life. For each of these three types we consider the degree of *concordance* in the operational perspectives of mothers and key professional workers at each of the three events previously described: the confrontation, the meeting of professionals and at key moments when circumstances change.

The results we present are aggregates of the individual cases, calculated by checking the content of transcripts with interviewees and comparing their responses. General levels of agreement were assessed and responses to questions designed to explore each of the five dimensions of operational perspectives analysed. The aim at this stage was to ascertain whether perspectives were concordant on each dimension and for each event. In ambiguous cases, the evidence was presented for adjudication to a wider group, including neutral observers.

For the first event, the confrontation, the proportions of families where there was concordance between the child's mother and the key professional for each of the five components of operational perspectives were as follows. Table 10.1 illustrates that at the confrontation stage, there was considerable discord between the operational perspectives of professionals and mothers. Indeed, in certain categories disagreement was twice, sometimes three times as frequent as agreement. This is hardly surprising in view of the evidence concerning the level of trauma experienced by accused families, which we have described in Chapter Six. Accusing a parent of child abuse causes a deep sense of violation; notwithstanding extremely sensitive work by many professionals, we, like Prosser (1992) uncovered extensive disagreements at the outset of the inquiry.

The greatest degree of discord related to the social dimensions of an operational perspective – not such a pessimistic result as it may seem, since it is in these areas that professionals are perceived to have greatest influence. Nevertheless, all three classes of parent were clearly unhappy about the power wielded by professionals and inclined to dispute the legitimacy of the abuse inquiry. Here, too, we found the highest level of discord between mothers and child protection staff. At the moment of confrontation, their competence to care for their own children suddenly under threat, parents experience a shocking loss of control over their own affairs. The professionals we interviewed were aware of the power differential that exists at this point, but they had no strategy for relieving parents' distress. On entering a household to investigate a suspicion of abuse, child protection workers do not know what to expect: the intervention might lead to the rescue and removal of a

Table 10.1 **Concordance of operational perspectives of mothers and the key professional worker at the confrontation**

The dimensions of operational ▼ perspectives	Degree of Concordance among different types of family*			Degree of concordance overall*
	Multi-problem families	Specific problem families	Acutely distressed families	
A. Psychological				
Interpretations of situations, events and phenomena	●○○	●○○	●○○	●○○
Self perception and emotional responses	●○○	●○○	●●○	●○○
Experience and expectations	●○○	○○○	●●○	●○○
B. Social				
Power relations with others	○○○	○○○	●○○	○○○
The way private information becomes public	○○○	●○○	●●●	●○○
Number of families	14	9	5	28

* Concordance among families ○○○ = 0–25% ●○○ = 26–50% ●●○ = 51–75% ●●● = 76–100%

child in danger; far more likely it will be just another routine inquiry without substance or significance; but at the outset there is only one procedure, and the likelihood is that it will create emotional tension and mutual mistrust not easily remedied.

With the exception of the five acutely distressed families, the professionals' handling of private information was also a source of disquiet on the part of parents. Many mothers, especially those from multi-problem families, are used to telling outsiders about their private lives. They freely discuss their health and even aspects of their social and sexual behaviour. The difficulty arises because of the sudden change in context a suspicion of abuse brings about. Information about an affair, some lingering disagreement or even an innocent tipple suddenly assumes new significance. In reality, professionals are skilled interpreters of anxieties and confidences, but parents do not necessarily know this. As the day of confrontation fades into night, mothers worry about what they might or should have said and contemplate the possible advantages of keeping quiet altogether.

The preceding Table also demonstrates that there was greatest correspondence in the operational perspectives of professionals and parents from acutely distressed families experiencing a temporary breakdown. For example, in four of the five cases, the handling of private information was perceived by both parties to be satisfactory, tending to reflect the emphasis of the social work in such cases, which is to provide resources to sustain a family through what is perceived as a short-lived crisis. The concern is seldom wholly to do with the suspicion of abuse.

Operational perspectives in those families where the intervention related to the specific issue of whether or not the child had been abused were most out of tune with the professional view. On the whole such parents had little experience of police or social work scrutiny and they considered themselves independent and not to be in need of help. Whether or not the suspicion was well-founded, they felt they were leading respectable lives and so regarded the inquiry as a serious threat. Had they been able to see themselves two years on, they would have realised there was little need for alarm. Nevertheless, the seriousness of the disruption an inquiry can inflict on such families at the confrontation stage should not be underestimated.

The Professionals Gather

We next look at the meeting, the moment when professionals assemble formally, sometimes with the parents, to discuss the suspicion in more detail. As we have seen, the meeting can often be considered routine and contributions from outside agencies are few; in other cases it will be far more significant and have the effect of determining whether a child's name should be placed on the protection register. Twenty-two cases progressed to such a meeting. The following Table indicates the level of correspondence between the operational perspectives of children's mothers and key professionals.

Compared with what was found at the point of confrontation, at the time of the meeting operational perspectives between mother and key worker were in closer agreement, and the general picture was considerably more encouraging than that painted by Prosser in his scrutiny of very contentious cases. Among our families the previous pattern of concordance was reversed: here agreement was twice as frequent as disagreement and there was a significant improvement in the social component categories, particularly with respect to the handling of private information, where there was a higher level of accord than on most psychological dimensions. This improvement was particularly marked among multi-problem families.

Discordance was still considerable in three areas: interpretations of whether or not abuse occurred, perceptions of the appropriateness of emotional responses and the power relations between professionals and parents. This discrepancy was especially marked among acutely distressed

Table 10.2 **Concordance of operational perspectives of mother and key professional worker at the moment when professionals gather**

The dimensions of operational perspectives	Degree of Concordance among different types of family*			Degree of concordance overall*
	Multi-problem families	Specific problem families	Acutely distressed families	
A. Psychological				
Interpretations of situations, events and phenomena	●●○	○○○	○○○	●○○
Self perception and emotional responses	●○○	●●○	○○○	●○○
Experience and expectations	●●○	●●○	●●○	●●○
B. Social				
Power relations with others	●●○	●○○	○○○	●○○
The way private information becomes public	●●○	●●●	●●●	●●●
Number of families	11	7	4	22

* Concordance among families   ○○○ = 0–25%   ●○○ = 26–50%   ●●○ = 51–75%   ●●● = 76–100%

families; their perceptions were now more at odds with those of the investigating professionals. For them, the abuse investigation brought to breaking point the accumulated stress of a number of problems and so could not be regarded as just another familiar intrusion or as an inquiry into a specific event. Yet, despite their discomfort at this stage, as we shall see, these families were likely to benefit from the help and advice they were offered.

As we described in Chapter Eight, one factor in particular caused discord at the time of the meeting. Our research was conducted before the admission of parents to case conferences became routine, and in many cases planning meetings and informal gatherings took place without their knowledge. When mothers discovered that such discussions were occurring, a rift in their relationship with the professionals was almost inevitable, particularly if the suspicion concerned sexual abuse and parents were excluded because of police anxieties about the disclosure of evidence. Some, though not all, aspects of the operational perspectives of specific problem and acutely distressed families were still noticeably discordant for the same reason.

We have observed that the operational perspectives of mothers do not necessarily accord with those of other family members, a phenomenon particularly common among specific problem families. In these families around the time of the meeting we found a surprisingly high degree of concordance between mothers' perspectives and those of child protection workers, except with regard to the substance of the allegation. However inside the families the picture was more complicated: a mother, her partner and their children might present a united front to a child protection meeting, but at home, behind drawn curtains, a review of the condition of family life was likely to take place. In those circumstances the mother was likely to be less charitable in her attitude to the possibility of the father having abused the children, especially if there was a question of her having to choose between the likelier truth of allegations and denials.

Nevertheless, greater concordance between operational perspectives is to be welcomed, not least because it lends support to the argument that the shock damage suspicion causes will have healed somewhat by the time the professionals assemble. It also suggests that sensitive handling of families can bring into closer step previously conflicting viewpoints. Supporting parents throughout an investigation and making them feel a participant in the case meeting, even if the nature of the evidence makes such conditions difficult to engineer, can only be beneficial.

Moments when perceptions change

Finally, we consider the impact on operational perspectives of fresh information or significant later events, the range of possibilities extending from the introduction of a new social worker to further abuse allegations. Something of the kind occurred in 17 of the cases included in the intensive study. It will be seen that at this relatively advanced stage, across the three types of family examined, there was a much greater degree of correspondence between the operational perspectives of professionals and mothers. On all fronts over half the families were now in agreement with the professionals' views, and, as the Table shows, in some areas consensus was almost complete. This situation in which concordance was now three times more frequent than discord was markedly better even where previously the combination of circumstances seemed extremely inauspicious, for example with respect to the interpretation of behaviour and the perceived legitimacy of the inquiry.

To an extent, the higher level of concordance uncovered later in an inquiry was to be expected. From the parents' perspective, it could be argued that most investigations began so badly that any change could only have been for the better. The degree of improvement, however, also reflected the quality of the help families received from social services and other welfare agencies: in many cases not only were the families possibly abusive, many were also needy

Table 10.3 **Concordance of operational perspectives of mother and key professional worker when circumstances change***

The dimensions of operational perspectives	Degree of Concordance among different types of family			Degree of concordance overall*
	Multi-problem families	Specific problem families	Acutely distressed families	
A. Psychological				
Interpretations of situations, events and phenomena	●●●	●●○	●●○	●●○
Self perception and emotional responses	●●○	●●○	●●●	●●○
Experience and expectations	●●●	●●●	●●●	●●●
B. Social				
Power relations with others	●●●	●●○	●●●	●●○
The way private information becomes public	●●○	●●●	●●●	●●○
Number of families	9	4	4	17

* Concordance among families   ○○○ = 0–25%   ●○○ = 26–50%   ●●○ = 51–75%   ●●● = 76–100%

and, as we have shown, the offer of bedding, the provision of housing benefit or access to day-care facilities could do much to lessen parents' animosity towards professional intrusion into their private lives.

Some change may also have been the natural result of lengthy interaction. The better families and investigators know each other, the more likely they are to agree; concordance is a measure of familiarity and successful negotiation. But, equally, some parents may have felt they had something to gain by adopting the 'right' perceptions. As research studies of the mentally ill and offenders in custody have shown, expressing the right views at the right time can accelerate release. It was precisely to accommodate the complexity of the relationship between perception and motive that we needed to develop the concept of an operational perspective in the first place.

Over time, family members also re-assess their attitudes to each other. The first accusation frequently results in parents blaming each other or even their children for their predicament. Having had the opportunity to mull things over, mothers will occasionally acknowledge their own abusive behaviour, a shift in perspective which will have a considerable impact on the operational perspective of professionals. Those undertaking the investigation may also change course: frequent visits to a family will make plain what should have been evident from the start, that an allegation of abuse is seldom other than symptomatic of underlying problems attributable to poverty, poor parenting, negligible social skills or disintegrating relationships.

But, lest we become too sanguine, there are exceptions to the general pattern of improvement and for a sizeable group, something like a quarter, there were serious disagreements. In the previous Chapter we dealt with the case of the Claytons, a specific-problem family where perspectives become increasingly discordant both inside the household and between the family and social services. We encountered similar patterns in some multiple-problem families. For example, in the case of the James family, one not previously discussed, the suspicion of abuse paved the way for a procession of minor disasters. A single mother of three children by different fathers, was accused by a neighbour of leaving them unattended. The report was followed-up during a regular social work visit with the result that the mother protested her innocence. The social worker was not altogether convinced by her explanation, but was all the same certain that child protection procedures were of little use in the particular circumstances of the case. Nevertheless, to cover herself, she convened a planning meeting. The story might have ended there, but in the meantime the mother found out about the meeting and, in a state of panic, brought all three children to the social services office and asked for them to be adopted. This was not the outcome she wanted but at that moment her operational perspectives were so out of step with those of her social worker that she began to behave in a self-destructive way.

One of the five acutely distressed families we studied was another exception to the general pattern of improvement. Darren and Karen Jones had two children, an infant and a baby. Struggling from crisis to domestic crisis they nevertheless chose to manage without direct support from social services, a preference rooted in their own care histories. A particularly serious case of nappy rash worried the health visitor to such an extent that she decided to call a child protection meeting, as a result of which a gulf was created between the operational perspectives of professionals and the family. The children's names were not registered but greater scrutiny of the family situation, combined with increased anxiety on the part of the parents led to a dramatic change of circumstances. One Saturday night Darren was extremely violent to Karen. The police were called and a second child protection conference was quickly convened. This time the children's names were registered, deepening the distrust parents felt for social services. Most noteworthy about the case was that with respect to the psychological dimensions of operational perspectives, there was relatively slight disagreement between professionals and parents. On this foundation it proved possible to base work that led to a positive case outcome. The children remained with their parents and their names were eventually taken off the protection register.

Families' assessments of the situation two years later

This analysis of the data obtained from the 28 families from whom we were able to elicit an opinion leads us to conclude that, in general, the operational perspectives of parents, though initially distorted by the stress of confrontation and suspicion, gradually shift to a position less at odds with those of the investigating professionals. Most families eventually establish a workable relationship with their social worker and the other key professionals involved.

Case analysis using operational perspectives has limitations, however, in that it does not pretend to indicate the depth of conviction with which views are held or, thus, the likelihood of their enduring for any length of time. We therefore conducted a series of follow-up interviews two years later to discover what, in retrospect, parents felt about the intrusion into their lives. The replies were surprisingly complimentary. As many as 22 of the 28 families had come to regard the intervention as having been of some benefit, either materially or in terms of its effect on family relationships. None had welcomed the accusation, but in two-thirds of the cases it was said to have had the effect of clearing the air and making possible some form of beneficial intervention in difficult lives. The most critical were the specific-issue families where there is a tendency strenuously to deny any allegation of abuse and to resist what they see as social work interference.

While this picture may be encouraging, replies to subsequent questions indicated that the rapprochement between parents with professionals occurred despite deep-seated disagreements about the extent and nature of the abuse. The gap narrowed, but at the end of the investigation nearly half the mothers who expressed a view still disputed the professionals' judgement. Disagreement was particularly marked in cases of suspected sexual abuse - among families prominent in the specific problem group - but was evident across the board, as Table 10.4 shows.

The nature of the disagreement varied according to the type of family and nature of the accusation. Among multiple problem families and in cases of neglect, the extent of the abuse was the main source of contention. For families faced with a specific problem, particularly those dealing with an accusation of child sexual abuse, it was the legitimacy of the allegation. Acutely distressed families on the other hand nearly always agreed that some abusive behaviour had occurred but could not accept the conclusions reached by professionals about its context and/or causes, at least in the early stages.

Thus the situation after two years was still one of wide variation. A few families admitted the abuse and co-operated fully; some struggled on,

Table 10.4   **Agreement between mother and key professional over the extent and nature of the abuse at the three events**

Event	Multi-problem family		Specific problem family		Acutely distressed family		Total	
	Agree	Disagree	Agree	Disagree	Agree	Disagree	Agree	Disagree
Confrontation	2	12	1	8	2	3	5	23
Gathering of professionals	5	6	2	5	2	2	9	13
Change in circumstances	5	4	1	3	3	1	9	8
Two years after confrontation	10	4	2	7	4	1	16	12

concealing tensions and rows from outsiders; others were consistently antagonistic; but most cases fell somewhere in between. It was common for generally sympathetic attitudes to be tested by specific disagreements, particularly about the extent and context of the abuse, matters on which social workers were compelled to take a serious view.

What alters parental perceptions of a child abuse investigation?

The enduring feature of the 28 families participating in our two year follow-up study was not the suspicion of abuse but their need of help and support. What parents wanted most was relief from poverty and the resources to be able to lead an uncomplicated life. To that end, they quickly learned - if they did not already know - how to use perspectives functionally. For example, admitting some measure of culpability was frequently found to be a way of obtaining help, the more so if the likely future risk to the child was considered to be minimal. This message can be regarded as encouraging by professionals involved in child protection work. They might feel manipulated but, on the other hand, it is crucially important that they should be able to establish a working relationship with families.

Determining exactly what parents want and need is made more difficult when, as often happens, deprived and vulnerable families couch their instrumental needs in expressive language. So, mothers who actually want better accommodation will say 'I need somebody to talk to when I get depressed', and fathers who use excessive physical control are likely to complain 'Look, I've been under a lot of pressure at work'. In the end, the new flat, the new cooker or the marriage counsellor are most likely to improve the situation, but these ordinary enough requirements can easily be overlooked in the midst of the bureaucracy and emotion of an abuse investigation. Greater understanding of these processes could encourage social workers to re-assess their own operational perspectives and acknowledge the benefits of the natural bargaining process that is part of work with families. It would also help to moderate the views of some professionals we interviewed who seemed to wish simply that there were more effective ways of coercing parents into agreeing with their diagnosis.

A further complicating factor, as Dingwall and colleagues (1983) have shown, is a tendency on the part of social workers to perceive the situation of the family and, in particular, that of the child to be better than it really is. Familiarity with child protection work can induce a high tolerance of poor child rearing practices and produce a situation where workers are too easily persuaded that, provided the child is adequately protected, the family is functioning satisfactorily. This distortion, arising from an emphasis on child protection, is mirrored in Waterhouse's (1992) research in Scotland. She found that the physical care of a child is the chief yardstick by which child protection professionals measure the quality of parenting behaviour. Yet in reality under-control is more evident among these families than the over-control that raises the spectre of abuse.

By focusing on the physical care of the child, professionals may overlook the functional, practical problems most important to the parent. Even when these were identified, social workers in the cases we studied sometimes paid small attention to detail. Thus, there was a tendency to try to deal with a bundle of wants and needs at a single stroke and, under pressure, to neglect those aspects of the situation which most concerned the parents. For example, housing difficulties might be explored at the same time as the possibility of child protection registration, but in the event of a case conference the latter would take priority, leaving parents feeling confused and doubly abandoned, particularly if registration did result and it related to abuse unspecified by date or place.

Clear criteria and established routines would help parents to understand the intervention process, but, because it is at the vernacular level that operational perspectives are formed, any new procedures need to take account of the rules and conventions of the neighbourhood culture if they are to be effective. The move towards 'local patch' teams using good prevention packages might be expected to change the pattern of child protection work and improve the relationship between vulnerable families and professionals. In one of our participating local authorities there was such a scheme, but operational perspectives between parents and professionals were found to be less concordant than in the more centralised authority. Administrative reorganisation, therefore, may not by itself be sufficient to remedy the situations we have described.

Conclusions

In this chapter, we have assembled evidence on the three events identified by parents as pivotal in the child protection process. We have shown that parents' operational perspectives change over time. In general, the parents in our study became more content and in accord with the work of professionals on all fronts. Except in those cases where the accusation of abuse was specific and enduring, professionals and parents reached agreement about the extent and nature of the abuse which had occurred.

Nevertheless, in coming to this conclusion, we uncovered a complex interactive process by which the attitudes, preconceptions and prejudices of everyone involved in an investigation were negotiated. When the suspicion of child abuse was first raised, a diversity of viewpoints emerged. Parents rarely agreed with each other, individual children responded differently and the extended family, rarely consulted by professionals, regarded the whole business from a different perceptual angle. Much depended on the type of family, the context of the abuse, its meaning to the participants and their intentions.

We are left in no doubt that an abuse suspicion acts as a catalyst whose action severely disrupts family relations. The upheaval may become the vehicle of expression for other problems and, as we shall see in the following Chapter, the inquiry occasionally knocks the final nail into the coffin of an already collapsing marriage. Either way, an accusation that a parent has abused his or her own child is a potent force.

But, over time, individuals and families adapt and re-establish some form of equilibrium, so that at the conclusion of an inquiry, operational perspectives are markedly different. Striking a balance requires more than simply accommodating the intervention of professionals; parents must cope with the altered perceptions of other family members, especially those of older children who are frequently empowered by abuse inquiries.

We have focused on meaning, intention and interpretation where abusive behaviour is concerned, but we also acknowledge that there are some abusers who are downright dangerous. Thus, in considering child development, the concern must be to balance diverse risks and protective factors, but when a child has been sexually or physically assaulted and there is a definite risk that he or she will be re-abused, a professional must act quickly and may properly disregard the sensitivities of family members. In such circumstances we have to accept that, on occasion, achieving compatibility between the operational perspectives of an abusing relative and a responsible professional is impossible.

However, having looked at over 600 families in the extensive and intensive parts of this study, we find that fewer than ten cases belong in this dangerous category. In the vast majority, an understanding of the context, meaning and intention is essential, not only, as we shall see, in order to achieve a satisfactory outcome but to gain the family's confidence in the pursuit of more general welfare objectives. In a multi-problem family, physical abuse may be but one feature of a generally turbulent and violent lifestyle – the suspicion of abuse is unlikely seriously to affect relations between mother and father. In middle-class families, on the other hand, even the most minor physical assault on a child can imply a disturbance of a quite different order, sufficient to damage the whole fabric of family relationships.

These conclusions reinforce the points made at the end of the qualitative study, namely that discrepancies in perceptions often arise because in circumstances when clearly so much is relative, social workers are compelled to apply absolute criteria. The extent to which abuse is 'felt' and the degree of 'intentionality' again emerge as the two variables that determine the significance of abuse and these in turn affect the development of perspectives mapped in this Chapter.

In this context, parents who accept help almost always perceive it as control. Such a situation would seem to conflict with the principles applied in other types of child-care case following the implementation of the *Children Act, 1989*. For example, the emphasis placed on parental responsibility for children who are looked after is seldom translated to situations where children on the Child Protection Register continue to live at home. It might be argued that parental responsibility and participation are less important considerations where decision-making about abused children is concerned - although a study by Thoburn and colleagues (1993) does not support such a proposition. Whatever the truth of the matter, the contrast between the level of participation promised to the parents of children being accommodated and the degree of duress and upset parents experience during a suspected child abuse 'confrontation' is significant.

We are therefore bound to question whether such a confrontation is always necessary. Like Gibbons and colleagues (1993), we were not convinced that every case of suspected abuse we studied warranted the involvement of the child protection system, so considerable was the risk of seriously distorting parents' perceptions of the value of social work and, in the process, reducing the potential benefits. Recourse to Section 17 of the *Children Act* or even to voluntary supervision are alternatives worth considering, if only because they would be less likely to sour relationships between parents and professionals for a long time in the future.

Summary points

1 When the operational perspectives of those involved in child abuse investigations are compared, it is found that the perceptions of parents do not reflect those of their children nor does one parent share the perspective of the other. Further, changes in the perspective of one family member may not be congruent with changes in others.

2 Harmful intent of parents towards their children was not much in evidence; abuse was more a question of failings, negligence or over zealous and inappropriate controls. Even some sexual misdemeanour by parents could be viewed as love inappropriately expressed. Thus, the majority of parents found the concern of professionals bewildering and violating.

3 Professionals face a difficult task; there is less evidence of what *is* happening to the child than what *might be* happening. But the perspectives of parents do give a clue as to what they view as appropriate and important in child rearing and where stress in the family might be located.

4 There is considerable divergence between the operational perspectives of parents and those of professionals at the outset of an abuse investigation. But the distance between perspectives varies from family to family. Acutely distressed families collapsing in crisis are more in accord with professional perspectives than are families unknown to social services, where suspicions of abuse are thrust upon them by others.

5 By the time a meeting of professionals takes place, the 'operational perspectives' of both parents and professionals are coming closer together. The inclusion of parents in case conferences, the provision of clear information, the stressing that succour rather than punishment is on offer and that children are not at risk of precipitate removal all help bring perspectives of parents and professionals together.

6 It is not so much the type of abuse that affects congruence between parental perspectives and those of professionals, but more the context in which suspicion is aroused, who makes the accusation, who handles subsequent investigations and how professionals manage their role.

7 The extent to which abuse is 'felt' and the 'intentionality' behind it are two variables which determine its meaning. These will affect both parental and professional perspectives.

8 While professionals seek reassurance of a child's well-being through physical criteria, long exposure to a case can raise their threshold of tolerance. Thus, inadequate control, marital discord and the lack of affection can be missed. Poor parents often use expressive language to transmit instrumental messages, just as the more affluent can communicate expressive feelings in instrumental ways, such as sharing an American Express card.

Chapter 11

Operational perspectives, intervention and outcome

We followed the progress of the 30 families participating in the intensive study for two years from the moment they became aware that they were under suspicion for possible child abuse. No matter how brief or insubstantial the official investigation, there was a possibility that the effect of such severe scrutiny of private lives would be marked, and so in all 30 cases we compared the family's circumstances prior to the investigation with what existed two years later. Were they better or worse off? Was the child protected? Had new problems emerged? Finally we attempted to tackle the larger question this study has sought to unravel: did parents' operational perspectives on the way an investigation was conducted have any measurable effect on the outcome of the case? In short, did it matter what the parents thought?

As a result of the deliberations which led to the publication of the *Looking After Children* materials (Parker and colleagues, 1991), the value of monitoring the consequences of child-care interventions has come to be widely acknowledged; but it is also recognised that 'outcome' is a fearsomely difficult concept to define or evaluate, so multifarious are the factors that influence it. In simple terms, paying attention to outcomes helps to establish to what extent a situation at one moment is related to whatever may have happened at a certain prior moment and thus to judge whether a process, such as an abuse investigation, may be said to have done a family good or harm; but even the most cursory glance at the data set out in the preceding Chapters shows how complicated are the calculations that need to be made. For example, every intervention must be regarded as the 'outcome' of some prior situation, so that it becomes extremely difficult to distinguish between cause and effect. Furthermore, while we have attempted to demonstrate the importance in such conditions of evolving operational perspectives, we would be the first to concede that they do not make outcome any simpler to assess; we know that parents' perceptions of an investigation fluctuate and are sometimes at odds with the views of those trying to help them, but how are we to say what has the most bearing on outcome – first or last impressions or the extent of the variation between the two?

In order to answer this question, we considered three aggregations of factors that can be said to have a bearing on any child protection outcome. First is the abuse itself. Generally we found that families suffered as a result of the child's neglect or maltreatment. Second is the investigative process and any intervention associated with it. There is a certain presumption that the action of professionals will be of benefit to a family, but, as we have shown, negative effects are not uncommon. We estimate that in about 2% of all child protection cases investigated, there is severe conflict between parents' and child's interests, to such an extent that family welfare has to be sacrificed for the sake of the safety of the child. However, the research indicates that even in cases where separation is considered necessary, the destinies of children and families will continue to be entangled, a finding acknowledged in the *Children Act*, 1989 in the emphasis placed on participation, partnership and continuous parental responsibility. Child rescue situations, though important, are insufficiently common to call into question the validity of this approach. The third group of factors relates to the qualitative study previously discussed and to the mass of evidence which shows that the manner in which an intervention is handled influences the development of the operational perspective of parents and of other members of the investigated family.

We next considered the relationship between these three groups of factors in order to determine whether outcomes were more or less favourable in cases where, using the terminology developed in the previous Chapter, operational perspectives may generally be said to have been concordant or discordant. The framework for this relationship is illustrated in the following Diagram, where plus and minus signs indicate improvement (+) or deterioration (-) in family situation following the 'intervention' and concordance or discordance between parents' and professionals' operational perspectives.

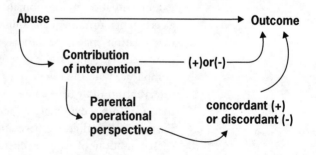

By using this model, the numerous possible influences on outcomes in cases of suspected child abuse can be simplified so that their pattern corresponds to one of the four permutations described below. In an ideal case, the uniformly negative impact of an abuse allegation is compensated by a beneficial intervention applauded by parents and professionals alike. Least encouraging are those instances where the intervention of child protection professionals makes matters worse and there is disagreement between participants on every front. With the two hybrids added, the four permutations possible are as follows:

	Abuse	Contribution of intervention	Parental operational perspectives
Combination One	–	+	concordant
Combination Two	–	+	discordant
Combination Three	–	–	concordant
Combination Four	–	–	discordant

Another dimension must be added to this very much simplified scheme to take account of the variety possible with respect to whom and to which outcome one is referring. As we have shown, improvement in the situation of a child may be at some cost to other members of his or her family, and a social worker may on occasion be content in his or her relationship with a household as long he or she is satisfied that the children are safe. Similarly, an abuse investigation is ostensibly concerned with whether or not a child is protected, but, given the vulnerable nature of many of the families in the study, observations concerning children's health, education and behaviour are also relevant. All these can be affected by how a suspicion is dealt with, and, as the evidence of previous Chapters indicates, gains in one aspect of family life are frequently offset by losses in another.

We therefore considered outcomes for each principal family member based on judgements of the overall situation made at the time of the first allegation and two years later. In doing so, we compared the interview replies from the two occasions, analysed responses relating to specific aspects of the family's circumstances and ascertained the views of the professionals concerned. Several aspects of family life were scrutinised and five incorporated: (1) living situations; (2) family relationships; (3) parenting behaviour and child development; (4) physical and psychological health; and, (5) whether or not the child was protected.

We began by classifying the 30 cases. First were those in which the abuse led to a negative outcome for family members and there was no intervening consideration, for example, where severe abuse necessitated the rescue of a child on terms which permitted only limited future parental contact or none at all. Next were situations in which the intervention influenced the effects of the abuse but parental perceptions were of marginal significance. Finally, we examined circumstances in which the operational perspectives of family members were a significant factor in determining their situation two years on, for example where a child in a family heavily supported by Social Services was re-abused and parents' non co-operation led social workers to remove the child.

1 *Abuse influences outcome independent of interventions and perspectives*

In this study, we came across no abuse so horrific that the intervention was intended to help no-one but the child, and the operational perspectives of parents were consequently rendered irrelevant to the outcome of the case. As Gibbons and colleagues (1993) have shown and as the evidence in Chapter Five confirms, the majority of cases of child maltreatment brought to the attention of welfare agencies, though unpleasant, are relatively minor. The severest physical abuse in this study involved a deliberate burn to an infant, and in most cases minor bruising was the worst visible sign of ill-treatment. Suspicions of child sexual abuse generally rested on slender evidence and in only three cases were professionals sufficiently concerned to remove a child under emergency proceedings. Without exception, members of the family were the focus of suspicion.

It is also encouraging to report that we did not discover any convincing example of a 'self-fulfilling prophecy' – in which a family's response to an unjustified intrusion could be said to be a factor in some subsequent maltreatment. As has been shown, there were cases where professionals' efforts were counter-productive, but none in which their action precipitated child abuse. This finding will not surprise those working in the child protection system but it has not, as far as we know, been previously demonstrated by research.

2 *Intervention mitigates the effects of abuse irrespective of parents' operational perspectives*

In two of the five areas of family life we studied – the nature and the quality of the families' living situation and the physical and psychological health of parents and children – the intervention of welfare agencies was found to have made a difference, irrespective of the operational perspectives of parents.

A child abuse investigation frequently precedes and in certain cases can be shown to precipitate a change of abode and a movement of family members between households. For example, of the 61 children considered 'at risk' in the 30 families we studied, 12 moved out of the house during the period of our follow-up study. But, in contrast to Prosser's (1992) findings with a more difficult group, only four moved to local authority accommodation; the rest transferred, sometimes several times, between the homes of close relatives. In such situations, the suspicion of abuse could be regarded as an additional unsettling feature in the lives of already troubled families. Twelve of the 30 moved house in the interval between initial investigation and our final visit, and, during the same period, nine families experienced the arrival or departure of a key adult, usually a father or step-parent.

Despite the upheaval that abuse accusations commonly inflicted on families, changes in living situations tended to be for the better, for example following the departure of an abuser or if a family was re-housed. Indeed, in

13 of the 30 cases, we considered that the household situation had benefited from professional intervention and in only one case were we driven to the conclusion that the welfare effort had made matters worse. The various living situations are summarised in the following Table.

Table 11.1 **The state of families' living situation prior to initial investigation and two years later**

	Type of family							
	Multi-problem		Specific Problem		Acutely Distressed		Total	
	0m	2y	0m	2y	0m	2y	0m	2y
Good	1	2	2	2	0	0	3	4
Average	1	4	4	4	3	3	8	11
Poor	13	9	3	3	3	3	19	15
	N=15		N=9		N=6		N=30	

As living situations improved, so did the health of family members, at least by their own account and as recorded in professionals' case files. Bearing in mind that the stresses of an investigation might be expected to undermine the well-being of both parents and children this was an encouraging impression. Nevertheless, it was disconcerting to discover that improvements in family health were usually made from a poor starting point. At the outset, the health of all but eight of the 30 mothers was poor and 12 spoke of serious illness. Their afflictions included chronic depression (6), heart disease (2), gynaecological problems (2), and cancer (2). In addition, five natural fathers or stepfathers and ten children had disabling chronic conditions, the most frequent of which in children were those aggravated by stress, such as eczema.

Improvements in health were found to be more or less directly linked to the instrumental aspects of the intervention. For example, ensuring that families received adequate social security benefits and were able to locate sources of respite care, or persuading older children to go to school so that they could claim free meals had the effect of improving the family diet and relieving the pressure on mothers and other children. These advantages in turn led to better health; indeed we found that half the 30 families benefited by this route. Changes in the incidence of health problems, major and minor, affecting mothers in different types of family are analysed in the following Table.

Table 11.2 **The number of mothers experiencing health problems prior to initial investigation and two years later**

| | Type of family | | | | | | | |
| | Multi-problem | | Specific Problem | | Acutely Distressed | | Total | |
Health problems	0m	2y	0m	2y	0m	2y	0m	2y
Yes	10	5	6	1	6	1	22	7
No	5	10	3	8	0	5	8	23
	N=15		N=9		N=6		N=30	

Since improvements in general health could be said to affect the quality of parents' operational perspectives, here was further confirmation of the value of whatever practical support social workers, health visitors and teachers were able to give vulnerable families. Regardless of how parents viewed their situation at the outset of an abuse investigation, most simply needed help. Against the distress the investigation caused, one must balance the contribution to their welfare, at least in these two areas, that the intrusion made possible.

3. *Interventions have an effect both on parental perspectives and outcome*
In other areas of family life, most notably family relationships, parenting behaviour and child development, the results of intervention were more variable, but more marked in relation to the development of parents' operational perspectives. The intimate nature of an abuse investigation was found frequently to change the dynamics of family relationships, to the extent that high levels of marital breakdown and discord were evident among the study group in the follow-up period. More encouraging was the finding that parents paid greater attention to the rearing of their children, understandably wanting to compensate for any perceived deficiencies.

Family relationships

Relationships in these families had seldom been comfortable – nor were they likely to be. Marriages and cohabitations were commonly described as a struggle against adversity and the quality of family life was constantly roughened by hardship. Bad enough to begin with, the domestic climate almost invariably worsened following the confrontation with the child protection system. Leaving aside seven cases involving single parents, relationships between the adults in all the remaining 23 households deteriorated.

As we have shown in previous Chapters, the suspicion of abuse will unsettle even the most stable relationship, so it is perhaps not very surprising that nine out of 23 marriages or cohabitations should have come to an end during the two year follow-up period. The indication that only two parents embarked on any new relationship during the same period is further evidence of the impact of the child protection system on the self-esteem of individuals. Several mothers said they had experienced enough emotional turmoil to last a lifetime.

What were the circumstances of the separations? In three cases, men left a household as a direct consequence of the abuse investigation: two were suspected of sexually abusing their children, the third was thought to have neglected and physically abused his seven year old son. In another two cases, the investigation hastened the collapse of already rocky marriages, and in the remaining two families, fathers were sentenced to prison custody for offences not related to the suspicion of abuse. It is noteworthy that in both these last cases, mothers regarded their partner's departure as final and, in combination with the end of the abuse inquiry, used the enforced absence as an opportunity to make a fresh start.

An abuse investigation will also have an impact on parent-child relationships. The psychological conditions in which the discipline, control and tending of children take place are altered: adolescents may recognise in the sympathetic presence of a social worker a chance to dispose of various anxieties; should they concern physical abuse the need for a partisan response is clearly urgent, but gripes about a lack of pocket money or of freedom to stay out late are rather less compelling. The point to make is that few parents can be expected to cope comfortably with the close attention paid to their regime by the child protection system, especially should their children seem to have been invited to join the ranks of the inquisitors. Under those circumstances, already fragile relationships between parents and adolescent children may deteriorate. In the same vein, an improvement in a mother's relationship with a child can sometimes result in a deterioration in the relationship between father and child, such may be the fineness of the balance.

We assembled evidence on the quality of family relationships from several sources and attempted to summarise the results by employing a methodology similar to that devised for the Dartington study of children returning from local authority care (Bullock, Little and Millham, 1993). Here, family relationships were examined on three dimensions: the spiritual/expressive, the functional and the structural. The results laid out in the following Table confirm how difficult it is to achieve any improvement in this area. Over the two-year period there is little change.

Table 11.3 **The quality of family relationships prior to investigation and two years later**

	Multi-problem		Specific Problem		Acutely Distressed		Total	
	0m	*2y*	*0m*	*2y*	*0m*	*2y*	*0m*	*2y*
Good	1	0	0	0	0	0	1	0
Average	2	5	2	1	3	3	7	9
Poor	12	10	7	8	3	3	22	21
	N=15		N=9		N=6		N=30	

Type of family (header spanning Multi-problem, Specific Problem, Acutely Distressed)

Family relationships were affected particularly by the process, intrinsic to any formal investigation, by which private information is passed openly between inquisitive strangers. Despite the efforts of child protection professionals to behave sensitively and maintain a degree of confidentiality, the existence of an abuse investigation tended to become quite widely known. All mothers and nearly all fathers knew that abuse was suspected, and in all but nine cases, members of the larger family, particularly grandparents but also aunts and uncles, were aware of the suspicion and the subsequent investigation. On the other hand, not every child considered to be a possible victim of maltreatment understood that an inquiry was under way: 11 remained oblivious, as did half the siblings in those families. Neighbours were aware of the investigation in 11 cases and in several they were much involved as counsellors.

It can be seen that as a consequence of raising suspicions of child abuse with parents a family's privacy and thus its sense of identity may be eroded. This experience is distressing for parents and counter-productive to professionals' efforts to help. The stigma associated with turning to social services for support is well enough documented; when such help is not only uninvited but tainted with the suspicion of child abuse, the harm done to families can be considerable.

Parenting and child development

If one next considers whether an investigation made any difference to the way in which parents brought up their children, the findings are more encouraging, since, despite the disruption caused, the quality of parenting certainly improved during the follow up period – at least in the eyes of the professionals. The introduction of family aides, the offer of family centre support and other forms of direct help were a clear factor. There was a measurable change in parenting behaviour in 17 cases and in all but three of those the change was for the better. Whether changes in parenting made any difference to a child's development was more difficult to determine, but there were indications that on certain criteria gains were made during the two year follow-up period. We collected information in interviews and from files concerning the child's health, education and relationships with parents and siblings and found that in each area some improvement was evident. It seems that parents give greater priority to key aspects of the child's life following the crisis of the confrontation. They are prepared to pay attention to aspects of their children's development long taken for granted.

A more independent estimate has been made in such cases by comparing a child's achievements with those appropriate to his or her developmental stage. As the following Table 11.4 indicates, the situation, as recorded by education, health and social services officials two years after the suspicion of abuse surfaced, was generally better than that which existed previously. Of the 61 children 'at risk' in the 30 families, 52 had reached their development stage satisfactorily compared with 44 at the outset.

Table 11.4 **Had children in the family reached a developmental stage appropriate for their age?**

	Type of family							
	Multi-problem		Specific Problem		Acutely Distressed		Total	
	0m	*2y*	*0m*	*2y*	*0m*	*2y*	*0m*	*2y*
Yes	28	30	14	16	2	6	44	52
No	7	5	6	4	4	0	17	9
	N=35		N=20		N=6		N=61	

Further, the behaviour of children in the family was said to have improved. Of the 30 children who exhibited problems at the point of investigation 17 had improved by the end of the follow-up period. Nevertheless, the deficiencies tended to persist and more might have been done to aid child development.

The general picture is one of progress in some areas and setbacks in others. Plainly, parents' operational perspectives are shaped according to how their cases are handled by professionals. The cast of their perceptions certainly matters because it has an influence on case outcome, at least in the areas of family dynamics, parenting skills and child development. The nature and style of interventions are also important considerations, since they have an independent impact on families' living situations and health. Investigations in which parents are treated sensitively can therefore be shown to be to the advantage of the family, and, in the great majority of cases, to the victims of child abuse.

We now return to evidence relating more directly to the suspected victims of abuse, to consider whether they were adequately protected as a result of the investigation and whether the quality of the intervention was a contributory factor.

Were the children in the families abused and did they need help?

In investigating the abuse histories of the 61 children at risk, we needed to distinguish between those cases where abuse had definitely occurred and those where there was a degree of doubt. Since clear definitions of acceptable parenting behaviour are so demonstrably lacking, it may be that parents judged to be innocent of one misdemeanour consider themselves by vague implication to be guilty of others (even to the extent of its becoming possible to argue that no-one is entirely blameless). Nevertheless, to be able to judge whether or not a particular child has been protected as a result of an investigation, it is important to know whether, by some common criteria, he or she was actually abused in the first place.

In the very broad sense just described, all 61 children considered to be 'at risk' in the 30 families had been abused or neglected in some way. But when one enquired if the abuse identified was precisely associated with the behaviour or circumstances that were the focus of the original investigation, the answer was frequently 'no'. Most children had been the victims of minor neglect and occasionally of physical punishment that went beyond acceptable bounds, but after carefully weighing the evidence, we concluded that only 20 of the 61 children had been abused in the manner of which their abusers were originally accused. These data are summarised in the following Table 11.5.

Failure to substantiate the original suspicion did not of course mean that the intervention was unnecessary. Our conclusion was that 30 of the 41 children with respect to whom the original suspicion of abuse was, by our definition, unfounded, required some support from social services. Thus, we separated the 61 children in the study into three classes:

a) had been abused as suspected; intervention required   N=20
b) not abused as suspected but intervention required   N=30
c) not abused as suspected; no intervention required   N=11

We next considered what happened to these children during the investigation and found that the child protection services erred on the side of caution.

Table 11.5 **Family type, category under which abuse was originally suspected and whether suspicion was founded**

	Category of abuse suspected			Whether the suspicion was well founded		
	Emotional	Physical	Sexual	Yes	No	Total
Multi-problem	2	21	12	13	22	35
Specific problem	2	9	9	4	16	20
Acutely distressed	2	4	0	3	3	6
Total	6	34	21	20	41	61

In relation to the majority (N=46) a protection meeting was called and as a consequence the names of 29 were registered. Had clear criteria been applied and the protection system been solely concerned with preventing abuse, then we might have expected most of those 'abused as suspected' to have been registered, provided there was a danger of significant harm. Similarly we would have expected no further action to be taken with respect to the less risky cases. However, as the following Table 11.6 indicates, there were some marked discrepancies between those expectations and the actual outcome. For example, two children not abused and, in our estimation, requiring no intervention, were conferenced and 13 of the 30 who needed help but who had not been abused were registered. Thus, it emerged that the relationship

Table 11.6 **Researchers' interpretation of child's situation and the decisions made by the child protection system**

	Decisions made			
Researcher's interpretation	No Action	Case Conference; Not Registered	Case Registered	Total
Abused as suspected; intervention required	2	3	15	20
Not abused; intervention required	4	13	13	30
Not abused; no intervention required	9	1	1	11
Total	15	17	29	61

between suspicion, confirmation, intervention and outcome was extremely fluid and subject to much negotiation during the investigation process.

Was the child protected?

It will be recalled that scrutiny of the situation of the 61 children in our study led us to conclude that the original accusation of abuse was well-founded in the case of only 20 cases but that all the children could be said to be 'in need' as defined by the *Children Act*, 1989. We were not convinced that interventions were strictly necessary in every case, but with respect to 41 children the investigation had the effect of reducing or ending the abuse, including all those children considered 'abused as suspected'. Such a reckoning is encouraging.

However, among our study group some new incidents of abuse were reported during the two year follow-up period. As the following Table indicates, 16 of the 61 children were reliably believed to have been re-abused. Given such a high-risk group it is probably a low figure, the more so if one takes into account the finding that, as before, the maltreatment was usually relatively minor.

Table 11.7 **The number of children thought to be re-abused during the two year follow-up by type of family**

Re-abused	Multi Problem	Specific Issue	Acutely Distressed	Total
Yes	13	2	1	16
No	22	18	5	45
Total	35	20	6	61

If a broader measure of success is used and one enquires whether a child was protected and living at home two years after the first suspicion of abuse, the findings are less clear-cut. It is pleasing to report on the one hand that when the research fieldwork ceased, all but three of the 61 children were living in the household of a family member; many had moved house but nearly all were 'at home'. Given such a vulnerable group, this was a considerable achievement. On the other hand, we found that 11 of the 58 children at home were not adequately protected against the threat of abuse by the initial investigation or the subsequent intervention. The children and their families benefited in several other respects, for example in terms of accommodation, parenting skills and child development, but, if one applied the strict criterion of further abuse, however minor, one was forced to conclude that the protection proved inadequate.

Abuse, interventions, perception and outcome

We began this Chapter by describing the factors that as far as the families were concerned might influence the outcome of a child abuse investigation. Generally speaking, the accusation of abuse had a damaging effect on family functioning, but we hypothesised that the intervention could permit a mediating process and, should the operational perspectives of professionals and parents coincide, that some benefit was likely to result. We now consider to what extent the hypothesis holds true.

The following Table 11.8 compares the four input permutations listed earlier with the components of family outcome discussed in this Chapter: living situation, health, relationships and parent skills. It will be recalled that inputs could be wholly beneficial, for example when agency intervention brought about an unqualified improvement and parents regarded the process entirely approvingly. Alternatively, the procedure could prove entirely counter-productive, so that the intervention did substantial damage and the operational perspective of parents was wholly unfavourable. In between these extremes were two other hybrid permutations. The outcome factors chosen related to two areas where we found parental perspectives to be not particularly important – family living situation and the health of its members, and to two more where operational perspectives were a significant influence,

Table 11.8 **The relationship between patterns of abuse, intervention, parental perspectives and family outcomes**

Abuse	Intervention	Operational Perspectives	Living Situations		Health		Relationships		Parent skills		
			Pos	Neg	Pos	Neg	Pos	Neg	Pos	Neg	
–	+	concordant	5	5	9	1	10	0	9	1	N=10
–	+	discordant	7	3	6	4	0	10	3	7	N=10
–	–	concordant	2	3	1	4	4	1	4	1	N=5
–	–	discordant	0	5	0	5	0	5	1	4	N=5
											N=30

Negative outcome includes situations where no improvement in family functions was found.

the quality of family relationships and parenting skills The classification of the relationship between abuse, intervention and operational perspectives was assessed in relation to each of these four areas of family outcome.

Apart from a few exceptional cases, the research findings supported our original hypothesis. A helpful intervention, which usually consists in the coincidence between instrumental support for the family and concordant operational perspectives, will nearly always lead to a more satisfactory outcome with respect to family relationships and parenting skills and is also of benefit to living situations and family health. In cases where domestic difficulties may be considered overwhelming, where serious abuse is denied or help is rejected, parental perceptions are usually at variance and even high quality intervention has minimal effect. Thus, the general conclusion must be that it is worth professionals paying attention to parents' views because not only are they changeable and responsive to skilful negotiation but, as the following Table illustrates, when operational perspectives of parents and professionals closely correspond, there is the additional bonus that the child is likely to be protected against abuse.

Table 11.9 **Patterns of abuse, intervention and parental perspectives in relation to whether or not the children in the 30 families were protected *and* living at home**

		Parents' operational perspectives	Child protected and living at Home	
Abuse	**Intervention**		*Yes*	*No*
–	+	concordant	10	0
–	+	discordant	9	1
–	–	concordant	0	5
–	–	discordant	0	5
			N=30	

Discussion

We have tried to separate the empirical evidence on what happens to families subjected to an abuse investigation from a discussion of the implications of these findings for the operation of the child protection system. The difficulty of gaining access to families at the outset limited the number of families and children whose circumstances we were able to monitor, but there is sufficient evidence here to permit comment on the strengths and weaknesses of the intervention procedures.

As we stated at the beginning of this Chapter, outcome is a difficult concept. A shortcoming of our research approach is that we have concentrated on family outcomes but have not been able to present data on the well–being of individuals within each family. We recognise that what is good for the parent may be bad for the child and vice-versa. The same criticism could be levelled at the child protection system as a whole, in that it is designed to alert several agencies to the needs of children at risk of abuse, but, as a consequence, may allow the immediate needs of children to displace the chronic needs of the whole family. At a time when the operation of the *Children Act,* 1989 is highlighting the extent of parental responsibility and the need to support vulnerable families, efforts to protect abused children could become inconsistent with the general approach to those more simply defined as being 'in need'.

The evidence also calls into question the usefulness of the child protection profession's preoccupation with categories of abuse. We have found it more helpful to consider types of family: the *multi-problem* families whose very existence is a struggle, the *acutely distressed* parents in whose lives one extra problem can tip the balance between survival and collapse. We believe that these families could be helped by less stigmatising support strategies. For the third group, *the specific problem* families, in which the extent and nature of abuse is the single and extremely urgent problem, child protection approaches seem appropriate. Indeed, from our scrutiny of the long-term outcomes of families, it emerged that with the exception of a few sexual abuse cases, the category of the suspected abuse had little or no bearing on what happened.

Professionals are inclined to assume that desired outcomes will be secured by following an appropriate administrative route. The balance of our evidence should serve to remind them that no particular course of action can guarantee that a child will be protected or that any other aspect of family functioning will improve. However, by the same token, it is clear that when an investigation is going badly, there are opportunities to rectify and improve the situation. In many of the cases described in earlier Chapters there were moments when the operational perspectives of parents and professionals might have been brought more closely into line.

Looking at outcomes from another point of view, as time passes we find that the problems faced by families, while varied at the outset, tend to become more alike. Despite any slight improvement, they endure the same disadvantages that thrust them towards the child protection system in the first place, with the difference that the confrontation will have left its mark. Long after the investigators have gone, the families exhibit caution and unease in their dealings with social services, but, on the whole, families do benefit in instrumental ways from the intervention: child care is marginally better and the majority of children are not separated from their families.

Lack of clarity about the aims, objectives and functions of the child protection system does not help to diminish the queasiness and the sense of unfinished business that beset the relationship between parents and professionals following a child abuse inquiry. Among professionals there is no common view as to what constitutes a satisfactory outcome, and, as we have seen, parents are often confused by the curious conjunction of the investigator and the carer in the behaviour of the professionals . The child protection service has been formalised to aid inter-agency planning but, in the process, has become a sophisticated bureaucracy. It manages to afford protection to the majority of those who come to its notice, but many families pay a high price. Disruption, lingering suspicion and resentment, the disintegration of adult and adolescent relationships can too easily become the side-effects of child protection work. Since the majority of cases investigated are minor, the cost in terms of human disturbance and misplaced resources may be considered unnecessarily high.

The great strength of the child protection system lies in its capacity to offer vulnerable families instrumental help and to keep children at home with the parents or other relatives. Its failings become most evident when the intervention becomes quasi-judicial, appearing to rule on the culpability of families and the degree of threat they may pose. We are led to ask whether the children involved in minor abuse cases could be classified as 'in need'. Should the protection service become more specialised in order to deal only with those at greatest risk? It is to these practice and policy issues that we turn next as we conclude the study.

Summary points

1 The study has contrasted family situations prior to any investigation for child abuse with that which existed two years later. Were they better or worse off? Have new problems emerged? Was the child protected? Examination of the 'outcomes' of a professional intervention poses problems. Parental perceptions of outcome may not match those of professionals, neither may they accord with more objective criteria, such as marital breakdown or the removal of children or adults from the family.

2 Horrific abuse is relatively rare, as is the removal of children from families, hence from the outset there is the possibility of a benign outcome to cases. However, any investigation of suspected child abuse precipitates movement of family members in and out of households. This turbulence may involve the victim and siblings.

3 Regardless of parents' perspectives on the intervention, the living situation in terms of accommodation and child care resources of nearly half the families improved as a result of the work of child protection professionals.

4 The physical and psychological health of family members was poor with 22 mothers displaying at least one difficulty. Their health improved as a result of intervention, leading to consequent advances in psychological functioning.

5 The intervention of child protection professionals inextricably influenced family functioning. Although at the outset few parents enjoyed idyllic liaisons, suspicions of abuse unsettled family relationships. Nearly half of cohabitations and marriages had ended by two years after the suspicion. In addition, the quality of relationships within the wider family and immediate neighbourhood fluctuated.

6 During the two year follow-up, half the parents improved their child rearing skills as a result of intervention and fewer children in the family remained below a developmental stage appropriate for their age.

7 All of the children 'at risk' had been abused in some way but the suspicions of child protection agencies were unfounded in the majority of cases. Nonetheless, we felt that some form of intervention was necessary in 50 of the 61 cases. Those that required the most help were not always those that benefited and some who received services were not necessarily the most serious cases.

8 Two thirds of the children were protected from abuse and remained at home or in the care of relatives. Of the 16 children who were re-abused, maltreatment was of a minor character.

9 The evidence appears to confirm the initial hypothesis proposed in this study. That is to say, where instrumental intervention coincides with concord between professionals and parents, outcomes on several dimensions are satisfactory and the child is highly likely to be safe and living at home.

10 The function of the child protection system is not only to safeguard children at risk of abuse but also to shield professionals and their organisations from criticism. Preoccupation with the putative damage done to the young can elbow aside the violation experienced by parents, siblings and wider family. In terms of outcome, the voicing of suspicion may be more abusive and long term in its consequence than the bruise which prompted investigation.

Chapter 12

Conclusions

This study has explored the incidence of suspected child abuse and the experience of families caught up in the process of suspicion. It has concentrated on parental perspectives during the early stages of a child abuse investigation and demonstrated that parents' perspectives have an influence on subsequent management of cases and on their outcome. Although not the focus of this study, the experience of other close family members has also been glanced at. Their perspectives interact with those of parents, modifying or confirming family strategies of managing the suspicion. Plainly, more needs to be known about the impact of suspicion upon the wider family, particularly upon siblings and others intimate with the victim.

During the 1980s there were several child abuse scandals in the United Kingdom, some concerned with the death of children. Other incidents revealed social workers and health professionals to be either over zealous or dilatory in their protection of children at risk. As the furore died away, official inquiries were set up, but subsequent critical reports did little to allay public concern. Questions were asked; how widespread was child abuse? Was it increasing? Were the procedures for referral, investigation, protection and assistance adequate? What was the experience of parents?

In response, the Department of Health initiated a programme of research studies to give a comprehensive view of the situation. Some studies were to look at agency practice, some to highlight orthodox control and sexual behaviour in families, some to examine the abuse behaviour itself and its consequences for children. This study is part of that package of research, summarised in a Department of Health publication (1995) and explores the perspectives of parents suspected of child abuse: how do they deal with suspicion and with accusations that all is not well with their child?

Problems of definition

The study faced many problems of definition, for example concerning what constitutes a 'perception', a 'suspicion' or a 'referral'. Even the term 'child abuse' may not be very helpful in aiding any research investigation or mounting protection strategies, as it is too vague and all-embracing a concept. We have seen that a number of problems have a bearing on the maltreatment of children and that abuse should be defined in the wider context of nurture, control and development of a particular child. Not only do perceptions vary on what constitutes child abuse, but the type and severity of violation also differ. In addition, time changes what families and societies view as abusive behaviour. In the same way, professional opinion can be out of step with public opinion and professionals may disagree with one another. Thus estimates of the incidence and nature of child abuse will vary considerably and emotive claims should be viewed with considerable caution.

While there has been an increase in the identification of various forms of child abuse in recent years, an increase in number does not necessarily reflect greater incidence. Indeed, there is evidence that identification has expanded at the minor end of the child abuse continuum and dwindled at the more serious end. Hence this study has had to clarify firstly, what is child abuse and secondly, what can be defined as 'serious'.

Definition is particularly important in deciding where the line should be drawn beyond which adult and family behaviour becomes unacceptable and enquiries become necessary. Such a decision will determine the size of the problem, its nature and trend. Definition will also affect the zeal with which professionals explore the issue. We have seen, however, that most suspicions of abuse come to nothing and even confirmation usually reveals but minor damage to children. In such situations parents wonder what all the fuss is about, they feel picked on, harassed and humiliated. Parents certainly do not define their behaviour as 'child abuse'.

Defining 'suspicion' has also posed problems. Here, too, a combination of issues may fan concern that something is wrong. Suspicion gathers force, it has a momentum of its own, it ebbs and flows. In this study we have viewed suspicion as 'the partial or unconfirmed belief that something is wrong or someone guilty'. We have seen that there are key moments in a child protection investigation, such as when suspicion enters the public domain, when an accusation is made, when professionals gather and when fresh evidence comes to light. During these events the perspectives of parents on child protection procedures are fashioned in such a way as to determine how they will respond to any investigation.

We found there to be psychological and social influences on perspectives: psychological influences are those such as personality, previous experience, motivations and expectations; social influences include the power relationship in the interaction between parent and professional, the ways suspicions are made public, who alerts the authorities and who confronts the parents. These perspectives are fashioned and change at key moments as the career of suspicion gathers momentum. To understand these various aspects of perception we use the term 'operational perspective' and have looked at their formation, development and use.

At any one moment it is possible to entertain a variety of perceptions because one can select, interpret and organise what is smelled, felt or seen in very different ways. Memory, experience and likelihood all influence how circumstances are interpreted. For example, a rumbling in the kitchen may presage an earthquake, herald the arrival of the Messiah or signal the protests of an overloaded pressure cooker. Perceptions of the acrid tremor would vary were we in San Francisco, Jerusalem or Manchester. Social class, religious persuasion and ethnicity might also influence the selection and interpretation of the event.

How we perceive an event determines what comes next, what 'operational perspective' we employ. It would be churlish to greet the bringer of salvation with a fire blanket and irrelevant to fall on one's knees in contrition before a blazing chip pan. Parents faced with an accusation of child abuse behave in equivalent fashion: they have rapidly to accommodate the event, interpret its meaning and manage the suspicion. They have to present themselves convincingly to their accusers, to the wider family and to the neighbourhood, hour by hour. In Becker's terminology 'they have to get by', to tackle social workers, to cope with the haunting fear of the police and still push the trolley jauntily around the supermarket as if nothing has happened.

At the outset, in the context of suspicion, parents and professionals are unlikely to share similar operational perspectives. We hypothesised that as time passes, to facilitate a successful outcome, the operational perspectives of parents and professionals must come together. We suggested that several opportunities for change present themselves at successive points in the investigation.

The contexts in which suspicion arises

This study has two dimensions, first an extensive scrutiny of child protection services in one local authority, involving, in all, 583 children and, second, an intensive study in two local authorities of 30 families, with their 61 children, who were suspected of abuse.

What did the extensive survey tell us about parental perspectives when under suspicion for child abuse? Particularly important are the findings that most suspicions of abuse are not substantiated on investigation and that even when abuse has occurred it is highly likely to be minor. Should concern be sufficient to merit a child's inclusion on the Protection Register, even then most of these children stay at home. These facts should be used to allay parental concerns at the outset of any investigation, because research demonstrates that parents are fearful that the precipitate removal of their children is imminent. This anxiety hinders co-operation, sharing and understanding of the role of social workers and other professionals in child abuse work.

Of the 583 cases where suspicion was sufficiently strong to merit recording, fewer than one third of the children eventually had their names placed on the Child Protection Register. Since about 24,500 children are added to registers in England each year and a similar number removed, this would suggest a national picture of nearly 100,000 serious investigations annually. In addition, many less pressing cases are dealt with but not recorded, a finding supported by other recent research. Thus a considerable burden is placed upon professionals by child protection work, much of it unacknowledged. The bulk of this load falls upon social services since it is they who are expected to initiate and co-ordinate investigations.

These investigations extend to children of all ages, although reports of abuse decline as children get older. Younger children are more at risk of neglect and physical abuse than are adolescents who tend to predominate in sexual abuse investigations. Sexual abuse accounts for half of referrals involving girls but only a quarter of those involving boys. We have found that some children such as the physically ill are more prone to abuse than others. In addition, those who display behaviour problems at school are frequent among victims.

Abuse is suspected in several different types of family but some factors seem common to all. Some form of family reconstitution or major change in adult membership is important. Thus suspicion usually falls upon close family members, particularly on those males recently recruited to the home. In 70% of cases involving child abuse parents are the chief suspects. Mothers and fathers equally come under the spotlight for physical abuse but in situations of neglect and emotional abuse, mothers predominate. In suspicions of sexual abuse, fathers, co-habitees and males outside the nuclear family are likely to be the chief culprits. However, there is growing evidence that siblings are not uninvolved in cases of sexual abuse, neither are mothers entirely innocent and unaware bystanders. Sexual abuse by strangers, however, is not frequent.

The extensive data led to a useful classification of abusing families, which proved valuable in understanding information from our intensive study of 30 families. We identified, firstly, multi-problem families who are well known to the social services and whose difficulties are manifold. The adults in these families are highly likely to have been abused themselves as children. These families are in the majority, forming 43% of those in the extensive study. Secondly, there are specific problem families who come to notice because of a particular suspicion. Such families have rarely previously been the recipients of welfare interventions or police concern. Ostensibly these families live well-ordered lives and cross class boundaries. Such families are not rare, forming 21% of those we studied. Thirdly, we identified acutely distressed families which share some of the characteristics of the multi-problem family group but are distinct in the degree and frequency of accidents, misfortune and trauma they experience. Able to cope in normal circumstances, these parents collapse, their children become an impossible burden and a break-down occurs which results in abuse, usually physical maltreatment or neglect of younger children. These families comprise 13% of the study group.

Fourthly, a minority of families are infiltrated by outsiders, intent on the abuse of children. These are common in sexual abuse situations. In a fifth group, children are abused outside the family, although the perpetrator is frequently known to the child.

Of the 583 cases of suspicion investigated by social workers and others in our extensive scrutiny, 28% of the children were registered, 34% were not registered but their progress was monitored, 16% were investigated and referred to another agency for additional assessment, such as to child guidance or hospital, thus postponing a decision and in 22% of cases no further action was deemed necessary. Of those children registered, slightly less than a third were removed from home. Even then, reunion remains the most likely outcome for these children. Despite parents' fears to the contrary, three quarters will eventually return and the majority will go back rapidly. However, some cases do linger away from home, for example, incest cases, situations where mothers have been indifferent or party to the abuse and cases of very serious physical injury.

If social services, police, hospitals or probation are involved in the initial referral, there is a stronger chance of registration than when health visitors or G.P.s raise the alarm. Schools, although providing an important source of referral, are a less coherent influence upon registration. When a male parent or infiltrator is the suspected abuser, there is more likelihood of registration, as is the case when someone with a record of child abuse or violence is present in the family. Sexual abuse is more likely to lead to registration than other forms of violation. Families' previous history can influence case conference decisions on what to do next. Turbulent families well known to social services are at high risk of having their children registered. A criminal history and a previous record of child abuse all increase the chances of a child's name being placed on the Child Protection Register.

Suspected child abuse comes to light in a variety of ways. It can surface when someone in the family or the immediate neighbourhood reports a suspicious situation. It can arise when abuse is noticed by a professional in the course of other duties, such as by a doctor or teacher. Abuse can also be suspected when an event or some aspect of child behaviour alerts concern, such as the child running away or an adolescent's suicide attempt. These referral processes have considerable impact on parental perspectives as suspicion emerges and an accusation is made.

Building on this extensive work, we followed up in detail 30 selected families and their 61 children from the point of initial confrontation for a period of two years. Although the circumstances of abuse differ markedly, parents tend to perceive any voiced suspicion in much the same way. They behave as we all do when confronted with something unexpected and violating. Faced with an accusation of serious misdemeanour, outrage and denial are our most familiar responses, as these are both well tried and successful strategies of immediate defence. A denial at least gives one time to organise a coping strategy and we decide that a low profile, and taciturn and grudging interaction with those in power are the best way forward. These perspectives are understandable in the innocent and even more so in the guilty. Unfortunately, accusers in situations of child abuse view these parental perspectives and their strategies of survival as confirming guilt or, at least, as indicating that parents have something to hide.

But behind tearful, public denial and recrimination, other perspectives lie hidden. Parents will entertain guilt over past neglect and indifference, regret their moments of over-vigorous control and obloquy, remember giggles behind closed and locked bathroom doors: all these anxieties are revived with new and awful meaning. Understandably, to the outside observer, parents, particularly mothers, present contradictory and unconvincing explanations.

In situations where parents are ignorant of the gathering suspicion of abuse, the impact of any accusation is very considerable. Parents feel violated and angry; they reject any suggestion of abuse, and worry that the confrontation will be the prelude to the removal of the child by social workers. They are resentful that much investigation has gone on behind their backs. At the outset it is difficult for social workers to distinguish the anguish and anxiety of the innocent from the fear and remorse of the guilty. It goes without saying that social workers need sensitivity, tolerance and awareness in their initial confrontation with parents because 'operational perspectives' are formed at the outset and tend to endure. Also, the impact on the family threatens to be long-term.

Parents not only have to manage suspicion from without, they have to cope with suspicions from within. There are differences between what they feel and what they say they feel. Mothers may come to suspect others in the family, partners may resent the disclosures of mothers or step-children. Siblings are dismissive and resentful of the publicity. Supposed victims may retreat into denial rather than endure more scrutiny. A spirit of wholesale recrimination may invade the family home.

The professional, burdened with many abuse investigations or preoccupied with other cogent problems, may easily lose sight of how violating to families are accusations of and investigations into child abuse. Child abuse procedures have a momentum of their own, fuelling parents' feelings of powerlessness and vulnerability. A cry for help from parents tends to incline all those involved to a more benign perspective than does suspicion aired by a stranger outside the family. Nevertheless, most cases generate feelings of trust betrayed that may extend beyond the household to the wider family and neighbourhood.

We have seen that families and professionals are unlikely to share similar 'operational perspectives' at the outset and parents must be given time to ponder, reflect, seek counselling and external advice. Unfortunately, many mothers have few confidantes they can trust. If the 'operational perspectives' of parents and professionals are to come together, deep wounds need to be healed.

Outcomes

Our task in this study was to see whether at key moments parents' operational perspectives shift towards those of professionals and whether such changes make any difference to long-term outcomes for the children and families.

We have seen that over time the cold hostility of parents may warm, but a long-term wariness of professionals can remain as a legacy of the initial suspicion and accusation. This is a problem, because many families continue to need help with difficulties well outside the abuse issue. In the same way, while not the focus of this study, suspicions of abuse have repercussions among the child's siblings and the extended family. The accusation acts as a detonator to that volatile mixture of love, hate and indifference which binds families together and we have seen that as bonds are loosened, families fall apart.

Changes in the operational perspectives of parents occur at three key moments during the abuse investigation. These are, firstly at the initial confrontation, secondly at the gathering of professionals or thirdly when situations change or new information comes to light. Certain influences are difficult to predict, such as the departure of a close family member, whereas others, such as a change in social worker, can be engineered.

Our follow-up study found that the hostile parental perspectives which surrounded the voicing of suspicion by professionals seldom endured. Moreover intervention often brought other benefits. When families were scrutinised two years after the initial confrontation significant changes had occurred in their circumstances and in their attitudes towards the statutory authorities, four-fifths of these changes for the better. We have seen that the living situations of the majority improve, for example their finances brighten, physical and mental health improve and an increase in parenting skills helps children reach the majority of their developmental milestones.

Evidence would also suggest that the child protection system, for all its faults, does protect the majority of children at risk. Scandals in recent years have been generated as much by inappropriate, precipitate and over-zealous interventions as by dereliction of professional responsibility. While it is probably impossible to protect a minority of children from occasional violence, from rejection and indifference, an awareness of external scrutiny does encourage caution as family temperatures rise. The need for continued supervision in many cases is demonstrated by the re-abuse of one quarter of the children we scrutinised. Although these incidents were minor, concern over parenting skills ought not to evaporate; failure to substantiate a suspicion does not necessarily mean the exercise has been a waste of time.

Nevertheless, it is easy to forget how great is the upheaval in family life and how damaging to interpersonal relationships are accusations of child abuse. We have seen that, in the majority of cases, there is little foundation for the suspicion and professional attention rapidly moves elsewhere. But an accusation that is all in the day's work for professionals such as health visitors, social workers and others, is a cataclysmic life event for parents and wider family. Not only must parents and families manage external suspicion but they must also manage the feelings of disloyalty, betrayed trust and malevolence within the family. The severity of this stress is witnessed by the frequent disintegration of marital relationships, the movement of family members and the relocation of children subsequent to an abuse accusation. These are high prices to pay for a bruise or children witnessing an unsuitable, spicy video. While relationships within the family break down because of feelings of suspicion, jealousy and violated trust, potent catalysts are also created by changes in the relative power and roles of family members. Fathers' controlling, protecting, all providing roles are compromised; mothers' tending, nurturing and affective care is devalued. Children are suddenly powerful, their voice, behaviour and welfare are of wider concern. Privacy gives way to scrutiny, taciturn confidence to endless, unconvincing explanation.

But change is not one way. Just as parental perspectives on professionals may become more benign, so professionals change in their attitudes towards the families. In many cases there is renewed concern over abuse and suspicions are subsequently confirmed. In others, the unease simmers, some professionals even come to re-evaluate the meaning of abuse and to appreciate the problems faced by families and the efforts made, particularly by mothers, to refute any further suspicions. While suspicions of abuse were often unconfirmed, some intervention was deemed necessary in most cases and the child protection services acted on the side of caution.

There is also the considerable bonus in that, not only are the majority of children protected by the system we have so painfully devised over the years, but most remain in a context which they view as 'home' rather than experience precipitate removal by social workers. Professionals are keenly aware that the upheavals associated with their interventions are likely to be more damaging to the child than the experience of minor abuse. Nevertheless professionals should consider, in addition, parental perspectives at all stages of the suspicion process and must cope with the hostility and sense of violation that parents display, because, where agreement is reached with parents, children are much more likely to be protected from abuse than where disagreement and dispute characterise relationships.

Few protection plans, short of the removal of a child to a place of safety, can guarantee a child's security but opportunities for improvement in professional–parental relationships are not infrequent and we have seen how beneficial commonly shared perspectives are in fashioning a satisfactory outcome for the child. In addition there are very few families who are so violated by their experiences at the hands of professionals that they cannot accept the proffered olive branch. There were no cases in this study where the perspectives of parents should have been ignored or where the efforts of social workers to win over parents were pointless and counter productive. As many of the families for a variety of reasons are likely to stay in contact with social services, as their children are likely to remain at risk, professionals need to accommodate parental perspectives and to work with them.

This study is part of a programme of research initiated by the Department of Health into a wide range of child abuse issues. The conclusions of these studies are likely to have considerable impact on child protection procedures and even lead to some revision of *Working Together*. Plans are already afoot to tease out the practice and policy implications of the research studies so far completed and for their adequate dissemination. Thus any comments on the wider implications of this study, concerned as it has been with a very narrow issue, i.e. parental perspectives when under suspicion of child abuse, may be precipitate and inaccurate. Nevertheless if only to stimulate discussion, some points immediately spring to mind as topics to be aired.

The importance of schools

Once again in this study, as in so many the Unit has undertaken, the role of the school emerges as important. It is a significant agent of referral for suspected abuse and, once the child is registered, the schools are in a prime position to monitor any subsequent progress. Our evidence suggests that there are difficulties in the relations enjoyed between schools and other parts of the child protection system. It is also evident that schools' potential for alerting professionals to situations of child abuse and in assisting in child protection is underestimated.

Our evidence gathered from a variety of sources would suggest that schools vary greatly in their ability to cope with problems of child abuse. There are considerable differences in referrals for suspected abuse between schools in geographical areas where strong similarities might be expected. In the same way there are variations in procedures within schools. For example, it is not unusual for classroom teachers to be unaware of those children whose names are placed on the Protection Register or for whom concern is growing. This is because school principals and those teachers designated with special responsibility for abuse and pastoral care issues vary considerably in their handling of confidentiality. Many do not communicate their concerns and knowledge downwards.

Because signs of distress in children are behavioural, particularly so in child abuse situations, it is frequently difficult to distinguish between abuse driven difficulties and those of general naughtiness or poor self control. After all, if every 11 year old's rude drawing was sufficient to alert child protection procedures, education in most schools would rapidly come to a halt. Moreover, teachers are reluctant to report their own failure to control. Is every footloose and fancy free child in Miss Smith's class abused? Or is it just Miss Smith?

There are also structural factors in schools that hinder child protection procedures. Teacher–pupil relationships have to be worked at, classrooms are private territories in schools into which even superiors venture with a degree of caution. Teachers will, for a variety of reasons, be very hesitant to set the abuse procedures in motion because they are highly disrupting to classroom routine. The process violates the trust of parents, disturbs the child–teacher relationship, may easily come to the notice of other children and staff, and certainly inflicts stressful distraction on the teacher.

Any investigation will call aspects of professional conduct into question, particularly in the classroom, where a climate of trust and empathy has to be created before children will feel safe enough to express their anxieties. One wonders whether many classrooms are capable of providing that asylum of compassionate understanding that abused children need. Worse, it is often the case that those children most at risk are not particularly loveable on other criteria: they are frequently in trouble, and, possibly mercifully from the school's point of view, frequently absent.

Once again in a profoundly important area of child care one finds that a gap exists between educational services and other aspects of child and adolescent care. Such barriers are found in the careers of children with special needs, with young delinquents and with those difficult children excluded from school. Abuse can now be added to that depressing list where our system fails our children.

When and how to intervene

As the volume of child protection work grows, there have been questions raised about the point at which the Child Protection system should come into play. Is the threshold of concern fixed too low, particularly as the majority of suspicions are groundless or concern abuse that is minor? This study suggests that whatever the administrative procedures followed in the early stages of child abuse, all initial suspicions will be explored by Child Protection professionals in much the same way. In addition, the number of abuse concerns does not necessarily reflect the levels of social work involved, because one serious abuse situation that proceeds as far as the High Court will occupy more time than dozens of others that wither away during early investigation. All suspicions of abuse have to be adequately explored because at the outset one cannot distinguish whether the incident represents the tip of the iceberg or not.

In drawing the threshold of abuse beyond which certain procedures come into play, it is important to identify which threshold is under scrutiny. Most practice concern has been with whether to investigate, call a conference or place a child's name on the register. This study emphasises another important threshold: the point at which the confrontation of parents becomes necessary. Is it at the moment of initial suspicion? Is it at the point of referral? Is it when social workers ring round or pay a low-key visit in an initial investigation? Is it when the child or parent is formally interviewed? Unfortunately any of us in day to day contact with children, uncertain, untrained in abuse matters and fearful of the consequences of inaction or indifference to a suspicion may choose to inflict child protection procedures on parents. It is professional anxiety not procedural guidelines that keeps the thresholds low in child abuse.

Perspectives are adversely affected when parents realise that a great deal of exploration and cross checking has gone on behind their backs, quite apart from the rights issues that such a strategy raises. Nevertheless, those families which are chaotic and already well supported by social workers might be approached without the awesome accusation of a specific incident of child abuse; this would help in more than one third of incidents. We saw, for example, how the acutely distressed families could have benefited as much from Section 17 interventions. The real problem in handling suspicions of child abuse occurs in those families unused to social work interventions or where family members have a history of child abuse, a murky past which has been undivulged to close partners or friends. In these situations, whatever the threshold of intervention employed, the social worker is highly unlikely to find 'welcome' woven into the doormat.

Child protection in the wider context

It is frequently suggested that social workers' preoccupation with child abuse has been at the expense of the care made available to other clients in need. This reproach is difficult to substantiate because of the considerable improvements made since the Maria Colwell case over the decade, in welfare provision for children and adolescents. Whether some would have done better were the considerable resources currently ploughed into child protection more evenly distributed is an open question. It is true that a gathering realisation of the widespread and varied nature of child abuse has changed the ethos of much child-care, it has certainly changed practice in residential homes and specialist schools, not necessarily for the better. On the other hand, increased awareness of an issue may be no bad thing – we have seen that most children are adequately protected from abuse by the system we now have in place. It has also sweetened the professional image of social workers whose role now can be identified as one of protecting children.

Naturally one would not expect a child protection system, however fashioned, to be without debit. It is concerned with investigating specific instances of abuse, focusing, of necessity, chiefly on the victim, which runs counter to one that emphasises the needs of the whole family, parental participation and shared care and the child's school and neighbourhood contexts. The capital of trust and co-operation this latter approach builds up in families at risk can so easily be squandered by an insensitive abuse inquiry.

It is a principle of the *Children Act*, 1989 that although strong powers are required to make it possible to remove children when necessary, most vulnerable children can best be protected by supporting their families. Apart from emergency procedures, child protection is not dealt with in a separate section. Duties are incorporated into wider requirements to provide for children and families. It is hoped that this research offers new evidence on what can be achieved in a difficult area of practice.

References

ALLPORT, F.H. (1924), *Social Psychology*, Boston, Houghton Mifflin.

AGATHONOS-GEORGOPOULOU, H. (1992), 'Cross-cultural perspectives in child abuse and neglect', *Child Abuse Review*, 1, 2, pp. 80–89.

ARGYLE, M. (1964), *Psychology and Social Problems*, London, Methuen.

ARGYLE, M. (1969), *Social Interaction*, London, Tavistock.

BASW (1985), *The Management of Child Abuse*, Birmingham, BASW.

BAUMEISTER, R.F. (1982), 'A self-presentational view of social phenomena', *Psychological Bulletin*, 91, pp. 3–26.

BEBBINGTON, A. and MILES, J. (1989), 'The background of children who enter local authority care', *British Journal of Social Work*, 19, pp 349–368.

BELL, M., and SINCLAIR, I. (1993*), Parental Involvement in Initial Child Protection Conferences in Leeds*, University of York.

BECKER, H.S. (1958), 'Problems of inference and proof in participant observation', *American Sociological Review*, 23, pp. 652–659.

BECKER, H.S. (1963), *Outsiders*, New York, Free Press.

BENEDICT, R. (1938), 'Continuities and discontinuities in cultural conditioning', *Psychiatry*, 1, pp 161–167.

BENTOVIM, A. (1987), 'The diagnosis of child sexual abuse', *Bulletin of the Royal College of Psychiatrists*, 11, 9, pp. 295–299.

BERGER, P. and LUCKMAN, T. (1971), *The Social Construction of Reality*, London, Allen Lane.

BERRIDGE, D. and CLEAVER, H. (1987), *Foster Home Breakdown*, Oxford, Blackwell.

BERTHOUD, R. (1976), *The Disadvantages of Inequality*, London, Macdonald and Janes.

BESHAROV, D.J. (1982), 'Towards better research on child abuse and neglect: making definition issues an explicit methodological concern', *Child Abuse and Neglect*, 5, pp. 383–90.

BESHAROV, D.J. (1987), 'Statement to the Select Committee on Children, Youth and Families', *American Enterprise Institute for Public Policy Research*, Washington DC.

BILLINGTON, R., STRAWBRIDGE, S., GREENSIDES, L. and FITZSIMONS, A. (1992), *Culture and Society: A Sociology of Culture*, London, Macmillan

BLAU P.M. (1964), *Exchange and Power in Social Life*, New York, Wiley.

BOK, S. (1978), *Lying: Moral Choice in Public and Private Life*, New York, Harvester.

BOK, S. (1982), *Secrets: On the Ethics of Concealment and Revelation*, New York, Pantheon.

BOND, C.F. and FAHEY, W.E. (1987), 'False suspicion and the misperception of deceit', *British Journal of Social Psychology*, 26, pp. 41–46.

BOSWELL, J. (1988), *The Kindness of Strangers,* London, Allan Lane.

BOTTOMS, A.E. and McCLINTOCK, F.H. (1973), *Criminals Coming of Age: A Study of Institutional Adaptation in the Treatment of Adolescent Offenders,* London, Heinemann.

BOURNE, P. (1970), 'Psychological aspects of combat', in Abram, H.S. (Ed.), *Psychological Aspects of Stress*, London, Thomas.

BOWLBY, J. (1965), *Child Care and the Growth of Love*, Harmondsworth, Penguin.

BOWLBY, J. (1973), *Attachment and Loss: Vol. 2, Separation: Anxiety and Anger*, Harmondsworth, Penguin.

BOWYER, J., BULLOCK, R., HOSIE, K., LITTLE, M. and MILLHAM, S. (1989), *Community Service Volunteers Independent Living Scheme,* Bristol Papers, 10, Bristol University.

BRAZIL, E. and STEWARD, S. (1990), *Parents Share their Experiences of Child Protection Procedures and their Views on Parent Participation in Conferences*, Report to Lewisham Social Services Department, London.

BREWER, C., and LAIT J. (1980), *Can Social Work Survive?* Temple Smith, London

BROWN, C. (1986), *Child Abuse Parents Speaking: Parents' Impressions of Social Workers and the Social Work Process*, Bristol University School of Advanced Urban Studies.

BROWN, M. and MADGE, N. (1982) *Despite the Welfare State,* London, Heinemann.

BROWNE, K. and SAQI, S. (1987), 'Parent-child interaction in abusing families: its possible causes and consequences', in Maher, P. (Ed.), *Child Abuse: The Educational Perspective*, Oxford, Blackwell, pp 77–103.

BROWNE, K., DAVIES, C. and STRATTON, P. (1988), *Early Prediction and Prevention of Child Abuse,* London, Wiley.

BROWNE, K. and SAQI, S. (1988), 'Approaches for screening for child abuse and neglect', in Browne, K., Davies, C. and Stratton, P. (Eds.), *Early Prediction and Prevention of Child Abuse,* pp. 57–86.

BULLOCK, R., LITTLE, M. and MILLHAM S. (1993), *Going Home: The Return of Children Separated from their Families*, Aldershot, Dartmouth.

BURNS, L. (1992), 'Views of families attending case conferences', *Child Abuse Review*, 5, 3, pp. 20–24.

CLYDE, The Lord (1992), *Report of the Inquiry into the Removal of Children from Orkney in February 1991,* London, HMSO, House of Commons Papers 195.

COHEN, S. (1972), *Folk Devils and Moral Panics*, London, MacGibbon and Kee.

CONNELLY, C.D. and STRAUSS, M.A. (1992), 'Mother's age and abuse', *Child Abuse and Neglect*, 16, pp.709–719.

CORBY, B. (1987), *Working with Child Abuse: Social Work Practice and the Child Abuse System*, Milton Keynes, Open University Press.

CORNISH, D.B. and CLARKE, R.V. (1975), *Residential Treatment and its Effects on Delinquency*, London, HMSO.

CREIGHTON, S.J. (1988), 'The incidence of child abuse and neglect', in Browne, K, Davies, C. and Stratton, P. (Eds.), *Early Prediction and Prevention of Child Abuse,* pp. 31–42.

CRITTENDEN, P. (1988), 'Family and dyadic patterns of functioning in maltreating families', in Browne, K, Davies, C. and Stratton, P. (Eds.), *Early Prediction and Prevention of Child Abuse,* pp.161–192.

DALE, F. (1991), 'The art of communicating with vulnerable children', In Varma, V.P. (Ed.), *The Secret Life of Vulnerable Children,* London, Routledge.

Dartington Social Research Unit, (1985), *Place of Safety Orders: Evidence to the DHSS Child Care Law Review Committee.*

DE LISSOVOY, V. (1979), 'Towards the definition of an abuse provoking child', *Child Abuse and Neglect,* 3, pp. 341–350.

DENZIN, N.K. (1978), *The Research Act,* New York, McGraw Hill.

Department of Education and Science (1988), Circ.4/88 *Working Together for the Protection of Children from Abuse: Procedures within the Education Service.*

Department of Health (1989), *An Introduction to the Children Act 1989,* London, HMSO.

Department of Health (1989), *The Care of Children: Principles and Practice in Guidance and Regulations*, London, HMSO.

Department of Health (annually), *Children and Young Persons on Child Protection Registers: year ending 31 March, England.*

DHSS, Social Services Inspectorate (1986), *Inspection of the Supervision of Social Workers in the Assessment and Monitoring of Cases of Child Abuse when Children, Subject to a Court Order, have been Returned Home.*

DHSS. (1988), *Working Together; A Guide to Arrangements for Inter-Agency Co-operation for the Protection of Children from Abuse,* London, HMSO.

DE YOUNG, M. (1988), 'The indignant page: techniques of neutralization in the publications of paedophile organizations', *International Journal of Child Abuse and Neglect,* 12, 4, pp. 583–591.

DINGWALL, R., EEKELAAR, J. and MURRAY, T. (1983), *The Protection of Children: State Intervention and Family Life,* Oxford, Blackwell.

DOBSON, C. (1992), 'The dilemmas of investigating child abuse', *Child Abuse Review,* 5, 3, pp. 13–16.

DOUGLAS, M. (1970), *Witchcraft, Confessions and Accusations,* London, Tavistock.

ERIKSON, E.H. (1950), *Childhood and Society,* New York, Norton.

ETZIONI, A. (1969), *The Semi-Professions and their Organisation: Teachers, Nurses and Social Workers,* New York, Free Press.

FARMER, E. and OWEN, M. (1993), *Decision Making, Intervention and Outcome in Child Protection Work,* Report submitted to the Department of Health, University of Bristol.

FINKELHOR, D. (1979), *Sexually Victimized Children,* New York, Free Press.

FINKELHOR, D. (1984), *Child Sexual Abuse - New Theory and Research,* New York, Free Press.

FINKELHOR D. (1986), 'Abusers: special topics', in Finklehor, D. (Ed.), *A Sourcebook on Child Sexual Abuse,* Beverly Hills, Sage.

FINKLEHOR, D. and BARON, L. (1986), 'High-risk children', in Finklehor, D. (Ed.), *A Sourcebook on Child Sexual Abuse,* Beverly Hills, Sage.

FISHER, M., MARSH, P. and PHILLIPS, D. with SAINSBURY E. (1986), *In and Out of Care: The Experiences of Children, Parents and Social Workers,* London, Batsford.

FOUCAULT, M., (1977), *Discipline and Punish,* London, Allen Lane

FOX HARDING, L. (1991), *Perspectives in Child Care Policy,* London, Longman.

FREUD, A. (1965), *Normality and Pathology in Childhood: Assessments of Development,* London, Hogarth.

FRIEDMAN, S.B. and MORSE, C.W. (1974), 'Child abuse: a five year follow-up of early case findings in the emergency department', *Paediatrics,* 54, pp. 404–410.

GARBARINO, J. and GILLIAM, S. (1980), *Understanding Abusive Families,* Lexington, Lexington Books.

GARBARINO, J., GUTTMANN, E. and SEELEY, J. (1986), *The Psychologically Battered Child,* San Francisco, Jossey-Bass.

GELLNER, E. (1974), 'The new idealism: cause and meaning in the social sciences', in Giddens, A., (Ed.), *Positivism and Sociology*, London, Hutchinson.

GIBBONS, J., GALLAGHER, B., BELL, C. and GORDON, D. (1992), *Family Health and Development Project*, report submitted to the Department of Health, Social Work Development Unit, University of East Anglia.

GIBBONS, J., CONROY, S. and BELL, C. (1993), *Operation of Child Protection Registers*, Report submitted to the Department of Health, Social Work Development Unit, University of East Anglia.

GIL, D.G. (1971), 'Violence against children', *Journal of Marriage and the Family*, 33, pp. 637–648.

GIOVANNONI, J.M. and BECERRA, R. M. (1979), *Defining Child Abuse*, New York, Free Press.

GLASER, B.G. and STRAUSS, A.L. (1967), *The Discovery of Grounded Theory*, Chicago, Aldine.

GOFFMAN, E.G. (1963), *Stigma: Notes on the Management of Spoiled Identity*, Harmondsworth, Penguin.

GOMES-SCHWARTZ, B., HOROWITZ, J.M. and CARDARELLI, A.P. (1990), *Child Sexual Abuse: The Initial Effects*, Beverly Hills, Sage.

GOUGH, D. (1988), 'Approaches to child abuse prevention', in Browne, K., Davies, C. and Stratton, P. (Eds.), *Early Prediction and Prevention of Child Abuse*, pp.107–120.

GUSFIELD, J. (1989), 'Constructing the ownership of social problems: fun and profit in the welfare state', *Social Problems*, 36, pp. 431–441.

HMSO (1984), *The Second Report from the House of Commons Social Services Committee*, session 1983–4; HC360–1.

HALLETT, C. and BIRCHALL, E. (1992), *Coordination and Child Protection: A Review of the Literature*, Edinburgh, HMSO.

HAMMERSLEY, M. and ATKINSON, P. (1983), *Ethnography: Principles in Practice*, London, Tavistock.

HARRÉ, R., CLARKE, D. and DE CARLO, N., (1985) *Motives and Mechanisms*, London, Methuen.

HAUGAARD, J.J. and REPUCCI, N.D. (1988), *The Sexual Abuse of Children; A Comprehensive Guide to Current Knowledge and Intervention Strategies*, San Francisco, Jossey-Bass.

HIGGINSON, S. (1990), 'Distorted evidence', *Community Care*, 17th. May.

HOBBS, C. (1992), 'Paediatric intervention in child protection', *Child Abuse Review*, 1, 1, pp. 5–17.

Home Office, Department of Health, Department of Education and Science and Welsh Office (1988) *Report of the Inquiry into Child Abuse in Cleveland 1987.*

Home Office (1988), *The Investigation of Child Sexual Abuse,* Circular 52/88.

Home Office, Department of Health, Department of Education and Science and Welsh Office (1991), *Working Together Under the Children Act 1989: A Guide to Arrangements for Inter-agency Co-operation for the Protection of Children from Abuse,* London, HMSO.

Home Office, (annually), *Criminal Statistics for England and Wales*, London, HMSO.

HUDSON, F. and INEICHEN, B. (1991), *Taking it Lying Down: Sexuality and Teenage Motherhood*, London, MacMillan.

HYMAN, C.A. (1978), 'Non-accidental injury, a report to the Surrey County Area Review Committee on Child Abuse', *Health Visitor,* 51, 5, pp. 168–74.

JONES, D. and MCGRAW, J. (1987), 'Reliable and fictitious accounts of sexual abuse to children', *Journal of Interpersonal Violence,* 2, pp. 27–45.

KAPLAN, S. (1977), *The Dream Deferred*, New York, Vintage.

KEMPE, C.H., SILVERMAN, F.N., STEELE, B.B., DROEGEMUELLER, W. and SILVER, H.K. (1962), 'The battered child syndrome', *Journal of American Medical Association,* 181, pp. 17–24.

KEMPE, R.S. and KEMPE, C.H. (1978), *Child Abuse,* Cambridge, Harvard University Press.

KORBIN, J.E. (1981), *Child Abuse and Neglect: Cross Cultural perspectives*, San Francisco, University of California Press.

KORBIN, J.E. (1991), 'Cross-cultural perspectives and research directions for the 21st. Century', *Child Abuse and Neglect,* 15 (supp.1), pp. 67–77.

LA FONTAINE, J. (1988), *Child Sexual Abuse*, London, ESRC.

LAMBERT, R., MILLHAM, S. and BULLOCK, R., (1975), *The Chance of a Lifetime? A study of Boarding Education,* London, Weidenfeld and Nicolson.

LEMERT, E. (1962), 'Paranoia and the dynamics of exclusion', *Sociometry,* 25, pp. 2–25.

LEVINSON, D. (1989), *Family Violence in Cross Cultural Perspective*, London, Sage.

LITTLE, M. (1990), *Young Men in Prison*, Aldershot, Dartmouth.

LITTLE, M. and GIBBONS J. (1993), 'Predicting the rate of children on the Child Protection Register', *Research, Policy and Planning*, 10, 2, pp. 15–18.

LITTLEWOOD, R. and LIPSEDGE, M. (1982), *Aliens and Alienists: Ethnic Minorities and Psychiatry,* Harmondsworth, Penguin.

LOFLAND, J. (1971), *Analyzing Social Settings: A Guide to Qualitative Observations and Analysis,* San Francisco, Wadsworth.

London Borough of Greenwich (1986), *Parental Participation in Child Abuse Review Conferences: A Research Report,* Planning and Research Department.

LYNCH, D., STERN A., OATES, R. and O'TOOLE, B. (1993), 'Who participates in child sexual abuse research?', *Journal of Child Psychology and Psychiatry,* 34, 6, pp 935–944

LYNCH, M.A. (1975), 'Ill health and child abuse', *Lancet,* 2, pp. 317–319.

MARGOLIN, L. and CRAFT, J.L. (1990), 'Child Abuse by Adolescent Caregivers', *Child Abuse and Neglect,* 14, pp. 365–373.

MARGOLIN, L. (1991), 'Child sexual abuse and non related caregivers', *Child Abuse and Neglect,* 15, 3, pp. 365–371.

MATZA, D. and SYKES, G. (1957), 'Techniques of neutralization: a theory of delinquency', *American Sociological Review,* 22, 6, pp. 664–670.

MEASOR, L. (1985), 'Interviewing in ethnographic research', in Burgess, R.G. (Ed.), *Qualitative Methodology and the Study of Education,* Lewes, Falmer Press.

MECHANIC, D. (1978), *Medical Sociology,* New York, Free Press.

MELLANBY, A., PHELPS, F. and TRIPP, J. (1992), 'Sex education: more is not enough', *Journal of Adolescence,* 15, 4, pp.449–466.

MENZIES-LYTH, I. (1988), 'The functioning of social systems as a defence against anxiety', in Menzies-Lyth, I., *Containing Anxiety in Institutions,* London, Free Press.

MERTON, R.K. (1957), *Social Theory and Social Structure,* Glencoe, Free Press.

MILLHAM, S., BULLOCK, R. and CHERRETT, P. (1975), *After Grace-Teeth: a Comparative Study of the Residential Experience of Boys in Approved Schools,* London, Human Context Books.

MILLHAM, S., BULLOCK, R., HOSIE, K. and HAAK, M. (1986), *Lost in Care: The Problems of Maintaining Links between Children in Care and their Families,* Aldershot, Gower.

MILLHAM, S., BULLOCK, R., HOSIE, K. and LITTLE, M. (1989), *Access Disputes in Child-Care,* Aldershot, Gower.

MORAN-ELLIS, J., CONROY, S., FIELDING, N. and TUNSTILL, J. (1991), *Investigation of Child Sexual Abuse:* Department of Sociology, University of Surrey, Guildford.

NSPCC (1989), *Listening to Children,* London, NSPCC.

NSPCC (1990), *Protecting Children into the Nineties,* NSPCC Annual Report, London.

National Children's Home (1992), *The Report of the Committee of Enquiry into Children and Young People who Sexually Abuse Other Children,* London, NCH.

NEWSON, J. and NEWSON, E. (1976), 'Day-to-day aggression between parent and child', In Tutt, N., (Ed.), *Violence,* London, HMSO, pp. 90–109.

PACKMAN, J., RANDALL, J. and JACQUES, N. (1986), *Who Needs Care? Social Work Decisions about Children,* Oxford, Blackwell.

PARKER, R. (1988), 'An historical background', In Sinclair, I., (Ed.), *Residential Care - the Research Reviewed,* London, HMSO.

PARKER, R. (1990) *Away from Home: A History of Child Care,* Barkingside, Barnardos.

PARKER, R., WARD, H., JACKSON, S., ALDGATE, J. and WEDGE, P. (1991), *Looking After Children: Assessing Outcomes in Child Care,* London, HMSO.

PARTON, N. (1985), *The Politics of Child Abuse,* London, Macmillan.

PINCHBECK, A. and HEWITT, M. (1973), *Children in English Society,* London, Routledge and Kegan Paul.

PLESS, I.B. and DOUGLAS, J.W.B. (1971), 'Chronic illness in childhood: epidemiological and clinical characteristics', *Paediatrics* 47, pp. 405–414.

PLOMER, W. (1973), *Kilvert's Diary,* London, Cape.

Plowden Report (1967), *Children and their Primary Schools: Report of the Central Advisory Council for Education,* London, HMSO.

POLANSKY, N. A. (1981), *Damaged Parents - An Anatomy of Child Neglect,* Chicago, University of Chicago Press.

POTTER, J. and WETHERELL, M., (1987) *Discourse and Social Psychology: Beyond Attitudes and Behaviour,* Sage, London

PRITCHARD, C. (1991), 'Levels of risk and psycho-social problems of families on the at risk of abuse register: some indicators of outcome two years after case closure', *Research, Policy and Planning,* 9, pp. 19–26.

PRITCHARD, C. (1992), 'Children's homicide as an indicator of effective child protection: a comparative study of Western European statistics', *British Journal of Social Work,* 22, pp. 663–684.

PRITCHARD, C. (1993), 'Re-analysing Children's Homicide and Undetermined Death Rates as an Indication of Improved Child Protection', *British Journal of Social Work,* 23, pp. 645–652.

PROSSER, J. (1992), *Child Abuse Investigations: The Families' Perspective,* Essex, PAIN.

QUINTON, D. and Rutter, M. (1988), *Parenting Breakdown: Making and Breaking of Inter-generational Links,* Aldershot, Gower.

RAW, M. (1989), 'Psychology of disasters', *British Medical Journal,* 298, p. 71.

ROBERTS, J. (1988), 'Why are some families more vulnerable to child abuse?', in Browne, K., Davies, C. and Stratton, P. (Eds.), *Early Predictions and Prevention of Child Abuse*, pp. 57–86.

ROBIN, M., (1989), 'False allegations of child sexual abuse: implications for policy and practice', in Hudson J. and Galaway B., *The State as Parent: International Research Perspectives on Interventions with Young Persons,* Dordrecht, Kluwer, pp. 263–280.

RYAN, T.S. (1986), 'Problems, errors and opportunities in the treatment of father–daughter incest', *Journal of Interpersonal Violence* 1, 1, pp.113–24.

SCHATZMAN, L. and STRAUSS, A. (1955), 'Social class and modes of communication', *American Journal of Sociology*, 60, pp. 329–338.

SCHATZMAN, L. and STRAUSS, A. (1973), *Field Research: Strategies for a Natural Sociology*, New York, Prentice-Hall.

SHAW, R. (1987), *Children of Imprisoned Fathers*, London, Hodder and Stoughton.

SHEMMINGS, D. and THOBURN, J. (1990), *Parental Participation in Child Protection Conferences, Report of a Pilot Project in Hackney Social Services Department*, Norwich, University of East Anglia.

SHIREMAN, J., GROSSNICKLE, D., HINSEY, C. and WHITE, J. (1990), 'Outcome study of protective services: comparison of interviews and records as data sources', *Child Welfare*, 69, pp.167–179

SKINNER, A. and CASTLE, R. (1969), *78 Battered Children*, London, NSPCC.

SMITH, M. and GRAHAM, P. (1989), *Self-concepts and Cognitions about Sexuality in Abused and Non-abused Children*, Report summitted to the Department of Health.

SMITH, M., BEE, P., GOODMAN, C., HEVERIN, A. and NOBES, G. (1993), *Parental Control within the Family,* Report for the Department of Health, Thomas Coram Research Unit.

SMYTHIES, J.R. (1956), *Analysis of Perception*, London, Routledge and Kegan Paul.

SROUFE, L.A. and RUTTER, M. (1984), 'The domain of developmental psychopathology', *Child Development,* 55, pp. 17–29.

SUMMIT, R. (1991), 'Preventing child abuse', Paper given at the First National Congress on Prevention of Child Abuse and Neglect, Leicester.

THOBURN, J. (1980), *Captive Clients: Social Work with Children Home on Trial,* London, Routledge and Kegan Paul.

THOBURN J., LEWIS, A. and SHEMMINGS, D. (1993), *A Study of Client Participation in Child Protection Work*, Report to the Department of Health, Social Work Development Unit, University of East Anglia.

THOENNES N. and TJADEN, P.G. (1990), 'The extent, nature and validity of sexual abuse allegations in custody/visitation disputes', *Child Abuse and Neglect*, 14, pp. 151–163.

THOMAS, W.I. (1931), *The Relation of Research to the Social Process,* Washington DC, Brookings Institute.

VALENTINE, C.W. (1930), 'The innate basis of fear', *Journal of Genetic Psychology*, 37, pp. 394–419.

VERNON, M.D. (1962), *The Psychology of Perception*, Harmondsworth, Penguin.

WADSWORTH, M.E.J. (1991), T*he Imprint of Time: Childhood History and Adult Life*, Oxford, Clarendon.

WAHLER, R.G. and HAHN, D.M. (1984), 'The communication patterns of troubled mothers in search of a keystone in the generalization of parenting skills', *Journal of Education and Treatment of Children*, 7, pp. 335–350.

WARD, H. (1990), *The Charitable Relationship: Parents, Children and the Waifs and Strays Society,* Ph.D. Thesis, Department of Social Policy and Planning, University of Bristol.

WATERHOUSE, L. (1992) *Child Abuse and Child Abusers*, London Jessica Kingsley.

WHYTE, W.F. (1982), 'Interviewing in field research', in Burgess R.G. (Ed.), *Field Research: A Sourcebook and Field Manual*, London, Allen and Unwin.

WILKINS, R. (1990), 'Women who sexually abuse children', *British Medical Journal,* 300, pp. 1153–1154.

WINCH, P. (1958), *The Idea of a Social Science*, London, Allen Lane.

WINNICOTT, D.W. (1958), *Collected Papers*, London, Tavistock.

WOODS, P. (1986), *Inside Schools: Ethnography in Educational Research*, London, Routledge and Kegan Paul.

WRESSELL, S.E., KAPLAN, C.A. and KOLVIN, I. (1989), 'Performance indicators and child sexual abuse', *Psychiatric Bulletin*, 13, pp. 599–601.

Forthcoming complementary studies include:

Child Protection Practice: Private Risks and Public Remedies
Elaine Farmer and Morag Owen (The University of Bristol Team)
HMSO 1995. ISBN 0 11 321787 0

The Prevalence of Child Sexual Abuse in Britain
Deborah Ghate and Liz Spencer (Social and Community Planning
Research)
HMSO 1995. ISBN 0 11 321783 8

Development After Physical Abuse in Early Childhood: A Follow-Up Study of Children on Protection Registers
Jane Gibbons, Bernard Gallagher, Caroline Bell and David Gordon
(University of East Anglia)
HMSO 1995. ISBN 0 11 321790 0

Operating the Child Protection System
Caroline Bell, Sue Conroy and Jane Gibbons (University of East Anglia)
HMSO 1995. ISBN 0 11 321785 4

Inter-agency Coordination and Child Protection
Christine Hallett (The University of Stirling)
HMSO 1995. ISBN 0 11 321789 7

Working Together in Child Protection
Elizabeth Birchall (The University of Stirling)
HMSO 1995. ISBN 0 11 321830 3

Paternalism or Partnership? Family Involvement in the Child Protection Process
June Thoburn, Ann Lewis and David Shemmings (University of East
Anglia)
HMSO 1995. ISBN 0 11 321788 9

Printed in the United Kingdom for HMSO
Dd300357 5/95 C7 G559 10170